Marx, Engels, and Marxisms

Series Editors
Marcello Musto
York University
Toronto, Ontario, Canada

Terrell Carver
University of Bristol
Bristol, United Kingdom

Assistant Editor
Babak Amini
London School of Economics and Political Science
London, United Kingdom

The Marx Revival The Marx renaissance is underway on a global scale. Whether the puzzle is the economic boom in China or the economic bust in 'the West', there is no doubt that Marx appears regularly in the media nowadays as a guru, and not a threat, as he used to be. The literature dealing with Marxism, which all but dried up twenty-five years ago, is reviving in the global context. Academic and popular journals and even newspapers and on-line journalism are increasingly open to contributions on Marxism, just as there are now many international conferences, university courses and seminars on related themes. In all parts of the world, leading daily and weekly papers are featuring the contemporary relevance of Marx's thought. From Latin America to Europe, and wherever the critique to capitalism is reemerging, there is an intellectual and political demand for a new critical encounter with Marxism. **Types of Publications** This series bring together reflections on Marx, Engels and Marxisms from perspectives that are varied in terms of political outlook, geographical base, academic methodologies and subject-matter, thus challenging many preconceptions as to what "Marxist" thought can be like, as opposed to what it has been. The series will appeal internationally to intellectual communities that are increasingly interested in rediscovering the most powerful critical analysis of capitalism: Marxism. The series editors will ensure that authors and editors in the series are producing overall an eclectic and stimulating yet synoptic and informative vision that will draw a very wide and diverse audience. This series will embrace a much wider range of scholarly interests and academic approaches than any previous "family" of books in the area. This innovative series will present monographs, edited volumes and critical editions, including translations, to Anglophone readers. The books in this series will work through three main categories: *Studies on Marx and Engels:* The series include titles focusing on the oeuvre of Marx and Engels which utilize the scholarly achievements of the on-going Marx-Engels Gesamtausgabe, a project that has strongly revivified the research on these two authors in the past decade. *Critical Studies on Marxisms:* Volumes will awaken readers to the overarching issues and world-changing encounters that shelter within the broad categorisation 'Marxist'. Particular attention will be given to authors such as Gramsci and Benjamin, who are very popular and widely translated nowadays all over the world, but also to authors who are less known in the English-speaking countries, such as Mariátegui. *Reception Studies and Marxist National Tradition:* Political projects have necessarily required oversimplifications in the 20th century, and Marx and Engels have found themselves 'made over' numerous times and in quite contradictory ways. Taking a national perspective on 'reception' will be a global revelation and the volumes of this series will enable the worldwide Anglophone community to understand the variety of intellectual and political traditions through which Marx and Engels have been received in local contexts. **Aims of the Series** The volumes of this series will challenge all the 'Marxist' intellectual traditions to date by making use of scholarly discoveries of the Marx-Engels Gesamtausgabe since the 1990s, taking on board interdisciplinary and other new critical perspectives, and incorporating 'reception studies'. Authors and editors in the series will resist oversimplification of ideas and reinscription of traditions. Moreover their very diversity in terms of language, local context, political engagement and scholarly practice will mark the series out from any other in the field. This series will involve scholars from different fields and cultural backgrounds, and the series editors will ensure tolerance for differences within and between provocative monographs and edited volumes. Running contrary to 20th century practices of simplification, the books in this innovative series will revitalize Marxist intellectual traditions. **Series Editors:** Terrell Carver (University of Bristol, UK) Marcello Musto (York University, Canada) **Assistant Editor:** Babak Amini (London School of Economics, UK)

More information about this series at
http://www.springer.com/series/14812

Frederick Harry Pitts

Critiquing Capitalism Today

New Ways to Read Marx

Frederick Harry Pitts
School of Economics, Finance and Management
University of Bristol
Bristol, UK

Marx, Engels, and Marxisms
ISBN 978-3-319-62632-1   ISBN 978-3-319-62633-8   (eBook)
DOI 10.1007/978-3-319-62633-8

Library of Congress Control Number: 2017951139

Cover illustration: Paul Jackson / Alamy Stock Photo

Printed on acid-free paper

This Palgrave Macmillan imprint is published by Springer Nature
The registered company is Springer International Publishing AG
The registered company address is: Gewerbestrasse 11, 6330 Cham, Switzerland

To Elsie

ACKNOWLEDGEMENTS

This book collects together work completed over several years and there are many people without the direct input of which the book, nor the doctoral thesis on which it draws, would not have happened: most of all my PhD supervisor and constant source of intellectual support Ana Dinerstein; second supervisor Jeffrey Henderson; my viva panel of Werner Bonefeld, Gregory Schwartz and Theo Papadopoulos, who gave me incisive and indispensable feedback on the doctoral thesis on which a large swathe of this work is based, alongside transfer examiner Kevin Doogan; from my time at the University of Exeter, Timothy Cooper, who supervised earlier postgraduate work that fed into the project, and Nick Vaughan-Williams and Andrew Schaap, whose MA unit based around a close reading of *Empire* in late 2009 set in motion an interest that culminates in the second part of this book; various other sympathetic colleagues and collaborators who have provided encouragement, read bits of the book in their various iterations, or with whom I've had the chance to discuss some, if not all, of its ideas, including Matt Bolton, Jon Cruddas, Paul Thompson and Patrizia Zanoni, as well as audiences and respondents who provided feedback on the presentation of works-in-progress at numerous conferences and workshops; Terrell Carver for providing support to this project in his capacity as one of the editors for this book series, and John Stegner at Palgrave for his support and perseverance with the production process, as well as the anonymous reviewer who provided useful feedback on earlier draft versions of the chapters collected here. The usual disclaimers apply.

There are also a number of organisations whose institutional support was invaluable: the Department of Social & Policy Sciences at the University of Bath, where most of the research and thinking that went into the book was conducted, the School of Sociology, Politics & International Studies at the University of Bristol, where I have been fortunate enough to teach some of the central themes of the book to an inspiring and enthusiastic group of postgraduate students who are deserving of my thanks in their own right, and the South West Doctoral Training Centre (now the South West Doctoral Training Partnership), under which the doctoral research represented in these pages was conducted, and in the offices of which my colleagues have tolerated me as I far outstayed my welcome. Financially, the research that went into the book benefitted from various funders including the Economic and Social Research Council (grant number ES/J50015X/1), EU COST Action IS1202 Dynamics of Virtual Work, Bath Alumni Fund, among other sources of revenue.

The book draws on elements of material or formulations published in an earlier iteration in existing articles, working papers and chapters: Chaps. 2, 5, 7, 8, 9 and 10 contain material derived from 'Creative Industries, Value Theory and Michael Heinrich's New Reading of Marx', *tripleC: Communication, Capitalism and Critique*, 13(1), 2015; 'The Critique of Political Economy as a Critical Social Theory', *Capital & Class* 39(3), 2015; 'A Crisis of Measurability? Critiquing Postoperaismo on Labour, Value and the Basic Income', *Capital and Class*, 2016; and 'Beyond the Fragment: The Postoperaist Reception of Marx's Fragment on Machines and its Relevance Today', *School of Sociology, Politics and International Studies Working Paper Series*, University of Bristol, 2016. Chapter 3 draws on 'Review of Christian Lotz, *The Capitalist Schema: Time, Money and the Culture of Abstraction*' in the *Marx and Philosophy Review of Books*, 2015, available from: http://marxandphilosophy.org.uk/reviewofbooks/reviews/2015/1594. Chapter 4 draws from 'Follow the Money? Value Theory & Social Inquiry', *Ephemera: Theory & Politics in Organization*, 14(3), 2014. Finally, in addition to those works listed above, Chap. 9 also draws on 'Form-Giving Fire: Creative Industries as Marx's "Work of Combustion" and the Distinction Between Productive and Unproductive Labour', in E. Fisher and C. Fuchs, eds., *Reconsidering Value and Labour in the Digital Age*, London: Palgrave Macmillan, 2015. I would like to thank the publishers of these works for permission, where applicable, to replicate elements of them here, and the editors and reviewers of those earlier works for their comments, criticisms and suggestions.

A number of the chapters in their various iterations benefited from presentation and discussion at conferences, workshops and other events over the course of the last five years. Needless to say, any flaws or faults remaining are mine and mine alone.

Chapter 4 was first presented at The Politics of Workers' Inquiry, an ephemera conference at the University of Essex, on 2nd May 2013, and again at the International Initiative for Promoting Political Economy conference at the International Institute of Social Studies in The Hague, 9th July 2013. I would like to thank David Bailey for inviting me to talk about the resulting paper that appears, in part, as Chap. 4, at the Conference of Socialist Economists Midlands Reading Group, University of Birmingham, on 14th September 2015.

Chapter 6 was illuminated by a brief conversation, at Plan C's Fast Forward festival in Edale in September 2015, with Mark Fisher, who I cannot claim to have known but who, in the few minutes we spoke, changed the way I thought about issues covered in that chapter and those that follow. Chapter 7 was presented in earlier iterations at a publication workshop hosted by the International Initiative for Promoting Political Economy at the University of Westminster in September 2016, as a working paper receiving detailed feedback from Stuart Shields and Juan Grigera. Its argument was also recapitulated at a special symposium on Marx's Fragment on Machines at the International Labour Process Conference, University of Sheffield, 5th April 2017. Thanks to Paul Thompson for organising.

Chapter 8 was presented in an earlier form at the London Conference in Critical Thought, at Royal Holloway, University of London, on 7th June 2013. Earlier versions of Chap. 9 were presented at two events under the auspices of the EU COST Action for Dynamics of Virtual Work. a workshop on Marx's Theory of Value in the Digital Age at the Open University of Israel on 16th June 2014, organised by Christian Fuchs and Eran Fisher, with useful comments from Kylie Jarrett and Bruce Robinson, among others; and a conference, The Transformation of Labour in a Digital Global Economy, at Hertfordshire Business School on 5th September 2015. Thanks to Ursula Huws and Andrea Fumagalli in particular for their feedback on the paper presented. Chapter 9 also profited from comments at two others conferences: Historical Materialism at SOAS, University of London, on 9th November 2014, and Capitalism, Culture and the Media, a conference at the School of Media and Communication, University of Leeds. Thanks to David Hesmondhalgh for his feedback at the latter. Finally, the discussion of Marx's Capital in Chap. 9, along with a lot else in this book, owes a lot to a programme of reading groups hosted by the Critisticuffs/ Kittens collective in London over 2013, from which I learnt a great deal.

Overviews of the whole project, including early results of an empirical study exploring the theoretical implications, have been given in a number of invited presentations. These include a workshop on Marx's critique of political economy at the Academy of Management conference in Anaheim, California, on 5th August 2016, for which I would like to thank Patrizia Zanoni; a special session on Value and Employment Relations at the Work, Employment and Society conference, University of Leeds, 7th September 2016, for which I would like to thank Matt Cole; and a seminar in the Fairness at Work Research Centre Seminar Series, at Manchester Business School on 22nd February 2017, for which I would like to thank Jenny Rodriguez. I have also had the opportunity to spend time discussing some of the book's arguments with Jon Cruddas, Maurice Glasman, Adrian Pabst and others at a series of seminars at the Houses of Parliament and Churchill College, University of Cambridge, over the course of 2016 and 2017, for which I would like to thank the Graduate School at the University of Bath for their financial support in attending.

Finally, I would like to thank my partner, my parents, my parents-in-law and our growing family for their indispensable moral, material and emotional support with work they always implicitly understood I had to do, even when they didn't quite understand what it was I was doing. This book is dedicated to their newest addition, welcomed into the world between manuscript submission and proofs.

CONTENTS

CHAPTER 1

Introduction: Marxian Value Theory in New Times

At the end of the last decade, Steffen Boehm and Chris Land observed that '[t]he question of measure has become a hotly debated topic' among heterodox Marxists. This debate centred on the claim 'that today's labour is "beyond measure" or "immeasurable"' (2009, p. 90). On one side were postoperaists like Hardt and Negri (2001, 2004), who argued that the rise of 'immaterial labour' (Lazzarato 1996) based on creativity, communication and cognition had sparked a 'crisis of measurability' simultaneous with a crisis in the law of value and the redundancy of the Marxian theory of value that conceptualises it. On the other were those autonomists like Caffentzis (2013) who argued for its persistence on the basis of a defence of the traditional labour theory of value (hereafter LTOV).

Taking a different route through these questions, this book brings new theoretical resources to the understanding of what is at stake in this debate. The debates Boehm and Land recount from the time pre-existed the Anglophone ascendancy of the New Reading of Marx (NRM), a revisionist reading of value theory based on new exegetical work on Marx's manuscripts. The NRM overhauls how we think about the relationship between value, labour and their measure, providing the tools to overcome any purported crisis of measurability associated with changes in the immediate form of labour.

This renewed and critical Marxism finds a way past the impasse of autonomist debates around the crises of measurability and the law of value to craft an account of why measurement still matters in contemporary capitalism. The book comes at a time when the uptake of postoperaist

© The Author(s) 2018   1
F.H. Pitts, *Critiquing Capitalism Today*, Marx, Engels, and Marxisms.
DOI 10.1007/978-3-319-62633-8_1

ideas in popular left 'postcapitalist' literature is gathering apace. The idea that capitalism can fall apart owing to a collapse in its capacity to capture value in existing frameworks of measure is the source of much 'wishful thinking' (Thompson 2005). But rethinking value, labour and how they are measured, the NRM offers us thinking that is not wishful, but critical. This book shows how.

1.1 New Directions in Marxian Value Theory

The book sits at the theoretical meeting point of two revisionist strands that challenge the traditional understanding of value, but in different ways. They lay divergent stresses on certain parts of Marx's output. In common, they reject the ideological monoliths erected of Marx's work in the last century. They emphasise instead what is unfinished, fragmentary and open to reconstruction. They do so distinctly, however. One cites empirical reasons for its specific and selective reading of Marx. The other does so exegetically.

The first is postoperaismo. In the Italian 1960s and 1970s, its forerunner, operaismo, focused on the factory as the locus of capitalist society. Postoperaismo, however, situated the factory in society as a whole. This theoretical switch was informed by an empirical understanding of changes afoot in production. They focused on the shift towards 'immaterial labour' (Lazzarato 1996). This rises with the service sector, creative industries and so-called knowledge economy. Postoperaists brought this empirical understanding to a reading of Marx's *Grundrisse* (1993). The *Grundrisse* were a series of notebooks for what would later become *Capital* (1976a). Their availability in English and Italian offered elements of an unorthodox Marx. Specifically, postoperaists seized on one part of the *Grundrisse*, the 'Fragment on Machines'. The scenario Marx paints in this led postoperaists to posit a crisis in the law of value his wider theory describes. Significantly, they use a revolutionary new Marx derived from long-unpublished notebooks to suggest his key theory's exhaustion. From the Fragment, they derive a vision of an incipient communism realised in the shell of capitalism. This vision, we shall see, wields political influence today. A new generation of postoperaist-inspired dreamers begin from the same few pages of Marx.

The second is the NRM, with which we can also associate a descendent, Open Marxism, with which we will also engage in this book. Postoperaismo cites empirical reasons for its specific and selective reading of Marx. But the NRM takes an exegetical approach. It originates in Germany, around the same time as operaismo. Scholars under Adorno's tutelage began scrutinising Marx's published and unpublished manuscripts (Bellofiore and Riva 2015). This close study showed the progression of Marx's value theory as it appears in *Capital*. Constantly revised and honed, in the procession of working drafts new complexities shone through. This exegesis extracts from the development of Marx's work a reconstruction of his value theory. The central insight is that value relates not to expended concrete labour as in orthodox accounts. Rather, it relates to abstract labour. This is a category of social mediation expressed in money. It springs from the exchange of commodities by means of money in the sphere of circulation. Thus, for the NRM, the *Grundrisse* here plays a much lesser role than *Capital*. And there is less consideration of empirical factors than we find in postoperaist literature. Focus falls instead upon the general laws of how capitalism proceeds through a series of social forms.

Thus, both postoperaismo and the NRM radically challenge received Marxist wisdom around value. The former comes to bury it using the *Grundrisse* and new empirical facts. The latter, bearing the first volume of *Capital*, buries only one form of it – the labour theory of value (LTOV). In its place, it establishes an alternative 'value theory of labour' (Elson 1979). On one hand, postoperaismo foretells the demise of the law of value and its theory. NRM, on the other hand, maintains their persistence, in radically rethought forms. The two schools are seldom treated together. This book is an occasion to do so.

1.2   The New Reading of Marx

The NRM can be thought of as something like 'the critique of political economy as a critical social theory' (Bellofiore and Riva 2015). As a critical social theory, and not a theory 'of' society, the critique of political economy assaults what Adorno and Horkheimer call, in the *Dialectic of Enlightenment* (1972, p. 205), 'ticket-thinking' that thinks *about* things as given, rather than *through* them as forms of socially and historically grounded relations. As such it asks why the content of life under capital should assume the forms it does (Bonefeld 2014, p. 58). This differentiates it from extant mainstream and Marxist approaches. Taking inspiration from Adorno's 'Seminar Mitschrift' on the critique of political economy (1997), the NRM might best be described as adopting a Frankfurt School-informed perspective on Marx based on the exegetical revisiting of his manuscripts for *Capital*. This dispels the myth that Adorno had no value-theoretical or political-economic component to his work, a subject to which he increasingly turned his attention towards the end of his life (Bonefeld 2016b; see Jay 1973, p. 152; Habermas 1983, p. 109 and Braunstein 2011 for the opposing view).

At the NRM's inception were two students of Adorno, Hans-Georg Backhaus and Helmut Reichelt (see Backhaus 1992, 2005; Reichelt 2005). As Bellofiore and Riva explain, '[b]oth Backhaus and Reichelt date the birth of the NRM to Backhaus stumbling upon a copy of the first edition of *Capital* in the library in 1963' (2015, p. 25). However, Reichelt has claimed, this 'would have had no consequences if it happened to someone who had not attended Adorno's lectures on the dialectical theory of society'. This combination of Marxology and a commitment to the subject–object dialectic were to structure the NRM thereafter, and specifically its approach to the issue of social constitution and social validation, best synthesized in the work of Werner Bonefeld. In particular, this involves a turn to the section on the commodity fetishism as not incidental but central to Marx's work and the tradition of critical theory as a whole, after a fashion which saw, for instance, Althusser notoriously recommend that one could skip the first three chapters when reading *Capital* for the first time (2001 [1971], p. 52).

Instead of taking the relationship between labour and value at face value, as has traditional Marxism, it is *abstract* labour, and not concrete practical human activity, to which the NRM holds value to relate. This is a crucial difference between this new interpretation of Marx (which itself has its roots in the earlier work of Isaac Rubin (1972)) and the traditional orthodoxy of Marx-interpretation, which emphasises concrete, practical labour as the source of value, rather than the source of the particular thing that 'carries' value (Arthur 2013, p. 104). From this perspective, the commodity is more than just a product of labour. Commodity status, and the arbitration of the value that attaches to commodities, is taken to rest in exchange.

In this, the specificity of the concrete labour that contributed to the production of a given thing carrying value must be negated so as to render that thing equivalent and exchangeable with other things. Thus also the activity that grants this specificity – concrete labour – must be abstracted from it. It is money that renders this service. Money establishes a measure of abstract human labour in general, responsible for producing exchangeable things in general. The measure – money – brings this abstract labour into existence, in the exchange of commodities.

The 'labour-time' that is central here is not time worked but time represented in a certain amount of money – the 'socially necessary labour time' (hereafter SNLT) in which things in average conditions are produced

(Arthur 2013). The actual labour as it is worked succeeds or fails based on whether it produces goods above, beyond or in line with this socially necessary standard, which is expressed in the going price of a commodity. Whether the work that takes place is socially necessary or not is arbitrated in the successful exchange of the product of labour as a commodity by means of money. This can depend on whether other capitalists overproduced a given commodity, for instance. Marx writes that

> The labour-time socially necessary to produce [value-bearing commodities] asserts itself as a regulative law of nature. In the same way, the law of gravity asserts itself when a person's house collapses on top of him. (1976b, p. 78)

But, in generating the conditions for such a crisis, this is not as natural as it seems, but rather socially constituted through human practice – that is through the process of exchange, the social relation of value. Social necessity is not something specific to the labour itself – the validity of the economic category does not hold in abstraction from society – but is established socially through the abstract relation of all things with all other things, in monetary exchange. This socially validates the private labour that went into their production as social and value-producing. This is arbitrated in exchange. Value arises from the meeting of commodities by means of money. As Bellofiore and Riva write,

> It is not possible to determine prior to actual exchange the amount of the immediately private labour expended in production that will obtain the form of money; that is, that will be validated as mediately social. (2015, p. 31)

But the crucial step that the social constitution critique of economic categories makes is that these socially mediate forms are rooted in real relations of antagonism, coercion, domination and dispossession – in other words, in 'concrete society'. As Marx writes of the commodity fetish, the money form, whilst abstract, contains within it the concrete roots of its creation:

> It is precisely this finished form of the world of commodities – the money form – which conceals the social character of private labour and the social relations between the individual workers, by making those relations appear as relations between material objects, instead of revealing them plainly. (1976c, p. 78)

It is this focus on how the social forms assumed by the results of productive activity in capitalist society express the antagonistic social relations therein that is the focus of this book, a focus true to the original spirit of Marx's critique of political economy recast in its most forgiving light: as a critical theory of society.

1.3   THE RISE OF POSTOPERAISMO

Pressingly for the present time, in recasting Marx in this way, my book tussles with the legacy of postoperaismo, specifically as it has been popularised by Negri and his theoretical inheritors since the paperback publication of Hardt and Negri's *Empire* (2001). *Empire* was 'academia's version of a blockbuster', described as a once-in-a-decade 'intellectual event' (Passavant and Dean 2003, p. 2). Its analysis of world power chimed with the tumult of globalisation. After the first run sold out, Harvard University Press hastily unleashed a mass-market paperback edition (Vuillamy 2001). With *Multitude* (2004) and *Commonwealth* (2009), *Empire* came to constitute part of a loose trilogy, its arguments gaining new resonances as the decade progressed. The theorisation of 'multitude' as a political actor became a go-to idea for a generation of activists 'reared on their Hardt and Negri' (Mason 2011). *Empire*'s release secured peak visibility for the rich tradition of Italian *postoperaismo*, sparking a continuing debate about class, power, strategy and the changing face of labour at the commencement of the twenty-first century (Balakrishnan 2003; Passavant and Dean 2003).

Bringing to light Italian radical left discussions about 'immaterial labour' (Lazzarato 1996), it challenged conventional Marxist understandings of work in capitalist society. Importantly, it disputed the relevance of Marx's LTOV. However, as Kicillof and Starosta (2007, p. 31, n. 4) suggest, postoperaismo's autonomist lineage rarely addresses contemporary debates in Marxian value theory such as those covered in Part I of this book. Although Hardt and Negri's 'rejection of the contemporary relevance of the law of value' implies dialogue, postoperaismo in the wake of *Empire* seldom engages with cutting-edge re-readings of Marx's value theory in the NRM, and vice versa. This book bridges this divide.

The book takes as its starting point an argument posed by the postoperaists. Those making it include Antonio Negri, Carlo Vercellone and Christian Marazzi. The argument centres on the 'immaterial' character of contemporary labour. Immaterial labour, it contends, produces an immeasurable plenitude of value. This arises through the immanently self-organised cooperativity of labourers themselves. This takes place outside the confines of the capitalist working day. It happens spontaneously, without the need for capitalist imposition or control. Owing to this, the value it creates is beyond both capture and measure. This, postoperaists contend, creates a 'crisis of measurability' for capital (Marazzi 2008). This crisis renders the law of value obsolete. By extension, it renders the theory of value Marx uses to understand it obsolete in turn.

1.4 What Does It Mean to Be Critical?

I contest this perspective using an approach derived from critical theory. Whereas traditional theory 'presupposes what needs to be explained' (Bonefeld 2016b, p. 236) – society or economic categories, for instance – critical theory 'develops from actual, given relations of life the forms in which they have become apotheosized' (Marx, quoted by Bonefeld 2016b, p. 236). Bonefeld writes that Marx uses 'the critique of economic categories' in order to reveal 'their origin in the social relations of production', in hunger, violence and so forth. The distinction between traditional and critical theory impacts upon how we conceptualise the aims of research. It suggests that, instead of finding 'proof', the true commitment of critical research is to negate. Traditional theory 'analyses the empirical veracity of incomprehensible economic forces' (2016a, p. 65). Critical theory, on the other hand, negates 'the whole sphere [they] move in' (Adorno 1990, p. 197). Rather than seeking positivistic 'proof' of hypotheses or the 'correct answer' to research questions, my approach engages in a negative critique of the economic objectivity assumed by social relations in capitalist society. The aim is to capture, by means of an analysis of appearances, the essence that, according to Hegel, 'must appear' in those appearances (Adorno 1974). This is a critical and, crucially, dialectical operation, capable of dealing with a world outside proof, where things can be two things at once, and the true is a moment of the false and vice versa.

The means by which I unpick the appearances of economic objectivity is through a critical approach informed by the NRM, roughly comprising two strands. The first, including theorists like Michael Heinrich (2012) and Chris Arthur (2013), takes the law of value to relate principally to the abstraction of labour in the production and exchange of commodities. This differs from the traditionalist LTOV which stresses labour's expenditure. The NRM generates theoretical resources with which to critique the postoperaist conceptualisation of a 'crisis of measurability'. It reveals that postoperaismo employs a traditionalist application of the LTOV only to refute it. Postoperaismo has no conception of the process of abstraction by which labours enter into relation. Only by reducing Marxist value theory to the study of concrete labour and its measurement can it make the claim that the process it describes is in crisis. The second strand is Open Marxism, here represented in the work of Werner Bonefeld (2014) and John Holloway (2002, 2010). This describes how abstract labour stems, practically and historically, from antagonistic social relations of production. This facilitates a critique of the intersecting portrayals in postoperaist and bourgeois accounts of immaterial labour as an unconflicted space of unburdened creativity. We will return to this by means of Bonefeld's critique of certain aspects of the NRM in Chap. 5.

The NRM supplies the tools to perceive the practices and larger context in which the abstraction of labour occurs. The NRM provides resources for the study of the unfolding process of social validation whereby abstract labour time productive of value is ideally and retrospectively conjured at various points of the circuit of capital, culminating in the successful exchange of the commodified good or service. This necessitates close attention to the movements of measurement, valuation and abstraction that take place as the concrete specificity of performed labour is abstracted from in the simultaneous constitution of both value and its measure, value-producing abstract labour-time. In this book I suggest that, whilst this process culminates in the successful sale of a good or service as a commodity, there are tentative points within the realm of production at which this abstraction reveals itself in an anticipatory form, before it assumes the guise of a real abstraction in society at large.

The abstractions constructed around labour-time within the labour process are necessary for various reasons. Following the accounts of Arthur (2013) and Sohn-Rethel (1978) surveyed in Chap. 4, the practical abstraction of one unit of measure – time – above all others enables capitalist enterprises to complete several imperatives. It allows them and their investors and clients to compare like with like. It allows the commensuration of their work with other enterprises. It allows the rationalisation and restructuring of work and disciplining of workers. And it measures the speed with which a job is completed and the good or service it renders sent to market.

Open Marxism suggests how these processes connect with antagonistic relations of domination and resistance. By focusing on these antagonisms, the persistence of capitalist social relations in the new world of work is brought to light. This allows us to see contemporary labour – or so-called 'immaterial labour' – as a site of struggle. Problematising it in this way disrupts its appropriation as a harbinger of a more pleasurable and enjoyable future world of work. It still remains subsumed within the antagonistic social relations of capitalist production. It is still beholden to the abstract economic compulsions of the social rule of value.

The book thus brings clarification to a crowded theoretical field. Marx's value theory has for some time struggled against its adherents. Weaponised for worker power, its analysis wavers. Traditionally, it has been taken to theorise the link between expended labour-time and surplus-value. The rendition goes something like this. Workers, with every hour, create value. Part of this is necessary for the worker. What is not, accrues as surplus to the capitalist. Read this way, it wielded a long but limited efficacy in mobilising workers politically. Or, at least, it falsely reassured them they were more powerful than they were in reality. Today, as we shall see, a new generation of Marxisant theorists make similar claims under a cloak of false anti-productivism. But, luckily, other Marxes are available. It is the contrast between two such competing visions of Marx and his work that I explore here.

1.5   THIS BOOK'S CONTRIBUTION

Within the literature on Marxian value theory, the book stands as a significant contribution steeped in the most contemporary and radical re-readings of Marxian thought. My theoretical framework is broadly informed by a critical approach to Marxian value theory. I bring together in critical reflection two contemporary schools of Marxian scholarship. On one side, value-form theory, incorporating the NRM and, to a lesser extent, Open Marxism. And, on the other, postoperaismo. They have seldom entered into dialogue. My emphasis, in bringing them together in dissensus, is less upon a traditional 'labour' theory of value than upon the process by which different concrete labours are brought into a relationship of abstract equivalence with one another in the exchange of goods and services as commodities. Rather than focus purely upon the workplace as the arena in which value is determined, then, my argument situates the determination of value on a continuum which culminates with its measure in the moment of exchange, the point at which a price is assigned to something.

From this basis, my critique opens out onto the future of work, inducing pessimism as to postcapitalist alternatives based on reduced working hours or a basic income. In this, the study is motivated by the recent rise to prominence postoperaismo enjoys. It wields more influence on left political thinking than ever. This gives us cause to use the NRM as a sharp tool with which to cut through some of the wilful leaps of faith it makes. There is a pressing political necessity to once again uncover alternative ways of reading Marx. New orthodoxies have sprung up in place of the old, and postoperaismo is one.

More stimulating politically, postoperaismo has had a much longer Anglophone exposure than the NRM. It has filtered through into public discourse in a largely unspoken and often unknowing way. Postoperaist ideas weave themselves seamlessly into the fabric of left policymaking. Their popularisation in works such as Paul Mason's *Postcapitalism* (2015) and Nick Srnicek and Alex Williams's *Inventing the Future* (2015) carries them from the radical fringe to the mainstream. As I will show, this prospectus produces an impoverished analysis. But, more pressingly, it produces an impoverished politics. As Noys writes, 'theoretical interventions…also function…as forms of political practice' (2012, p. 4). From wrong-headed philosophical illusions stem perverted and unsuccessful modes of praxis. This is important now. Many of the impetuses of this new politics are present in Negri. By critiquing the latter, they provide resources for critiquing the former.

1.6   Ideology Critique as Social Critique

In the chapters that comprise this book, I interrogate the claims made by postoperaists about immaterial labour and the crisis of measurability as ideas the critique of which opens out upon the critique of the society they seek to grasp. This unity of theory and practice is suggestively delineated by Richard Gunn. According to Gunn (1989), rather than posing the question as to whether such-and-such is true, critical theory poses the question as to what truth itself *is*, and interrogates the validity of the categories upon which truth judgements are made. Therefore, philosophical questions can be said to deal with matters at a 'metatheoretical' level, or what Gunn calls a second- or higher-order type of reasoning. Distinct from this is the 'theoretical' level of the first-order, or empirical, kind of reasoning. The two work in conjunction. If first-order theory was to validate its own categories of truth, then, Gunn suggests, a 'vicious circularity' would result. The recourse to second-order 'meta-theory' bypasses this circularity. However, this does not avoid a second pitfall: *infinite regress*, whereby the second-order meta-theory itself needs validation from a third-order theory, and this by a fourth-order theory, and so on and on ad infinitum. Gunn contends that this dilemma can be circumvented in an alternative model of theorising, in which theorising is both theoretical and metatheoretical, and first- and second-order, '*at the same time*'. As Gunn suggests, this approach overcomes both vicious circularity and infinite regress, interrogating its own truth claims by questioning the validity of its categories and interrogating the validity of its categories at the altar of its truth claims (Gunn 1989, pp. 3–4).

It is exactly this mode of theorisation that is found in what Gunn calls 'Marx's theoretical 'totalisation'.' For Gunn, philosophy's separation of theory and metatheory into distinct spheres of intellectual activity was reconciled by Marx through his engagement with Hegel. The main grounds upon which this reconciliation is effected is by means of the denial that metatheory presents some separate 'conceptual realm' completely divorced from the first-order and empirical. Rather, from the Hegelian-Marxist perspective, practice is that to which theory *belongs*. The latter is a moment of the former. Gunn attributes to this Hegelian-Marxist reconciliation something he labels '*practical reflexivity*'. This is where theory reflects upon the validity of its categories with recourse to practice itself. In practically reflexive theorising, then, the theorising itself is included within the scope of the theorisation and is therefore its *object*, and the validity of its categories is self-analysed within the context of the social situatedness of its own existence as *practice*. Therefore, the three conceptual moves involved – theorisation of the object, theorisation of its presence within the object, and reflection upon the validity of its categories – are not separate stages of theorisation, but form a single simultaneous totality. Each element impacts upon the other, with consideration of the object immediately and at once consideration of the presence *within* that object as a 'totality of social practice'. Reflection upon the latter totality is therefore also reflection upon the truth criteria through which the social totality is understood. In this way, 'to raise metatheoretical questions is to raise social questions', and vice versa (1989, pp. 4–8).

It is the theoretical/empirical quality of the abstractions that concern us that requires a practically reflexive, dually theoretical and metatheoretical approach, whereby the categories of truth are taken to be categories of the object of study and vice versa (Gunn 1992, p. 23). Gunn discusses this approach in terms of the necessity of both *first*- and *third-person perspectives*, whereby the determinate abstraction is third-person as 'part of a determinate social world which. . .goes on existing whether it is theorised or not', and first-person in that it can be 'engaged with and understood' (1992, p. 21). It is such a mode of 'determinate abstraction' that makes possible immanent critique. As Gunn writes, '[d]eterminate abstraction's understanding of abstractions as *socially existing* allows it to mount an ideology-critique which is directly, and at the same time, social critique. To criticise ideas *just is* to criticise political relations; and conversely' (1992, p. 22). This is important now, at a time wherein postoperaist ideas are being mobilised politically, in the UK at least, like never before, and wielding an influence in policymakers in the process. By critiquing the ideas the world has about itself, we can critique that world in turn.

Critique need not be explicitly morally committed to one or another group of social actors, then, in order to constitute what Harry Cleaver calls a 'political' reading (2000) situated in the 'urgencies of the class struggle' that Gunn suggests are susceptible to an immanent method (1989, p. 14). In this reading, Marx's theory of value is a 'radical negation' of its object (Endnotes 2010). Rather than a 'positivistic presentation of capitalist categories', value theory must instead be thought of as 'their immanent radical critique' (Kurz 1999, pp. 1–2). Value critique conducted on such terms 'moves beyond a positive account of the concrete determination of profits, and becomes part of a critique of the very structure of possibilities in the existing society' (Wright 1981, p. 74). Thus, we can restate Gunn's assertion that ideology critique is immediately and at once social critique with the addendum that the reverse, too is true: social critique offers the possibility of revolutionary political critique. It is such a critique that ultimately constitutes the method employed to review the literature presented in this book.

1.7   CHAPTER OUTLINES

Following this introduction, in the first chapter proper, Chap. 2, I chart how, from a singular theory of value constituting a cornerstone of Marxist thought, today multiple and plural interpretations of this theory resemble shifting sands beneath it. The debate is complex, but strong polarisations may be derived from it that lend themselves to broad characterisations. This chapter maps these theoretical polarisations and the alternative positions of possible reconciliation that lie between them. First, the development of Marx's theory of value is surveyed. Second, its interpretations are grouped into two main overarching schools, traditional and value-form. The latter, it is suggested, presents a more satisfactory and consistent way forward for the Marxian theory of value. Tracing a tradition of thought stemming from the earlier work of I.I. Rubin, this section assesses the claim of the NRM for Marx's theory of value as an inherently monetary theory of value rather than the traditionalist 'labour' theory of value held by most orthodox interpretations of Marx's work.

Chapter 3 looks at what Christian Lotz calls the 'capitalist schema', drawing on the work of Kant, Sohn-Rethel and Adorno to theorise how our relationship with the world is ordered and mediated through monetary value. Proceeding further with a monetary theory of value outlined in Chap. 2, in Chap. 3 I set out what precisely is meant by this 'monetary' status, and the particular kinds of 'real abstraction' the exchange relation implies. In subsequent chapters, we will explore the antagonistic concrete social relations this monetary abstraction contains in their negation, owing, as we shall see, to the radical state of dispossession whereby we cannot live except through the wage.

Chapter 4 conceptualises Marxian value theory as a problem for social research to investigate. The chapter takes the positions developed in the previous chapters forward into a synthesis and reconceptualisation of value theory adequate to investigation through social research. It reflects upon how the theory of value developed might be taken as the basis of a programme of social research. It is argued that so conceptualised, value can only be encountered by the study of the 'totality of social relations' in capitalist society, inside the workplace and outside in the market. It thus suggests a way of conceptualising the theory of value as an object of research. It is contended that such research requires the study of the different 'modes of existence' that value takes over the course of the production of commodities and their circulation in society. An approach is put forward inspired by feminist research into the 'life trajectory of the commodity', which incorporates the full totality of capitalist social relations into a broad and wide-ranging study of the different modes of existence taken by value both inside and outside the workplace, in production and circulation.

To clarify the object of study in a programme of research around questions of value, labour and abstraction, in Chap. 5, I draw on Werner Bonefeld's Open Marxist critique of the NRM to advance an interpretation whereby the abstract unfolding of value theorised by the NRM is rooted in antagonistic social relations of production. The combination of the NRM's monetary theory of value and Bonefeld's 'ad hominem critique of political economy' (2014, 2016a, b) which sees the supersensible world of value through the sensuousness of the actual conditions of life sharpens a double-edged critical sword with which to cut open postoperaist ideas around the redundancy of the law of value and the 'crisis of measurability' sparked by the advent of so-called 'immaterial labour' in Part 2. I close Chap. 5 with a brief discussion of the role of class as the central contradiction contributing to crisis tendencies in Heinrich's rereading of Marx's crisis theory. Against traditional Marxist accounts that stress the falling rate of profit as the key explanator of crisis, centring class shifts our focus towards the constrained capacity to consume enforced by continually reproduced conditions of dispossession, and the propensity of capitalist enterprises to produce in excess of this, generating unsold inventories unable to attain commodity status in exchange. We pick this thread up again at the end of Chap. 9, considering the role of the 'immaterial labour' found in fields such as advertising in helping remedy the contradictions associated with capitalism's confined social basis.

Beginning Part 2, and moving to the critique of postoperaismo, Chap. 6 critiques the trajectory of Antonio Negri's work since the late 1970s. It identifies a shift from Marx to Spinoza as the source of a series of problematic positions. These relate to the understanding of the possibilities and production of change under capitalism. And they owe to the absence of a proper critique of political economy. My critique focuses on how Negri posits change as subject to the multitude's immanent relationship with global power. In so doing, he rejects dialectics, mediation and transcendence as analytical principles. Adopting the 'critique of political economy as a critical theory of society' (hereafter CPECTS), I argue that these are necessary to grasp the continuing dominance of capitalist economic categories. Contrary to Negri, human practice is imbued not with any immanent, revolutionary positivity. Rather, its results are abstracted from and turned against us. The forms they assume, in value, money and commodities, dominate its doers. This negativity Negri's neo-Spinozism lacks.

Chapter 7 critiques the purposes to which Marx's Fragment on Machines is put in postoperaist thought. Changes in labour lead proponents to posit a crisis of measurability and an incipient communism. I contest the postoperaist positing of the existing realisation of the Fragment. Postoperaists elide the persistence of the real abstraction of value, covered also in Chap. 8, and the social relations of production it expresses and proceeds through. I challenge the assertion that the crisis and redundancy of value associated with the Fragment is realised. This is because we still, in a contradictory way turned against us, subsist through the value-form. Where postoperaists see a 'communism of capital' (Beverungen et al. 2013) already existing, I contend that we live, work, starve and suffer still under its rule. This alternative strand of Marxist theorising brings its full horror home. But recognition of this negativity is necessary to develop the theoretical and practical tools to overcome it, conceptually and politically.

Chapter 8 critiques postoperaist conceptualisations of immaterial labour from the perspective of Marxian value-form theory. Critiquing the idea of the 'crisis of measurability' catalysed by immaterial labour and the contention that this makes redundant the law of value, it contests the novelty, immediate abstractness and immeasurable productivity postoperaists attribute to contemporary labour using the NRM. The chapter explores this theoretical conflict, asserting that postoperaismo refutes Marx's value theory only insofar as it holds a productivist understanding of value to begin with. The immaterial labour thesis brings into dispute only a traditional, orthodox LTOV. The conditions it describes leave intact the abstract law of value by which capitalism operates. Theorists of immaterial labour are correct to say that the LTOV is redundant. Indeed, it was ever thus. Capital has always struggled in its attempts to render human labour productive against a 'crisis' of measurability. But it is abstract labour that enters into and sustains the social relationship of value, more so than that expended in the realm of production. Thus, capital has always faced the immateriality of the process of abstraction as a potential crisis of measurability. In this way, the existence of immaterial labour poses no threat to critical reinterpretations of value theory such as the NRM. An approach to value oriented around the 'social validation' of abstract labour places little importance on the possibility or impossibility of the quantification of working hours (Heinrich 2012). This approach transcends the crisis of measurability posited in the postoperaist literature. It conceives of such a crisis as a permanent and in no way novel feature of valorisation.

Using this social validation perspective to explore a closer analytical case study of a sector central to the debates covered in Part 2, Chap. 9 takes on postoperaist claims about work in the creative industries as an immeasurably productive form of immaterial labour. In so doing I extend the insight, drawing on the presentation of the 'capitalist schema' in Chap 3, that the culture industry makes possible the exchange abstraction. I contest the implicit judgements of productive and unproductive labour made by postoperaists such as Andrea Fumagalli on this point, going further and stronger in the powers ascribed to fields in which 'immaterial labour' is hegemonic. These include advertising, branding and graphic design. In so doing, this chapter considers the role played in the production of value by the labour that takes place in the 'sphere of circulation'. It applies Heinrich's conceptualisation of 'social validation' to these sectors. This suggests that valorisation depends upon goods and services attaining commodity status by selling for money. Value is subject to this validation. The capitalist use of advertising, graphic design and branding guarantees the possibility of this validation. Using Heinrich, the chapter re-evaluates claims made about the creative industries and cognate fields in three main respects. First, it exposes as inadequate certain Marxist understandings of productive and unproductive labour and the place of circulation activities within this distinction. Second, it refutes claims as to the immeasurability of immaterial labour and the redundancy of the law of value. Third, it suggests that creative industries possess a significant role in a capitalist economy blighted by a necessity towards the overproduction of commodities. I argue that these practices, traditionally seen as peripheral to the production of value, may actually be indispensable to it. This claim is based on a rereading of the discussion of productive and unproductive labour found in Marx's most direct treatment of the question of circulation work as 'the work of combustion' in *Capital* Volume 2. I close the chapter by returning to the conceptualisation of crisis set out at the end of Part 1, in Chap. 5. I assess the extent to which 'circulation' activities like those found in the creative industries contribute to the attempts of capitalist enterprises to realise the latent value of overproduced inventories in times of crisis.

I conclude by linking this analysis into a wider challenge to currently popular ideas around technology and the future of work. Contemporary immaterial labour is taken to epitomise technological transformations on which the future is said to hinge. But the ascription of these powers to contemporary work misunderstands its continuing status within frameworks of capitalist valorisation, domination and exploitation. I suggest no utopia attends it. The optimistic 'postcapitalist' perspective rests on a misunderstanding of where value comes from, and what the relationship is between the economic activity that takes place in production and the abstract forms of economic objectivity this creativity results in. The critical Marxist account given here opposes the liberatory narratives presented in mainstream accounts of the rise of immaterial labour and the impulses of self-actualisation it is taken to reflect. It also opposes the resonant discourses present in postoperaist accounts and their modern proponents, which envision a world of work in which a creative multitude self-actualises unencumbered by the capitalistic demands of industrial factory labour. Postoperaist accounts of immaterial labour's liberatory potential, when applied to contemporary work, dovetail with mainstream accounts of changing capitalism. Addressing my work to this context, I close by critiquing utopian visions that see in immaterial labour a template. In its current form, whatever potential it possesses exists only in denial. Struggle must ensue to recapture creative human activity from this. Ultimately, I conclude, capitalist development will not deliver us utopia. Critical thinking, and not wishful thinking, is our only resource.

Bibliography

Adorno, T.W. 1974. Commitment. *New Left Review* I/87-88: 75–89.
———. 1990. *Negative Dialectics.* Trans. E.B. Ashton. London: Routledge.
———. 1997. Seminar Mitschrift of 1962. Appendix to Backhaus. In *Dialektik der Wertform*, 501–512. Freiburg: Ca Ira.
Adorno, T.W., and M. Horkheimer. 1972. *Dialectic of Enlightenment.* London: Verso.
Althusser, L. 2001 [1971]. Preface to Capital Volume One. In *Lenin and Philosophy and Other Essays*, 45–70. New York: Monthly Review Press.
Arthur, C. 2013. The Practical Truth of Abstract Labour. In *Marx's Laboratory: Critical Interpretations of the Grundrisse*, ed. R. Bellofiore, G. Starosta, and P. Thomas, 101–120. Leiden: Brill.
Backhaus, H.-G. 1992. Between Philosophy and Science: Marxian Social Economy as Critical Theory. In *Open Marxism Volume 1: Dialectics and History*, ed. W. Bonefeld, R. Gunn, and K. Psychopedis, 54–92. London: Pluto Press.
———. 2005. Some Aspects of Marx's Concept of Critique in the Context of His Economic-Philosophical Theory. In *Human Dignity: Social Autonomy and the Critique of Capitalism*, ed. W. Bonefeld and K. Psychopedis, 13–30. Aldershot: Ashgate.
Balakrishnan, G., ed. 2003. *Debating Empire.* London: Verso.
Bellofiore, R., and T.R. Riva. 2015. The Neue Marx-Lekture: Putting the Critique of Political Economy Back into the Critique of Society. *Radical Philosophy* 189: 24–36.
Beverungen, A., A.-M. Murtola, and G. Schwartz. 2013. The Communism of Capital? *Ephemera* 13 (3): 483–495.
Boehm, S., and C. Land. 2009. No Measure for Culture? Value in the New Economy. *Capital & Class* 97: 75–98.
Bonefeld, W. 2014. *Critical Theory and the Critique of Political Economy: On Subversion and Negative Reason.* London: Bloomsbury.
———. 2016a. Negative Dialectics and Critique of Economic Objectivity. *History of the Human Sciences* 29 (2): 60–76.
———. 2016b. Bringing Critical Theory Back in at a Time of Misery: Three Beginnings Without Conclusion. *Capital & Class* 40 (2): 233–244.
Braunstein, D. 2011. *Adornos Kritik der politischen Okonomie.* Bielefeld: Transcript Verlag.

Caffentzis, G. 2013. *In Letters of Blood and Fire: Work, Machines, and Value*. Oakland: PM Press.

Cleaver, H. 2000. *Reading* Capital *Politically*. Edinburgh: AK Press.

Elson, D. 1979. The Value Theory of Labour. In *Value: The Representation of Labour in Capitalism*, ed. D. Elson, 115–180. London: CSE Books.

Endnotes. 2010. Communisation and Value-Form Theory. *Endnotes #2: Misery and the Value-Form*. https://endnotes.org.uk/issues/2/en/endnotes-communisation-and-value-form-theory. Accessed 29 Oct 2016.

Gunn, R. 1989. Marxism and Philosophy: A Critique of Critical Realism. *Capital and Class* 13: 1–30.

———. 1992. Against Historical Materialism: Marxism as First-Order Discourse. In *Open Marxism Volume II: Theory and Practice*, ed. W. Bonefeld, R. Gunn, and K. Psychopedis, 1–45. London: Pluto Press.

Habermas, J. 1983. *Philosophical-Political Profiles*. London: Heinemann.

Hardt, M., and A. Negri. 2001. *Empire*. Cambridge, MA: Harvard University Press.

———. 2004. *Multitude*. London: Penguin.

———. 2009. *Commonwealth*. Cambridge: Harvard University Press.

Heinrich, M. 2012. *An Introduction to the Three Volumes of Karl Marx's* Capital. New York: Monthly Review Press.

Holloway, J. 2002. *Change the World Without Taking Power*. London: Pluto Press.

———. 2010. *Crack Capitalism*. London: Pluto Press.

Jay, M. 1973. *The Dialectical Imagination, A History of the Frankfurt School and the Institute of Social Research, 1923–1950*. London: University of California Press.

Kicillof, A., and G. Starosta. 2007. Value Form and Class Struggle: A Critique of the Autonomist Theory of Value. *Capital and Class* 92: 13–40.

Kurz, R. 1999. Marx 2000. www.exit-online.org. Accessed 7 July 2012.

Lazzarato, M. 1996. Immaterial Labor. In *Radical Thought in Italy*, ed. P. Virno and M. Hardt, 133–150. Minneapolis: University of Minnesota Press.

Marazzi, C. 2008. *Capital and Language*. Los Angeles: Semiotext(e).

Marx, K. 1976a. *Capital*. Vol. I. London: Penguin.

———. 1976b. The Critique of Hegelian Philosophy. In *Critical Sociology*, ed. P. Connerton, 51–72. London: Penguin.

———. 1976c. The Fetishism of Commodities. In *Critical Sociology*, ed. P. Connerton, 73–89. London: Penguin.

———. 1993. *Grundrisse*. London: Penguin.

Mason, P. 2011. Twenty Reasons Why It's Kicking Off Everywhere. *Idle Scrawl*, February 5. http://www.bbc.co.uk/blogs/newsnight/paulmason/2011/02/twenty_reasons_why_its_kicking.html. Accessed 29 Oct 2016.

———. 2015. The End of Capitalism Has Begun. *The Guardian*. July 17. https://www.theguardian.com/books/2015/jul/17/postcapitalism-end-of-capitalism-begun. Accessed 29 Oct 2016.

Noys, B. 2012. *The Persistence of the Negative: A Critique of Contemporary Continental Theory.* Cambridge: Cambridge University Press.

Passavant, P., and J. Dean, eds. 2003. *Empire's New Clothes: Reading Hardt and Negri.* London: Routledge.

Reichelt, H. 2005. Social Reality as Appearance: Some Notes on Marx's Conception of Reality. In *Human Dignity: Social Autonomy and the Critique of Capitalism,* ed. W. Bonefeld and K. Psychopedis, 31–68. Aldershot: Ashgate.

Rubin, I.I. 1972. *Essays on Marx's Theory of Value.* Detroit: Black and Red.

Sohn-Rethel, A. 1978. *Intellectual and Manual Labour: A Critique of Epistemology.* London: Macmillan Press.

Srnicek, N., and A. Williams. 2015. *Inventing the Future.* London: Verso.

Thompson, P. 2005. Foundation and Empire: A Critique of Hardt and Negri. *Capital and Class* 29 (2): 73–98.

Vuillamy E. 2001. Empire Hits Back. *The Observer.* July 15. http://www.theguardian.com/books/2001/jul/15/globalisation.highereducation. Accessed 29 Oct 2016.

Wright, E.O. 1981. Reconsiderations. In *The Value Controversy,* ed. I. Steedman. London: Verso.

PART I

The New Reading of Marx

CHAPTER 2

Value, Time and Abstract Labour

2.1 Introduction

In this chapter I will introduce the central themes of the re-evaluation of Marx's theory of value conducted within the New Reading of Marx (NRM). In so doing, I will run against the grain of traditional Marxism by reading labour and time through value rather than seeing the latter spring from the former. In this way we will start with the delineation of value and then seek its relationship with both the concrete and abstract guises of labour and their temporal measure to which workers are subject in the workplace. The relationship of this to the external context of the market, where value is ultimately arbitrated through commodity exchange, will be touched upon to be picked up again in more detail in Chap. 4. I will begin by situating the NRM's approach to Marx within extant approaches. I will then briefly set out the classical political economists' debates on value and labour – specifically those of Smith and Ricardo – as a foundation for understanding the significance of Marx's critique in this regard. Following this, I will give an outline of the core basics of Marx's theory of value, before turning my attention to the headline innovations of the NRM, posing them against the embodied labour theories of value found in the so-called 'Ricardian' approach of its Marxist forerunners and competitors. This, we shall see, centres on Michael Heinrich's theorisation of the 'social validation' of abstract labour-time as the key principle for explaining how labour can be taken to result in a value-bearing commodity. This validation is harboured in exchange, which changes the way we think about how labour relates to value. Rather than *direct* labour-time, then, we see that the NRM stresses 'socially necessary labour-time' (SNLT), a retrospective abstract social relation between all labours mediated by commodity exchange. We end by considering why, then, if value is ultimately arbitrated in exchange, time is such a central focus of management control, worker resistance and capitalist competition. Drawing on the work of Chris Arthur and Alfred Sohn-Rethel, we can see that the exchange relation that constitutes value holds sway in production as well as circulation, contrary to critics of the NRM who associate it with too 'circulationist' a standpoint.

2.2   VALUE IN THE NEW READING OF MARX

One might restrict a chapter on the theory of value simply to the presentation of a patchwork of the thoughts of Marx himself on the topic. However, Marx's work on the question of labour and value contains interlaced ambiguities which lend themselves well to varying interpretations, each with its own arsenal of quotations and passages to confirm its position. In this spirit, this chapter outlines some of the ways in which Marx's LTOV has been interpreted in the Marxist tradition.

Following Marx's advice that one can best understand the ape from the vantage point of its highest stage of development in the human being, Riccardo Bellofiore suggests that such a rule applies equally to reading Marx's oeuvre: '*the most developed is the key for the knowledge of the less developed*' (2009, p. 179). As such, in the three volumes of *Capital* (Marx 1976, 1981, 1992), one gains the greatest sense of the ultimate resolution of his life's thought. It is upon these texts that the foregoing discussion will be based, although its details and ambiguities will often be paraphrased through the words and ideas of thinkers following Marx. As Alfredo Saad-Filho writes of his own approach to Marx's work, selected quotations and evidence from Marx's output are given second place to the presentation and critique of 'other readings of his works' which 'may illuminate certain problems from different angles' (1997, p. 458). In the context of the internecine struggle between competing conceptions of Marx's thought, an approach claiming to be presenting his opinions and nothing else would only constitute the taking of one position or another in that struggle. The uncovering of numerous manuscripts, tentative notes and unpublished works have only served to reveal that Marx's project was a mere 'fragment' of what was possible, and has exposed 'Marxian theory as a radically open project' (Endnotes 2010). It is this radical openness that allows us to be free of constant reservations based upon what Marx did and did not say on this or that issue, and to move the debate forward into virgin areas of investigation and critique whilst still remaining within in a rich and multifaceted Marxist paradigm.

Far from its typical representation as a strictly 'labour' theory of value, monolithic, scientific and assured it its essential status in the intellectual repertoire of those situated in the Marxist tradition, Marxian value theory is subject to considerable critical dispute. This chapter maps the theoretical polarisations at play and the alternative positions of possible reconciliation that lie between them. The presentation of Marx's theory of value will open up into an outline and critique of the principal positions taken on value theory in the subsequent literature in the Marxist tradition. Plotting a spectrum of approaches, from the 'embodied labour' theory of value of traditional Marxism to the exchange-oriented perspective of value-form analysis, the discussion will focus chiefly upon the way in which the debate has been split along the lines of allegiance to either production or circulation as the means by which the determination of value can be explained.

Responding to the internecine debate represented in the spectrum of interpretations of Marx's theory of value, we will consider the question Heinrich poses: 'A Production or Circulation Theory of Value?' His answer is neither, and both; indeed, the question itself is revealed to be senseless, subject to a false choice (2012, pp. 53–55). Heinrich depicts as nonsensical the dispute over whether production or circulation ultimately determines the creation of value. As he asserts, '[v]alue isn't just "there" after being "produced" someplace', but is a 'social relationship...constituted in production *and* circulation, so that the "either/or" question is senseless' (2012, p. 54). Thus, rather than placing the object of its analyses squarely within either production or circulation, a critical Marxist theory of value situates itself in the circuit of capital as a whole.

This is largely about where in Marx's work one places emphasis, rather than a 'correct' interpretation. By outlining the monetary emphasis of the NRM's take on value theory, I will go deeper into the significance of 'social validation' for my understanding of the relationship between labour, time and value. I will use the work of Bellofiore to root this in an overarching 'monetary' theory of value, and the work of Chris Arthur and Alfred Sohn-Rethel to understand the relevance of time for the study of value in the workplace. The NRM, it is suggested, presents a more satisfactory and consistent way forward for the Marxian theory of value.

Thinkers associated with the NRM share an anti-substantialist approach to the theory of value that stresses the importance of abstraction and social validation. This has two aspects, according to Christian Lotz. The first is that, in the words of Marx, 'the value form must be a socially valid form' (Marx, quoted in Lotz 2014, p. 38, author's translation). By extension of the first, the second is Arthur's contention that '[v]alue has a purely social reality' (Arthur, quoted in Lotz 2014, p. 38). Lotz suggests that this is a key shared point of agreement and identification among thinkers associated with the NRM (Lotz 2014, p. 69, n. 21).

The theory of value I derive from the NRM proceeds as follows. To exchange as commodities, products of labour (whether goods or services) must have some kind of value on the basis of which they can relate with one another. This provides a metric for decisions about what quantity things can exchange in and for. But the labours specific to each good or service are heterogeneous and incomparable. Thus, the *concrete* specificity of individual labours must be *abstracted from*. This abstraction irons out the differences. It generates pure, undifferentiated homogeneous 'amounts' of labour. This then provides the grounds for like-for-like comparison. This undifferentiated labour is *abstract* labour. It is because of this that a good or service exchanges with other goods and services by means of money, attaining the status of a commodity.

Abstract labour does not so much take place itself, as come about by means of an invention. The process of abstraction by which this occurs stems from the concrete, private nature of performed labour. It is this latter labour that *does* take place in capitalist society. It becomes social and abstract only after its expenditure. First, a product of labour is confirmed as a commodity possessing value and exchangeability. Only then is the concrete labour-time that went into its production *validated* as a part of the total abstract labour time of society. It passes as *productive* labour that has helped bestow value upon a good or service. The good or service can then stand as a commodity in a relationship of equivalence and commensurability with the other commodities of the market. This unfolds by means of money. Marx (1861–63) writes that '[a] singer who sells her singing on her own is an unproductive worker, but the same singer when hired by an entrepreneur to sing in order to make money is a productive worker because she produces capital'. Thus, the singer may sing like a songbird with or without the capitalist turning her songs to profit. Whatever the exact nature of the end result of her labours, the essential task remains the same. But it is only when the capitalist exchanges her songs or performances for money that her labour becomes productive, properly capitalist labour. Thus, we may say that value productivity is determined in exchange.

Following this, I suggest that value does not consist in the amount of labour-time expended in production by any one labouring individual. It relates to the amount of time 'socially required for its production' (Marx 1976, p. 301). This is subject to a validation made after the concrete expenditure of labour. It is only through this validation that labour can be said to produce any value at all (Bonefeld 2010, pp. 266–7). In Chap. 4, we will explore the significance of this for how we can conceptualise the relationship between the workplace and economic life as an object of inquiry.

2.3   POLITICAL ECONOMY AND ITS CRITIQUE

First, I will survey the development of Marx's theory of value from its roots in Smith and Ricardo. It was the contributions of Adam Smith and David Ricardo that made possible that of Marx, whose 'critique of political economy' developed his own distinct and revolutionary theory of value. Marx's theory of value was formed from an encounter with classical political economy. Through the method of immanent critique, Marx's critique of political economy established the foundations of a new theory of value forged from the ruins of the old one. It is in this respect that any account of Marx's theory of value would be left incomplete without a prior examination of the political economy that preceded it.

Political economy's engagement with the question of value came at a time when the 'just price', reliably configured in the medieval absolutist world, had given way to the 'impersonal role of the market' and a world of non-absolutes in which the determination of value was seldom as clear cut (Dinerstein and Neary 2002, pp. 10–12). This political aspect provided the background for a more direct concern with the appearance of the surplus as a defining feature of the new capitalist mode of production. Salvatore Veca (1971) identifies the theory of value as a 'problem' facing the classical political economists, who treated the problem as a symptom of a capitalist economy in which the defining characteristic was the pre-eminent role of the surplus. Establishing the magnitude of this surplus thus became an issue of value and its determinations.

Despite the relativizing influence exerted by the rise of the market, the role of exchange in determining value was obscured in much political economy of the time. In line with his belief in the right of labour to its product, with John Locke arrived the perspective that value is determined by the labour embodied in an object's production. William Petty was the most notable advocate of a distinctly 'labour' theory of value, ruling out the determination of value in circulation and locating determination squarely within the realm of production. It was the *quantity* of labour expended on the production of an object which gave it its value. Whilst such an approach will possess a problematic status in subsequent thought, Petty's major contribution is to begin thinking of value-producing labour in terms of 'labour in general' rather than as the product of individual labours. The implication of the early 'embodied labour' position was that, as a body of potential labourers, 'society, i.e. population, was itself a form of wealth'. The importance of this perspective is that it throws the concept of value open to a wider social determination, as 'a mass of congealed or crystallized social effort' that attains its sociality not just through the interdependence of value creation but also of the social relations that stem from it. Value is not only created by means of the 'organization of society in that direction', but is also only 'value' through its recognition as such 'from the point of view of society as a whole' (Dinerstein and Neary 2002, pp. 10–12).

Whilst earlier political economy had investigated the *source* of value, the next phase of political economy sought to explore the determination of its quantity or measure. The first major contribution arrived in the work of Smith. Smith held that the value of a commodity was divided up between three revenues, rent, wage and profit, which accrued to three classes, landowners, wage-labourers and capitalists. In so doing, Smith disputed the position advanced by Locke et al. that value was an expression of the labour embodied in a commodity. This may have been so in pre-capitalist economies, when the value of a commodity would go straight to its producer. Yet this situation was no longer the case in a capitalist economy where value was shared between different interests who all contributed towards production, through cost or effort, and therefore were apportioned some element of the rewards. Smith therefore situated the determination of value not in the actual labour performed and embodied in the commodity, but in its *price*, without an effective means of describing the relativizing social process by which price is ascribed (Dinerstein and Neary 2002, pp. 12–13).

Despite this, however, it should be noted that Smith's work on value makes two important contributions. The first is that, like Petty, Smith offers a significant advance on previous political economy by looking beyond the purely *physical* dimensions of labour to its generalized role in the production process as a whole. In Smith, labour was not simply treated in its concrete guise, but as 'labour in general' (i.e. as *abstract* labour). The maintenance of 'physiocratic naturalism' based upon agricultural labour was unsustainable as the capitalist division of labour swept away such activity with new technological and organizational developments that fostered the increasing *interchangeability* of different concrete types of labour (Veca 1971, pp. 49–50).

Second, and most importantly, Smith's work was of some utility in drawing attention away from a narrow preoccupation with labour content and towards the sphere of social form, reinstating to political economy a consideration of exchange that had been missing from earlier accounts. For Smith, the value of a commodity depends not only upon the labour invested in its production (direct labour), but the labour invested in the production of other equivalent commodities (indirect labour). Thus, for Smith, exchange is all. However, as Veca asserts, the 'rules' of this exchange had to be located in underlying phenomena bearing determination upon its immediately apparent superficiality. Smith therefore sought to explore the very foundations of exchange. Surplus and exchange only *'function as if'* they are themselves these underlying, foundational phenomena (Veca 1971, pp. 49–50). Smith considered it correct to begin from this artifice, plunging deeper into the layers below in order to discover the context out of which the surface has sprung. Here is found the world of *labour*. However, this depth analysis was left incomplete, only to be taken up later by Ricardo and Marx.

Where Smith tentatively began a descent into the underlying determinations of value in the sphere of labour, his project was an inadequate and incomplete one, the threads of which were picked up by Ricardo (Veca 1971, pp. 48–9). Ricardo rejected Smith's reliance on 'observable empirical phenomena,...looking behind the obvious processes of social reality to what lay underneath', opening further the territory of 'social form' for political economy to plunder (Dinerstein and Neary 2002, p. 14). However, to celebrate Ricardo as a theorist of the social form and to malign Smith's analysis as having overlooked this aspect ignores the way in which the former restricted himself to production whilst the latter invited a greater awareness of the possible determination upon value of circulation.

Whereas Smith had opened up the theory of value to at least *some* determination in the realm of exchange, Ricardo situated determination of value squarely in the field of production once again, gaining a lasting association with the 'embodied labour' theory of value later taken up by orthodox Marxists. Ricardo dismissed the determining influence that Smith attributed to costs, wages and profit, identifying them instead as 'aspects of value itself'. Ricardo emphasized the origins of value in embodied labour, not only in its immediate form as labour expended but also as that labour congealed in the various forms of 'accumulated labour' such as machinery and other aids to production (Dinerstein and Neary 2002, pp. 14–15).

Thus, for Ricardo, 'the labour objectified in the commodity must be considered both as present and as past labour which has been stored in "utensils, tools and means" of production'. In the process of piecemeal advances made by the classical political economists in the understanding of value and labour, this marked the point at which the further theoretical elaboration demanded by Smith's initial forays was enacted, functioning at a 'higher level of abstraction' in order to go beyond the immediate appearances of transactions in the system of exchange to reach far back into the foundational determinations of value that existed, and continue to persist, in the past (Veca 1971, p. 57).

Ricardo's return to labour, according to Dinerstein and Neary, presented itself as a 'threat' to political economy and thus provoked a retreat *away* from labour as an explanatory factor in value (Dinerstein and Neary 2002, p. 15). It was Marx who rectified this, both returning to and surpassing Ricardo. Where Ricardo based value and price merely on the temporal amount of labour expended, he did not pose the question as to why and how products of labour become value-bearing commodities on this basis. It is this question that forms the springboard of Marx's analysis, and to answer it, he developed *Capital*, an account of value based around the concept of abstract labour (Fine and Saad-Filho 2004, p. 29).

2.4   OUTLINE OF MARX'S THEORY OF VALUE

In *Capital*, Marx counsels against situating value in the sheer amount of labour expended in a commodity's production. He notes that if this were the case then the commodity with the most value would be that produced by the most 'unskilful and lazy' worker. The labour-time that determines value is instead that *socially necessary* (Marx 1976, p. 129). Value exists, according to Marx, only as 'definite masses of crystallised labour time' (1976, p. 184). The emphasis here is upon the crystallisation by which this can be said to be so – and not upon any amount of actual concrete labour in time. Hence, value relates to abstract labour and not its concrete expenditure (Bonefeld 2010, p. 262). Thus, as we shall see in Chap. 8, any putative crisis of measurability based upon the latter is thus shown to be mistaken. It is an abstract measure of 'time taken' (Arthur 2013) that capital extracts as the socially significant datum of value production, expressed finally in monetary terms – and not the direct expenditure of the concrete labour from which it abstracts, as implied in the postoperaist treatment of Marx's theory of value critiqued in Chaps. 7 and 8.

In a footnote in *Capital* (1976, p. 188), Marx dispenses with the illusion that value relates to expended labour-time. The footnote envisions a national database logging the labour-time expended in commodity production. Individual contributions are calculated and recompensed in the form of a labour certificate. Marx critiques the scheme for its assumed comparison of like-for-like products of social labour-time. For Marx, the labour-time does not become social in production. It becomes social only in and through commodity exchange. As Elson writes, 'the labour-time that can be directly measured in capitalist economies in terms of hours. . .is not the aspect objectified as value, which is its social and abstract aspect' (1979, p. 136).

From this perspective, the main matter facing explanation in Marx's theorisation is the way in which exchange is organized through the bringing of different concrete labours and the use-values they create into a relationship of equivalence which allows their commensurability and interchangeability on the market. In a nutshell – the process by which the content of labour should result in a specific social *form*.

The LTOV is the means by which Marx attempts such an explanation. Outlining his method, Marx remarks that '[i]t is always the direct relationship of the owners of the conditions of production to the direct producers – a relation always naturally corresponding to a definite stage in the development of the methods of labour and thereby its social productivity – which reveals the innermost secret, the hidden basis of the entire social structure' (1981, p. 791). To apply this method to capitalist societies requires that one begins from that which is specific to them. This specific feature is the commodity. Rather than track back to find the origins of the form, Marx instead sought to delve deeper *inside* the form beneath its immediate appearance (Elson 1979, p. 142). Following this method, and beginning from the commodity as the most immediately apparent distinguishing feature of the capitalist system, Marx sets out from the proposition that the commodity has a dual character. Marx proceeds to split the commodity 'into two aspects, use value and exchange-value; further examining exchange-value, as a historically specific form of exchange relation, and establishing what this form of appearance must presuppose as a product of a socio-historical process' (1979, p. 160).

Commodities are defined as 'use values produced by labour for exchange' (Fine and Saad-Filho 2004, pp. 18–19). In every society, the products of labour can be said to possess a certain amount of use-value, whether this be food to be eaten, a coat to keep us from the cold, or education and healthcare to ensure our continued and prosperous existence. However, noting the way in which capitalist society is defined by the production, exchange and accumulation of commodities on a grand scale, Marx is provoked to move beyond the simplistic portrait of the products of labour as items of use. It is *exchange* value that provides the basis of the ability of one commodity owner to trade the commodity he or she owns for another, constituting and embodying a relationship of equivalence and interchangeability (2004, pp. 15–17).

In order to be exchanged, commodities must be brought into such a relationship so that two different commodities with different use-values can be compared in a like-for-like way. This equivalence is not merely established in the *individual* act of exchange. The examples used by Marx, such as that of the exchange of corn and iron, should be taken not as an indication that exchange so described refers to the individual act of trading corn for iron, but rather the 'whole process of exchange from which this one example has been abstracted' (Elson 1979, p. 152). Arthur sums this up well when he writes of the almost infinite interchangeability of all commodities with one another, an interchangeability from which no individual commodity can be isolated and allowed to stand on its own specific value (1979, pp. 67–81).

Equivalence is achieved through a social process encapsulating the individual exchanges of the totality of social actors, without any reference to 'rational social convention' (Elson 1979, p. 154). Where Smith attributed valuation and market exchange to what Heinrich (2012, pp. 45–7) describes as the '*rational considerations* of isolated individuals', Marx displayed a marked incredulity towards the individual thought processes of market actors, preferring instead to concentrate his analysis upon the set of social relations specific to capitalism in which social agents insert themselves. The values expressed in exchange have nothing to do with the fancies or determinations of those involved. There might, at first glance, seem to be some convergence between form approaches to value and marginalist accounts of valuation. But here the difference is clear. Rather than speaking of the buying and selling of commodities through the example a single act of exchange through which these subjective elements might be assessed, as does Smith, Marx instead deals with the entire totality of social relations in which exchange takes place. It is this totalising viewpoint which allows Marx to explore the way that the social organisation of labour within capitalist society is geared towards the commensuration of distinct labours in service of commodity exchange. Value theory is therefore principally an attempt to explain 'the specific social character of commodity-producing labour' (Heinrich 2012, pp. 45–7); namely: why and how a content should take a certain form. This is a key feature of Marx's thought we will return to repeatedly throughout this book.

In this sense, the equivalence of exchange constitutes an appearance which Marx digs deeper down into in order to unmask the network of economic and social relations underlying it. Once the equivalence of exchange is established as the necessary condition for the capitalist market economy, Marx turns towards the question as to what makes this equivalence possible.

How does Marx trace this possibility? The common element that all commodities possess is that they are the products of labour. This labour is criss-crossed and differentiated by the division of labour, which separates out working tasks, trades and distinct labour processes in the production of different commodities. Due to this division of labour, the products created need to be reconciled with one another in order to be exchanged. Different concrete labours, which bestow upon commodities their individual and specific use-values, must therefore be mediated and measured as human labour in general in order to constitute a common basis upon which distinct commodities can be traded. The undifferentiated, homogeneous representation of distinct concrete labours so established is an *abstraction* from each of the specific practices involved in the production of individual commodities and use-value. Therefore, the dual character of the commodity is mirrored in the dual character of labour. Where concrete labour determines use-value, it is *abstract* labour that forms the substance of exchange value.

This translation of concrete labours into abstract can also be thought of in terms of individual and social labour (Kay 1979, p. 56). In capitalist society individually performed concrete labour can be said to produce commodities through its existence as abstract social labour. On the principle that all labour occupies time, this 'human labour in general' can best be measured with recourse to labour-time (Fine and Saad-Filho 2004, pp. 19–20). However, it is not the individual expenditure of labour-time which is measured in the exchange relation. Rather, what determines value is the *socially necessary labour-time* (SNLT), which Marx defined as 'the labour-time required to produce any use-value under the conditions of production normal for a given society and with the average degree of skill and intensity of labour prevalent in that society' (1976, p. 129).

This SNLT is represented in the *money form*. Elson (1979, p. 139) notes that in the various equations contained within the pages of *Capital*, Marx never attempts to substantiate the value of a commodity with any figures drawn from labour-time. Rather, everything is presented through the numerical prism of money. The practical way in which the totality of individual exchanges previously described gives rise to an accidental, unplanned equivalence relies upon the role of money as a reference point for the equivalence of all commodities as parts of the social totality, an objective form of value to which all commodities can bear comparison and on the basis of which they can attain commensurability. In capitalist society, through 'social custom', this form of value – which becomes the universal equivalent – is money (Heinrich 2012, pp. 59–61; Marx 1976, pp. 180–1).

In order for money to act as the universal equivalent, it must be 'directly exchangeable' (Marx 1976, p. 147) on a basis unconnected to its individual use-value or the actual concrete labour expended in its production. This sets it apart from the other commodities with which it is exchanged. Its exchangeability arises not from its use-value but from its '*social* position as equivalent' (Elson 1979, p. 162). This social position comes about through the totality of exchanges, as Marx puts it 'the joint contribution of the whole world of commodities' (Marx 1976, pp. 159, 180). The specific role of money as the equivalent in capitalism 'crystallises out of the process of exchange' rather than by agreement (1976, p. 181; Elson 1979, p. 163). As Heinrich asserts, commodity owners by their very activity as such bring about money through necessity (2012, p. 63). Indeed, exchange could not take place without it. However, it is important to remember that money is not in and of itself the key component, but acts only as an expression of abstract labour and SNLT (2012, p. 64).

It is in this sense that we can attribute to Marx a *monetary* theory of value that moves beyond the *pre-monetary* theories that preceded it (Heinrich 2012, pp. 63–4). The debate about just how 'monetary' the Marxian theory of value is or should be is one which forms a central crux of the competing conceptualisations that have followed in the Marxist tradition, which we will now consider. The debate centres upon the distinction between the spheres of production and circulation. The sphere of production is where labour is expended in the production of commodities, and the sphere of circulation is where these commodities are exchanged. Whether one believes that value is determined in the former as an expression of actually expended labour, or in the latter where value constitutes a kind of 'social validation' which registers different concrete labours as abstract and the labour-time in which they were expended socially necessary, forms the key distinguishing feature of the different characterisations of Marx's theory of value.

2.5   FROM TRADITIONAL MARXISM TO VALUE-FORM THEORY

Alfredo Saad-Filho follows Philip Mirowski in differentiating between two contradictory versions of the theory of value in Marx. In the first, the *crystallised-labour* or *substance* approach, 'labour-time is extracted in production and buried in the commodity, where it subsists independent of any market activity until the commodity is consumed'. This approach is utilized by Marx to emphasize his point that exchange is not wholly responsible for value, and that labour matters too. This attention to labour plays itself out in Marx's preoccupation with exploitation. The second version of value theory in Marx is what Saad-Filho, following Mirowski, calls the *real-cost* or *virtual* approach. Here, value is determined by a '(changing) configuration' of production and circulation (Saad-Filho 1997, p. 457). From this ambiguity can be extrapolated two central strands of Marxian thought each with a competing interpretation of Marx's theory of value. The substance–virtual divide described by Mirowski corresponds to the distinction between traditional Marxism and value-form theories (Saad-Filho 2002). It is on the basis of this distinction that we will discuss the spectrum of positions occupied in the debate about labour and value.

Until the 1970s a 'Ricardian' consensus dominated the understanding of Marx's theory of value. This is best exemplified in what is known as the 'embodied labour' approach to the theory of value, which posits that value is determined by labour embodied in commodities during production. In the traditional interpretation of Marxism, Marx's economic theory is considered to differ little from that of Ricardo. The main focus of Marx's theory of value is held to be exploitation rather than exchange, with commodities, money and value purely incidental to this central preoccupation. Value is incorporated only as a means by which the rate of exploitation can be determined. This leads to a concern purely with the *magnitude* of value as represented in the 'amount' of abstract labour congealed in a commodity, rather than the substance or form of value in the shape of money. Concrete labour and abstract labour are treated as separate and in opposition with one another.

So too are their attendant values, use-value and exchange-value (Saad-Filho 1997, p. 459).

Such a perspective relies upon a reading of *Capital* whereby the first three chapters on commodities, value and money are portrayed as referring to a system of exchange that exceeds capitalism alone. It is suggested that it is only in Chap. 4 that *Capital* deals directly with capitalism, whereupon Marx begins to deal with surplus-value and exploitation. Saad-Filho suggests that this exposes a severe misunderstanding of Marx's method in *Capital*, whereby he proceeds from the 'cell-form' of the capitalist mode of production he wishes to study. This 'cell-form' is the commodity, from which are extrapolated successive new stages of understanding relating to exchange, value, the money form and abstract labour. This is an attempt to begin with the concrete in order to 'achieve a systematic and consistent reconstruction of reality in thought'. For Saad-Filho, whether or not the matters investigated in the first three chapters of *Capital* have existed for aeons, Marx's treatment deals only with their reality as facts of *capitalism* specifically. Therefore, all categories used in his analysis are specific to capitalism (1997, pp. 460–1).

Marx's critique of Ricardo points us towards the importance of a value-form analysis. Traditional Marxism makes the same mistake that Marx alleged of Ricardo, namely the complete ignorance of the realm of circulation. Ricardo was unable to conceive properly the nexus of money and commodities and therefore understand the relationship between value and abstract labour. Ricardo never stopped to question the relationship between labour, its duration and value, prohibiting him from the consideration of the 'form' that labour takes in determining exchange value – its specifically *capitalist* form. Ricardian Marxists therefore follow Ricardo in 'taking the mode of labour for granted' (Saad-Filho 1997, p. 460). What can broadly be labelled the *physiological* approach deepens the transhistorical treatment of labour and value found in Ricardian accounts. This approach argues that 'capitalist social forms can be traced back to some natural basis, which however does not exist in pure natural form'; rather, it 'always subsists through distinct modes of production'. Ultimately, it sees 'capitalist social relations as developed nature'. It is towards this analysis of the 'historical specificity of the capitalist mode of production' (Bonefeld 2010, p. 242) that value-form analysis is directed.

In the 1970s, the Ricardian consensus was challenged by such a focus on the 'the *historical specificity*' of the value form (Kicillof and Starosta 2007, p. 13). Where the earlier paradigm saw prices as determined by their labour content, value-form theories saw prices as determined by the 'social valida-tion' of labour in the marketplace (Kicillof and Starosta 2007, p. 30, n. 1). At the extreme end of responses against traditional Marxism has been the circulationist approach that originated in the work of I.I. Rubin (1972). Here, the reality of abstract labour and value is held to be constituted solely through the exchange of commodities for money. Removing the determi-nation of value from the 'objectification of productive activity' and into a separate realm of pure exchange and circulation circumvents the possibility of lapsing into the Ricardian labour-content analysis (Kicillof and Starosta 2007, p. 14).

Where the Ricardian 'embodied labour' approach places emphasis upon the quantitative magnitude of value whilst neglecting completely the money-form, the circulationist approach possesses an essentially *qualitative* appreciation focused specifically upon 'the commodity moment' and the form of value involved (money) and its relationship with production through the conduit of abstract labour. Rubin emphasized the specifically commodity-oriented characteristic of capitalism to the extent that he referred to the subject of his analysis as 'commodity-capitalism'. Rubin posited that producers are subject to a need to render the commodity they produce 'socially useful' so that it can be sold on the market. This 'imperative to sell' has been labelled the 'monetary constraint', whereby private and concrete labours are only, 'at best', 'potentially or only ideally abstract and social. Private and concrete labour is converted into social and abstract labour if and when its product is exchanged for money' (Saad-Filho 2002, p. 26). Important here is the idea that private labours are only 'at best', 'potentially' abstract and social. This is as against those perspectives which argue that the abstract side of labour is always present in the expen-diture that takes place in the production process proper. As Saad-Filho notes, such an account of abstract labour 'correctly restricts the concept to commodity societies', rather than eternalising it as a natural category, by virtue of the fact that here it only comes about through validation in market exchange. Saad-Filho points out that the abstract labour approach refutes the dual character of labour as the *simultaneously* concrete *and* abstract quality of labour in favour of a dual character which is staggered, with labour only becoming abstract 'when its product is exchanged for money' (1997, pp. 465–6).

Although numbering among those sceptical of accounts of value that foreground the sphere of circulation in their analyses, Saad-Filho commends the way in which such a perspective emphasizes the necessary appreciation of the role of money in value analysis, counselling against an analysis informed purely from the vantage point of production. As Saad-Filho notes, money is important in that economies of commodity exchange could not exist without it, and through price forms the only means by which value can appear and be expressed. Riccardo Bellofiore is perhaps the principal proponent of a specifically monetary, or 'circuitist' (2009, p. 191), paradigm of NRM value theory. He suggests that this moniker refers to the way in which the determination of value is considered to be subject to a process located within the entire circuit of production and circulation. Money is taken to be the element which unites this process. Therefore, the circuitist approach can also be seen as an extension and reformulation of the 'monetary theory of value' of the circulationist approach. The circuitist position holds that value is determined not solely in production, but through the social validation of expended labour, which takes place in circulation. There the one cannot be said to possess any determination without the other, with production and circulation consisting as 'moments of a whole' (Clarke 1980, p. 9). This whole is the capitalist circuit. This circuit will be central to the analysis of so-called 'immaterial labour' in the creative industries given in Chap. 9.

2.6   The Social Validation of Abstract Labour-Time

What this monetary theory of value shows us is that the value of a commodity is its 'social value', and as such does not consist in the amount of labour-time expended in its production by any one labouring individual, but rather its SNLT, the amount of time 'socially required for its production' (Marx 1976, p. 301). SNLT is an *ex*-post validation, synonymous with the social validation posited in circuitist accounts of value theory. Concrete labour can achieve use-value, but the dual character of labour entails that only abstract labour can provide the exchange-directed content of the commodity's value, in the shape of a certain mass of congealed, undifferentiated labour-time. The status of 'abstract labour time' is a validation made after the concrete expenditure of labour, and it is only through this validation that labour can be said to produce any value at all, the implications of which for the conceptualisation of how circulation relates to production we will explore in the final chapter of this book. As Bonefeld posits, concrete labour has a 'concrete temporality', which in order to stand as a portion of social labour productive of value must be rendered a component of the abstract, homogenous time of labour in general, the measure of which is socially necessary labour-time. In this way, '[c]oncrete labour time is compelled to occur within the time of its abstract measure. If it does not, it is nothing, valueless.' It is thus labour-time that constitutes the medium through which abstract labour sustains the equivalence of commodity exchange. In making possible undifferentiated generalized labour in the abstract whilst also measuring that very same abstract labour, time 'appears as the substance of the very same activity that it measures' (Bonefeld 2010, pp. 266–7). It is expressed as both substance and measure through the form of *money*, the abstractive functions of which we will survey further in the next chapter.

Thus, the NRM rests upon the key role of the exchange abstraction in effecting the social relation of value. But time is also crucial – insofar as it is socially validated as part of the SNLT of society as a whole. This concerns the movement between concrete and abstract labour. Heinrich suggests that abstract labour cannot be counted on the clock, like the hours expended in acts of concrete labour. Rather, abstract labour is not expended at all. Instead, as Heinrich asserts, abstract labour is a 'relation of social validation…that is constituted in exchange'. Exchange validates 'privately expended concrete labor' as 'value-constituting abstract labor'. According to Heinrich, this involves three 'acts of reduction' by which diverse concrete labours reduce to abstract labour (2012, pp. 50–1). In this reduction, they are socially validated as value-producing.

The first is that the labour-time expended on an individual basis must reduce to SNLT. Only that labour-time resulting in value under average conditions of production is socially necessary. This average only becomes clear in exchange. Successful exchange validates individual labour and the time in which it has taken place as socially necessary. They are thus conferred as part of the abstract social labour, which is the substance and measure of value (2012, p. 51).

The second way in which labour is validated as abstract and social is by meeting 'monetary social demand'. It is the combination of these two factors that determines the abstraction of labour in exchange. For instance, say production of a given commodity exceeds monetary social demand. The labour-time has been devoted to the production of one unwanted com-modity at the expense of others. The monetary social demand cannot accommodate it (2012, p. 51). Chapter 9 evaluates further this issue.

Third, the relative worth of individual concrete labour is only established through validation in exchange. Here, it becomes apparent whether differ-ent degrees of skill can be said to be productive of different amounts of value. The three movements identified by Heinrich establish the 'extent to which privately expended individual labor *counts* or is *effectively valid* as value-constituting abstract labor'. The three reductions, Heinrich contends, 'take place *simultaneously* in exchange' (2012, p. 52).

Value is thus not a property inserted into the commodity by labour. It is not a property possessed by the commodity at all. Value is instead something 'bestowed *mutually* in the act of exchange'. Marx himself points towards this mutual constitution of value. He suggests that outside their exchange with one another, the coat and linen have no 'value-objectivity'. It is only the relation between the two, in which the labours that produced them equalize and are abstracted from, that can endow them with any such objective value. A product of labour on its own, then, is neither value-bearing nor a commodity. The product of labour is only such when it enters into exchange. But whilst value is not determined prior to exchange, it does not originate 'coincidentally' solely through the exchange act itself. Rather, the '*individual* labor of the producer and the product' meet in a relationship of validation. Here, individually expended labours enter into relation with the '*total labor of society*'. Neither exchange nor labour is therefore seen as 'producing' value. Rather exchange is seen as mediating the relationship between individual and social labour (Heinrich 2012, pp. 53–5). But this is the crucial moment. In bestowing value upon abstract social labour through a process of social validation, it brings value into existence.

2.7   SOCIALLY NECESSARY LABOUR TIME

But if SNLT is subject to an ex-post validation, then why does concrete labour-time matter at all? I explore this question further in Chap. 4, but for now the understanding of SNLT as a practical abstraction lays down an important foundation for a fuller answer to this question.

In his study of time in the Taylorist factory, Alfred Sohn-Rethel shows how concrete labour-time need not relate to the abstract time of measurement at all. Sohn-Rethel draws upon examples from Frederick Taylor's early experiments in 'scientific management', centring on the reconfiguration of work time in search of greater productivity and efficiency. Sohn-Rethel, grasping that there is no 'inherent' (1978, p. 49) relationship between expended labour and its appearance in the value-form, analyses how the Taylorist restructuring of work-time and its measurement make this disconnect clear. The measure of time, Sohn-Rethel suggests, bears no reference to the actual duration it purports to represent.

Sohn-Rethel quotes Taylor as emphasising that the timing of work relates less to how long something *does* take as to how long it *should* take. Sohn-Rethel notes how, rather than anything objective, these standards are set largely as the result of a 'pretence' which then comes to structure things anyhow – 'the whole intention of Taylorism' and 'scientific job analysis'. The breaking down and measuring of work in units of time relates not to the reality of duration but to conformity with an ideal standard. It therefore disciplines the worker's use of time, rather than measuring it, and in turn abstracts from the worker's experience of their work and the time in which it passes.

Sohn-Rethel writes that 'the essence of Taylorism' is that 'the standards of labour timing are not to be mistaken for the empiricism of the work as the workers themselves do it'. Rather than corresponding to the experiences of workers themselves, and the time that they take to perform tasks, 'Taylor does not learn his time measure from the workers', but 'imparts the knowledge of it as the laws for their work' (1978, p. 154). Thus, the measure does not measure a pre-existing concrete reality, but rather brings into existence an abstract reality – or better, a real abstraction – that rules over and structures concrete practice and lived experience. This, as we shall see in Part 2, captures what the postoperaist foretelling of the crisis of measurability and the law of value do not: namely, that whether concrete expenditure of labour exceeds the quantifiable confines of the working day does not impact upon the ability to capture and measure value – because time measurement, and the arbitration of value that culminates in exchange, refer not to something outside themselves, but rather bring into existence that which they measure through the conferral of monetary worth or the standard of social necessity.

In describing how the empirical passing of work-time is translated into the ideal standard of SNLT, Sohn-Rethel distinguishes between three types of timing: empirical, coercive and synthetic.

Empirical timing measures, or purports to measure, the 'time of the act' itself (1978, p. 155). But this time is resistant to direct measurement. Concrete labour, 'as it occurs in society', Sohn-Rethel writes, 'is not of itself quantifiable...in terms of labour time unless the labour were identical in kind of the actual differences, material or personal, were disregarded' (1978, p. 168). This latter must be achieved so as to ensure the commensuration of diverse labours in a way that pre-empts their final commensuration in commodity exchange.

The achievement of this owes to a second kind of timing Sohn-Rethel labels *coercive timing*. This takes the empirical 'time of the act' and 'separates [it] from all its contents' (1978, p. 155). This is a practical step, which is what gives it its coercive character. As Sohn-Rethel suggests, any system of commensurating labour 'must have a character of causal reality in practice' and cannot be 'merely a calculation existing somewhere on paper'. In the labour process, this causal reality rests on 'an actual process of flow production'. Sohn-Rethel puts this in blunt terms, more readily associated with the cold, hard framework of the factory than with the more ephemeral modes of production the capture of which is attempted in the concept of immaterial labour: 'Only by a conveyor belt in motion does the calculated proportion of labour which it enforces on the workers assume the functional reality of social labour commensuration' (1978, pp. 170–2). Today, the factory form survives in the new technologies of workplace control which serve the same role as the conveyor belt in structuring labour within commensurable limits: computer programs for monitoring progress and recording hours, that translate the chaos of contemporary 'immaterial labour' into systematised techniques for the organisation and streamlining of tasks. The context of abstract labour and the practical abstractions necessary to its coherence impact upon the way concrete work itself is organised. The measure helps construct the measured.

The effect of this coercive timing is to open the way for a third kind of timing – one relating less to practice than to the conceptual abstraction the coercive instruments of the factory eventually make possible. This is *synthetic timing*. This, Sohn-Rethel points out (1978, p. 155), marks not only a logical extrapolation from the commensurating effects of coercive timing, but a chronological development in the tradition of scientific management, evolving in the work on bricklaying of Taylor's pupil, Frank Gilbreth. What the instruments of coercive timing produce is a quantifiable, abstract time emptied of specificity that can be grasped, manipulated and reconfigured by the 'scientific intellect' according to 'laws' immanent not within the activities 'measured' but stemming from that intellect itself. The intellect breaks the work down into units of a 'fictitious norm of labour timing', 'construed without consulting or watching the worker, even for new jobs which have never yet been practised'. In this way, a new-economy creative agency is no different than an old-economy factory. The factory form persists, over and above any change contended in its content, and with it certain abstract forms that in turn structure the work performed. This will become relevant in our discussion of the 'social factory' in Chap. 6.

Exemplified in what Gilbreth named the 'measured day-rate', this synthetic timing, facilitated by the coercive timing of factory discipline, translates human labour into a purely 'technological category' with no basis in the actual time and practice of human labour at all. It approximates, rather, machinery, and becomes comparable, insertable and adaptable in direct relation with that conceptual and, ultimately, practical proximity with the machine (1978, p. 155).

Sohn-Rethel's treatment raises a number of interesting issues. If the abstract labour-time validated ex-post as socially valid bears no relation to concrete labour-time, then why is it a continuing fact that workers must spend their days under the temporal jurisdiction of managers? If emphasis falls on the process of social validation of *abstract* labour time, then why is labour-time a key focus of management control, and the target of worker resistance? We can seek some answers first through reference to the work of Chris Arthur. Arthur (2013) suggests that time is central to capitalist enterprise, but only in an 'emptied out' form achieved through practical abstraction, a concept we will cover in more detail in Chap. 4, by which time becomes the measure first of concrete labour and then of abstract, via the implementation of organisational routines and measures.

Arthur begins from a statement of the obvious: 'In commensurating labour, time is what capital selects as its relevant parameter' (Arthur 2013, p. 120). But, the question is: why? As Arthur writes, despite the fact that 'concrete labours cannot be aggregated in any meaningful way', due to their qualitative heterogeneity, we are still confronted with the situation whereby capital makes precisely such a 'senseless aggregation ideally'. It does so only 'under the aspect of time'. We ask, therefore, with Arthur: 'How and why is it relevant to abstract from all the features of this collective worker the one dimension of time?' (2013, p. 112). If money is the measure of value, then how do we think about labour-time in both its concrete, lived experience and its abstract, quantitative guise? If abstract labour has no concrete existence or duration, why measure it in terms of time? In answering these questions, as political and practical as they are theoretical, I will first set out some foundations.

First, the wage is not paid for concrete labour time, but for the reproduction of labour power. It is not tied to any actual amount of time. Rather, it pays for the worker to live. Indeed, the very status of the wage in capitalist society is to allow the capitalist to gain a value greater than the value of the labour-power for which he or she has paid. This is not robbery, but a situation implied within the formal legal relationship of equality between buyer and seller established in the contract of employment. As such, the wage is not presupposed on a certain number of hours, even though the imposition of national minimum wages and so on may suggest as much. The wage also, as discussed previously, already abstracts from concrete labour. Through its price – the wage – the expenditure of labour power as concrete labour enters into a monetary framework of abstraction that measures and structures its practical existence. This measure need not capture the experienced concrete reality of the expended labour. It establishes its own reality, subservient to monetary quantification. This abstraction follows from the status of the wage itself, as a payment to live – that is, to reproduce one's labour power – rather than a recompense for labour itself.

Second, 'Essence must appear' (Adorno 1974), and value contains within itself and implies the categories of profit, surplus value and so forth – because at its foundation is the capitalist desire to turn a buck, which in turn incorporates popular dispossession from the means of living and the compulsion to sell one's labour power to survive, and the presence of a buyer for that labour-power later put to productive ends. The capitalist pursuit of surplus-value – as the social reproduction of the system itself – cannot be divorced from the realisation of value in commodity exchange. This completes the abstraction of labour which proceeds initially through its positing as value-producing, inter-mediately through the practical abstractions that take place in production (comparison, measurement, rationalisation) and, finally, through the commensuration of commodities, which brings isolated private labours into a relation of full equivalence with one another.

Third, labour time is posited as value-bearing and value-producing by being abstracted from as pure time carrying a monetary value. The wage helps achieve this, but the time it tallies with is an internal accounting mechanism rather than the thing for which the wage is paid. This accounting mechanism enables the practical abstraction of labour by means of its measurement – the measure positing its own reality, bringing the measured – value – into being in a preliminary, potential form from its latent origins in the buying and selling of labour-power. Why time? Time becomes the means by which this is effected by virtue of the imperatives of competition and turnover, of getting (more) goods to market as quickly and efficiently as possible, and also of commensurating labour processes in such a way that their procedures and outcomes are comparable with other such processes (see Arthur 2013).

Such a form of time abstracts from and posits as value-bearing and value-producing the labour it measures and disciplines, like the Taylorised time

Sohn-Rethel identifies: fictional, with little or no reference to the reality it describes, and only to the reality it creates. In this way, we come back to where we began: to the wage, which although auspiciously tied to an amount of hours, in fact pays for no hours at all, and guarantees subservience and social reproduction at a different level. Time – monetised, abstract time rather than time as lived and experienced duration – is a convenient fiction at every step of the way.

2.8   TIME IN THE CIRCUIT OF CAPITAL

If we look outward from the workplace to labour's imbrication in the circuit of capital, we can suggest some reasons why time reigns supreme in the workplace despite its significance, according to the letter of the law of value, pertaining less to concrete expenditure than its abstract social form.

This can be understood with reference to the theories of value discussed above. What the monetary theory of value of Bellofiore and others shows is that value is monetary from the start, with the finance that commences all rounds of production an advance on what does not yet exist. This induces pressure on capitalists to conform to certain abstract economic compulsions from the off, and puts all that follows under the sign of monetary value, and, thus, its appearance in the abstract time of pure measure that Sohn-Rethel identifies. As we see, for Arthur, the competitive and compulsive incitements placed upon capitalists to measure labour circulate around a time emptied of all content, the pure time taken by a given round of production. As SNLT, this takes on not only an ex-post existence but comes to structure the practice and experience of work itself.

In response to Arthur's posing of the question 'why time?', we can define eight 'c's, each representing a different aspect of why time offers itself as the measure par excellence of abstract labour: creation, competition, comparison, commensuration, circulation, counting, control and compulsion.

Creation This relates to the basic condition whereby the creation of a given thing – a good or a service – capable of bearing value takes up time, and uses labour. Note that this is different to saying that the creation of *value* takes time and labour. This is a question of the material process of producing a good or service that *has* value, potentially or actually. Arthur writes: 'Since labour is necessary to produce what has value, capital must time it… New value cannot be generated all at once, but takes time, because living labour takes time to produce what has value' (Arthur 2013,

p. 113). That this is so introduces a practical necessity to time whatever takes place in the workplace, for other reasons that we shall discuss shortly. What is important to remember, however, is that the concrete activity that creates the thing which *has* value is sublated and forgotten in the value form. The measurement of 'time taken' here need not refer to a concrete expenditure of labour, but is rather the outgrowth of things taking place in time in the first place, applied to ideal measurements of abstract labour's 'senseless aggregation' (2013, p. 112).

Competition   The imperative to time labour relates also to the competition between capitals. Labour must be timed because time is crucial in a given capital's competition with other capitals. The timing of labour allows comparison against other capitals and the rationalisation and speeding-up of processes to get goods to market before competitors (these points follow in further detail).

Comparison   Arthur suggests that '[t]he adding of concrete labours by time is required because this is the dimension in which the comparison of one process to another is undertaken by capital' (2013, p. 113). This takes two forms: internal and external. Internally, capitals can compare one labour process with another across time and space – departments, locations, years, quarters, shifts, days and so forth. Externally, capitals can compare themselves against one another in the competitive struggle to get goods to market and use labour and resources efficiently. The power of comparison afforded by time measurement is a self-fulfilling prophecy. The time something takes becomes the time taken (Arthur 2013, p. 113). Thus, the labour process itself – its structure, its pace, the everyday lived experience of it – becomes the residue of standards of comparison established in the past and henceforth updated. This generates the 'empty time' of SNLT.

Commensuration   Arthur writes 'there is no process through which the individual labourers commensurate their toil and trouble with that of others. The products have a unitary form as products *of capital*. Thus capitals commensurate *their* toil and trouble, namely the time they are tied up in the production process, the time taken to pump out labour from recalcitrant workers' (Arthur 2013, p. 106). Practically, then, measurement on the basis of time creates the conditions whereby labour can be abstracted from in the exchange of its product as a commodity along with all the other commodities and their labours by means of money as the universal equivalent.

Circulation Capital abstracts 'under the aspect of time', Arthur contends, 'because it needs to get the commodities out as quickly as possible' (2013, p. 112), and this is a question of time. Time is here a measure of success but also a disciplining tool to increase the speed and intensity of the labour process.

Counting As well as using time to compare and commensurate labour processes, capital uses concrete labour time more basically as a means of counting labour in terms of its duration. As Arthur writes, '[m]aterial labour...is *counted* as simple duration because that is what *capital* counts as effective in generating value' (2013, p. 114). The more time that is spent on something, or the closer the time spent on something to the going average, the better or more successful a given labour process is said to be. Time offers itself here as the go-to measure of this, associated as it is with the duration of activities and of bodies through space.

Control Measuring concrete labour through time allows the manipulation and disciplining of work and workers. Materially, as Arthur notes, 'only *concrete* labour is subject to reshaping' (2013, p. 114). It is not possible for capital to 'economise' on abstract labour. This is because the latter cannot be 'measured and minimised' in its practical occurrence, for it has no such concrete existence. Only concrete labour can be quantified and adapted in this way. Nonetheless, the measurement of concrete labour time does posit and refer to an abstract measure – the 'empty' pure motion through time of social necessary labour.

Compulsion Only concrete labour can be practically manipulated and reshaped. But the demands, expectations, means and frameworks through which this takes place are abstract. Perhaps, therefore, the central of our eight 'c's, and the one which constitutes a golden thread uniting the other seven, is *compulsion*. The choice of concrete labour time as the purported measure of labour – and the construction from this of an abstract, empty time of SNLT – is subject to abstract economic compulsions (see Bonefeld 2014) and social domination that exists both beyond and through the individual volitions of those involved, whether capitalist or worker. As

Arthur contends, 'each industry has its specific way of pumping out [concrete] labour, even if ideal demands are presented to it abstractly and require concrete interpretation by managers' (2013, p. 114). The 'ideal' and 'abstract' character of these demands relate to the monetary imperatives they imply, and the pressures that the monetary status of these imperatives place upon capitalist functionaries to enact all of what we have covered above: commensurate, compare, control and so forth. It coerces actors to bring their actions and measurements in line with the prevailing standard of SNLT – as we shall see, the standard of the 'time taken' for labour processes both in particular and in general.

In this way – and on this Arthur's analysis does not go far enough – concrete labour is not only measured, but distorted in practice and experience by an abstract framework of ideal demands and measures. The timesheet measures not the time something takes but what Arthur calls the 'time taken'. Reading Sohn-Rethel alongside Arthur's conceptualisation of SNLT, this shows that the measures of time used in the workplace construct a new reality rather than represent an existing one. The market-mediated forms of measure bring about the measured by restructuring the practices and experience of the raw material with which they work. SNLT is the theoretical key to the eight 'c's delineated above. It is the link between the measurement of concrete labour time as it happens and the abstract labour it is hypostatised into as part of the totality of private activities commensurated in the value-form.

Arthur suggests that, rather than themselves moving through a preordained objective time, the time itself – established by the abstract economic compulsion placed upon capital – moves through the worker, and 'takes the worker as its carrier'. This time is an empty time, elapsed time commensurable with other empty, elapsed time. The time something takes becomes, henceforth, 'the time taken', and thereafter the time that moves through the worker as its carrier. The labour process, therefore, represents nothing other than the 'trace' of this 'time taken' (2013, p. 113).

What makes this 'empty' abstract time researchable, as explored further in the next two chapters, is the practical and material effects it assumes both through its constitution in a set of decisions taken by human actors under the spell of real economic compulsion associated with the social reproduction of their 'actual conditions of life' (Bonefeld 2014) and the impact of the experiential and affective movement through this time in practice. Human agents, via the forms of real appearance through which they encounter these processes, are thus able to testify to their efficacy. As Arthur writes, in its materiality, and the concrete conditions of antagonism, exhaustion and domination it implies, both psychologically and bodily, this abstraction is a 'practical reality' rooted in real actions. But through these practices proceeds an empty time, 'unqualified by any natural rhythms' (Arthur 2013).

This tells us that the value-form is not something that owes its existence solely to the moment of exchange, but has a practical, and also tentative, existence in the sphere of production itself, that hinges on ultimate arbitration through social validation in and by the market. The account given at the beginning of this chapter of the differing viewpoints on the LTOV courtesy of traditional Marxism and value-form analysis portrays an intellectual field divided over one central issue: the relative determination of value in either the sphere of production or that of circulation. However, as the criticisms raised demonstrate, neither seems to provide a sufficient and convincing case in support of one or the other. Within value-form analysis, which has been displayed to possess a significant theoretical edge over its more traditional counterpart, there has arisen a willingness to engage with value theory in a manner which acknowledges the merits, correctives and essential revisions offered by circulationism whilst seeking to locate matters more proportionally in the field of production.

2.9   CONCLUSION

As regards the different conceptualisations of Marx's theory of value, in this chapter we have sought to plot the different positions on a spectrum delineated by whether or not the given approach emphasises production *or* circulation as the sphere in which value is determined. In the wake of selected value-form critiques of traditional Marxism, we have set out an alternative position that emphasises both production *and* circulation as parts of a totalising process of value determination. This theorisation of value, by making clear that value concerns not the quantification of immediate labour and its concrete expenditure but rather its abstraction through socially mediated forms of appearance, becomes a platform, in the second part of the book, to conduct a thoroughgoing critique of the postoperaist understanding of labour and value in contemporary capitalism. But first, it is necessary to draw out the specificity of the monetary exchange at the heart of the monetary theory of value so far presented here. Thus far the presentation of value, exchange and money has tended toward the positing of an abstract social totality hard to situate in concrete human practice. In order to get to the point where we can say more about the practical – and political – relationship between value and labour and the classed antagonisms that accompany it, we must first ascend a further level of abstraction so as to consider, through a radically revisionist synthesis of the Kantian schema, Marx's value theory and Frankfurt School critical theory found in one part of the NRM, the existence of value as a 'non-empirical reality' that both springs from practical life but is not apparent to those living it. This will allow us, in Chaps. 4 and 5, to first evaluate how we grasp value in and through labour, and, later, how the social constitution of class society is inseparable from the abstract rule of value. In so doing, we further square the circle of what appear at first glance two separate approaches assessed in this chapter: productionist and circulationist attempts to get to the heart of value. Thus unfolded, in Part 2 this understanding will be used to critique the voguish claims of postoperaismo as to value theory's untimely demise.

BIBLIOGRAPHY

Adorno, T.W. 1974. Commitment. *New Left Review* I/87-88: 75–89.
Arthur, C. 1979. Dialectic of the Value-Form. In *Value: The Representation of Labour in Capitalism*, ed. D. Elson, 67–81. London: CSE Books.
———. 2013. The Practical Truth of Abstract Labour. In *Marx's Laboratory: Critical Interpretations of the Grundrisse*, ed. R. Bellofiore, G. Starosta, and P. Thomas, 101–120. Leiden: Brill.
Bellofiore, R. 2009. A Ghost Turning into a Vampire: The Concept of Capital and Living Labour. In *Re-reading Marx: New Perspectives After the Critical Edition*, ed. R. Bellofiore and R. Fineschi, 178–194. London: Palgrave Macmillan.
Bonefeld, W. 2010. Abstract Labour: Against Its Nature and on Its Time. *Capital and Class* 34 (2): 257–276.
———. 2014. *Critical Theory and the Critique of Political Economy: On Subversion and Negative Reason.* London: Bloomsbury.
Clarke, S. 1980. The Value of Value. *Capital and Class* 10: 1–17.
Dinerstein, A., and M. Neary. 2002. From Here to Utopia: Finding Inspiration for the Labour Debate. In *The Labour Debate: An Investigation into the Theory and Reality of Capitalist Work*, ed. A. Dinerstein and M. Neary, 1–27. Aldershot: Ashgate.
Elson, D. 1979. The Value Theory of Labour. In *Value: The Representation of Labour in Capitalism*, ed. D. Elson, 115–180. London: CSE Books.

Endnotes. 2010. Communisation and Value-Form Theory. *Endnotes #2· Misery and the Value-Form.* https://endnotes.org.uk/issues/2/en/endnotes-communisation-and-value-form-theory. Accessed 29 Oct 2016.

Fine, B., and A. Saad-Filho. 2004. *Marx's Capital.* 4th ed. London: Pluto Press.

Heinrich, M. 2012. *An Introduction to the Three Volumes of Karl Marx's* Capital. New York: Monthly Review Press.

Kay, G. 1979. Why Labour Is the Starting Point of Capital. In *Value: The Representation of Labour in Capitalism,* ed. D. Elson, 46–66. London: CSE Books.

Kicillof, A., and G. Starosta. 2007. Value Form and Class Struggle: A Critique of the Autonomist Theory of Value. *Capital and Class* 92: 13–40.

Lotz, C. 2014. *The Capitalist Schema: Time, Money, and the Culture of Abstraction.* Lanham: Lexington Books.

Marx, K. 1861–63. *Economic and Philosophical Manuscripts.* http://www.marxists.org/archive/marx/works/1861/economic/ch38.htm. Accessed 29 Oct 2016.

Marx, K. 1976. *Capital.* Vol. I. London: Penguin.

———. 1981. *Capital.* Vol. III. London: Penguin.

———. 1992. *Capital.* Vol. II. London: Penguin.

Rubin, I.I. 1972. *Essays on Marx's Theory of Value.* Detroit: Black and Red.

Saad-Filho, A. 1997. Concrete and Abstract Labour in Marx's Theory of Value. *Review of Political Economy* 9 (4): 457–477.

———. 2002. *The Value of Marx.* London: Routledge.

Sohn-Rethel, A. 1978. *Intellectual and Manual Labour: A Critique of Epistemology.* London: Macmillan Press.

Veca, S. 1971. Value, Labor and Political Economy. *Telos* 9: 48–64.

CHAPTER 3

Money and the Exchange Abstraction

3.1   INTRODUCTION

The theory of value presented in the last chapter is not that traditionally conceived as a 'labour theory of value', but closer to what has been termed the 'monetary theory of value' found in the New Reading of Marx (NRM). This chapter will explore first the extent to which we can say the law of value is essentially monetary, using the work of Riccardo Bellofiore. We will then use this as a platform to go into more detail as to the philosophical and empirical implications of the monetary aspect of the exchange abstraction as the means by which all things are brought into relation with all other things. For this exploration, we take inspiration from a largely subterranean lineage of critical theory stemming from fragments of Marx's work but commencing fully with the Frankfurt School's rereading of Kant's schema, via the work of Adorno, Horkheimer and Sohn-Rethel, and, today, in the work of a leading theorist of the NRM, Christian Lotz. These theorists, across decades, associate the organising capacity Kant attributes to the mind with socio-historical practical action rooted in time and space: namely, the use of money in commodity exchange. Expressing labour in its abstract form, by using and thinking through the category of money we organise the chaos of reality in ways commensurate with commodity exchange. But this use of money is rooted in its coercive material status as the sole means by which we secure our subsistence in a society where our social reproduction is guaranteed in and through the wage. This means that we need to situate the 'non-empirical' nature of the value abstraction in a concrete set of social

© The Author(s) 2018   53
F.H. Pitts, *Critiquing Capitalism Today*, Marx, Engels, and Marxisms,
DOI 10.1007/978-3-319-62633-8_3

relations determined inside and outside labour – something this chapter prepares the way for and Chaps. 4 and 5 pick up in greater detail.

In this chapter, I first set out, in basic terms, the main contours of Kant's conceptualisation of the mental schema through which human agents interact with the world. Next, I discuss Lotz's recent account of what he terms the 'capitalist schema', a re-rendering of the Kantian schema in which determination rests in capitalist social forms and relations as opposed to transcendental mind. Next, I unwind the genealogy of this conceptualisation in the work of the Frankfurt School, with specific focus on Sohn-Rethel's theory of the 'social synthesis' established in money as a means of exchange. This strand of work stands central to the development of the NRM. Finally, I consider the understanding of schematic abstraction not as something only ideal and mental but rooted in practical, material human life. This gives us a foothold through which, in the next two chapters, to resituate concrete labour relations around labour, class and social reproduction – and their contradictions and crises – within what has been, up to this point, the presentation of the rule of value as an abstract, social and totalising force – in short, a non-empirical reality we seek to get behind.

3.2   A MONETARY THEORY OF VALUE

As seen in Chap. 2, the NRM presents a monetary theory of value. One of the chief proponents of such a monetary understanding is Riccardo Bellofiore. Bellofiore's account is distinguished by its attempt to reconcile the divide between theories of exploitation and theories of value that has opened up on the terrain of the debate over whether production- or circulation-oriented interpretations stay truest to Marx's original work. Bellofiore criticizes exchange-oriented versions of the theory of value for a '*total evacuation of labour*'. He states his aim to reinstate labour into such versions (which include that of Rubin and his followers) whilst simultaneously reinstating the exchange abstraction into production. The way that Bellofiore sets about this is by positing the existence of a 'monetary *ante*-validation' predating the production process, which renders everything that takes place subsequently '*tentatively* social'. This relies upon a conceptualisation of the capitalist circuit as an 'essentially *monetary*' one, with '*bank finance to production*' as its origin and basis (2009, p. 184). Money, here, holds a role over the whole course of capitalist production and circulation, validating before and after its inputs and outputs as value bearing. In this chapter, we will go deeper into this role through the prism of a strand of Marxian theorising that takes the Kantian schema as its central principle in order to explain the specific social and psychological aspects of the relationship between people and things by means of monetary exchange.

Money is the entry point by which we experience what I will later go on to define as the 'non-empirical' reality of value. This does not mean that we neglect the undertow of this non-empirical reality in the lived and practical life of labour. In the sense that money is the form in which abstract labour is represented, it is on the basis of abstract labour that Bellofiore seeks to 'unite' production and circulation. Abstract labour is both '*presupposed* to' and '*actualized* within' the act of exchange. The reason that commodities are exchanged for money, for Marx, is that they already possess some aspect of commensurability. However, Bellofiore does not follow so-called 'embodied-labour' theorists of value in attributing this commensurability to an abstract labour content that is immanent with the commodity and within production seemingly apropos of nothing. Rather, for Bellofiore the golden thread which links the idealized mental abstraction of abstract labour into its objectification in the commodity is *money*, present from the very beginning of the production process. It functions first as 'ideal money', the optimistic mental abstraction from different labours expressed in an idealized monetary form, and finally as 'real money', whereby the labour expended is abstracted from objectively. This transition can only be completed in the act of exchange, and not within the labour itself. In this way, through the conduit of money, abstract labour is both 'precondition' of final exchange and its 'result' (2009, p. 185).

For Bellofiore this is the real meaning of Marx's presentation of value as a 'ghost' that 'must *take possession* of a body to exist.' This host body is that of the universal equivalent, gold money, the concrete labour directly or indirectly expended in which functioning as the expression of the abstract labour that initially exists only as idealized potential – 'ideal money' – and then finds objectified form as 'real money'. This highlights capital's status as 'money begetting money' (2009, p. 185). It is this latter 'monetary' theory of value that the NRM encourages us to adopt. In so doing, it draws on a lineage of Frankfurt School-influenced theorising that centres on a radical re-envisioning of Kant's schema in order to understand the role of money in mediating and expressing our interaction with the world of things through commodity exchange. This began in the occasional dialogue between early members like Adorno, Horkheimer and, most notably, Alfred Sohn-Rethel, and has picked up most recently by Christian Lotz. First setting out the key principles of Kant's thought on this topic, we will start with Lotz and, over the course of the chapter, unfold a genealogy of this contentious rereading of Marx's theory of value through a Kantian lens in the work of the Frankfurt School.

3.3   THE KANTIAN SCHEMA

We will begin with some first principles as a reference point for the discussion of the Kantian schema on which this set of ideas depends. In his First Critique (2007), Kant suggests that the possibility of accessing objects and reality relies upon the capacity of reason to constitute them in some ordered, understandable way. This then structures what is possible for us to experience. Experience is possible only with the coincidence of concepts and empirical data. It is reason – by means of what Kant calls the 'schema' – that establishes this possibility. Human reason, for Kant, is the schematising force in this instance.

In delineating this schema, Kant offers considerable resources to think through the practices by which conceptual apparatuses are applied to make sense of the world. As we will see, those such as Sohn-Rethel and Horkheimer have reinterpreted Kant, resituating this ordering activity from the psyche to society. However, the framework Kant provides is important as a basis from which we make such speculations about the way in which things are abstracted from to serve as identifiable, exchangeable and commensurable in a world of irreconcilable particularity and difference.

As Kant writes, 'Thoughts without content are empty; intuitions without concepts are blind' (quoted in Bowie 2010, p. 11). In other words, the concept is needed to make sense of the world and our intuitions of it. Whereas intuitions are the product of perception, concepts are those of reflection working in conjunction with experience. The use of concepts to negotiate the world is supported by psychological evidence which suggests that much of what we perceive is 'structured by the conceptual structures we already possess' (Bowie 2010, p. 11).

Without concepts, we would be confronted with 'endless chaotic particularity'. As Bowie writes, 'what we perceive is always different from moment to moment,...and no two objects are absolutely identical' (Bowie 2010, p. 11). Yet the construction of similarity and sameness is necessary for us to interact with the world as it is, not least in the realm of exchange, for instance. Sameness is not a feature of the perceptual data we receive from the world. No two things can be shown to be identical. Kant's transcendental idealism therefore posits that there must be a mental framework through which the world can be structured and ordered in a way such that things can be grouped together and compared in categories. Therefore, objects as we perceive them – in their objectivity – 'follow our ways of thinking, rather than vice versa' (Bowie 2010, p. 11). Their objectivity derives from the objectivity of these mental processes.

Kant's notion of 'general rules for apprehending objects' (or 'categories' in the Kantian parlance) is one derived from Aristotle, who saw the onto-logical structure of the world as stemming from the way in which it was categorised and conceptualised. These 'categories' signify 'concepts' *of an object in general*, and which can be accessed only by reflecting upon per-ception rather than through perception itself. With reference to the discus-sion of sameness above, the quantitative categories of 'oneness' and 'manyness' are seen as central by Kant to the possibility of *synthetic* a priori knowledge – the possibility of having pure knowledge without experience (Bowie 2010, p. 12). For the critical theorists discussed in this chapter, this is not something innate to the human mind but forged socially and mate-rially through concrete human practice in capitalist society.

The reflection which delivers us categories is known by Kant as *judge-ment*. It is judgement that 'actively synthesises different bits of perceptual experience into a relationship with each other'. This synthesis is that from which the *synthetic* a priori is derived. Whereas the raw materials of cogni-tion are received passively, judgement marks 'the active application of categories and concepts to that material'. Of these categories and concepts, space and time are perhaps the most important for judging and ordering reality. The synthesis afforded by concepts and categories enables us to 'connect different moments of experience to make them intelligible' (Bowie 2010, p. 12).

The application of the categories is dependent upon the 'principles', which govern the conditions whereby a category can be said to be valid. In order to understand the world at all, however, Kant suggests that these principles must be satisfied so that we can apply the categories in the first place. The implication of this, as Scruton points out, is that 'the world must ordinarily appear to us in such a way that we *can* accept these principles'; put simply, the very possibility of self-consciousness demands that the world conform to the categories and their principles. This, for Kant, was his 'Copernican Revolution'. Rather than the outside world as the primary element of which human cognition attempted the capture, the capacities of human cognition are held to be the primary thing to which the external world must correspond. As such, the world of nature can be said to be *objective*: because experience is organised around the categories of space, time, substance and causality, any knowledge directly implies a world of nature. Therefore, '[o]ur point of view is intrinsically a point of view *on* an objective world', because the objectivity of this world relies entirely upon our having experienced it (Scruton 2001, p. 39).

As Bowie writes, for Kant '[t]he task of "reason" is to establish principles that make our thoughts coherent'. These principles are ideas which have a 'regulative' status, ordering our thoughts about the things around us. They are not 'constitutive', however, as that would pre-empt thinking about the things around us and would therefore be what Kant calls 'dogmatic' (Bowie 2010, p. 15). Thus, Kant sets out a distinction between *constitutive* and *regulative* functions of ideas. The constitutive seeks to describe the world as it really is. The regulative, on the other hand, regulates our experience as if it were a true representation of the world as it really is, in order to guide our hypotheses towards a greater degree of truth. The idea of an unconditioned perspective, when employed in a *constitutive* role, gives rise to illusion. However, when used in a *regulative* way, it may govern experience in such a way as to enable us to develop true knowledge of the world. The idea of order and totality upon which an unconditioned perspective is based, as Scruton suggests, 'lead[s] us to propose ever wider and simpler laws, in terms of which the empirical world becomes more intelligible' (2001, p. 69).

Kant's conceptualization of reason is reflected in his more general doctrine of *transcendental idealism*, whereby only the *appearances* of things-in-themselves can be known, rather than the things themselves. A debate ensued among Kant's followers as to the exact nature of the thing-in-itself. For Mendelssohn, the thing-in-itself was a distinct and separate entity from the appearance of it which is presented to human knowledge. However, J.S. Beck posited that the thing-in-itself and the appearance were one and the same object. It seems, according to Scruton, that the textual evidence available in Kant's oeuvre lends support to this second interpretation, that appearances are part of an object, the other part of which is the thing (Scruton 2001, p. 55).

Bowie too suggests that Kant believed his transcendental idealism to be a 'realism' of sorts, assuming as it does that 'objects do exist independently of our perceptions'. This objectivity, however, is one phrased 'in terms of *subjectivity*'. It is the 'conditions of possibility' of knowledge pertaining to the latter that objectivity depends upon. The importance of these 'conditions of possibility' is what makes Kant's epistemology 'transcendental'. Although subjectivity is commonly thought of as in some way arbitrary, subjective thinking is here marked instead by *necessity*. Yet this subjectivity works in conjunction with the objective to produce knowledge. Knowledge 'depends both on the impact of the world on us and on the ways in which the mind orders that impact' (Bowie 2010, p. 10). As we will see, there are elements of this understanding of appearance and essence in the epistemological foundations of the NRM. For now, however, we are concerned with how thinkers in this tradition – and more broadly the lineage of Frankfurt School critical theory – have conceived of the same nexus of concepts and categories theorised by Kant, but situated them not in the human mind but in society as a whole.

3.4   THE CAPITALIST SCHEMA

Coming at the recent crest of such undertakings, Lotz's conceptualisation of the capitalist schema (2014) marks a significant intervention into current reinterpretations of Marx's theory of value. Eschewing the Hegelian heritage of much value-form theory, Lotz gives a Kantian interpretation of the law of value. This states that the money form works along schematic lines. Money, for Lotz, establishes the conditions of possible experience and the social thinghood of objects. Lotz's undertaking gives the clearest exposition yet of the real abstraction by which all things enter into relation with all other things. In so doing, it builds upon earlier attempts to outline the schematic quality of the capitalist exchange relation.

Whilst situating his work in a 'Kantian tradition of philosophy' that entails a view of the world whereby 'everything we think and do is ultimately filtered through a schema that – behind our backs – structures every reference and makes the relation between subject and object possible', following Sohn-Rethel and Horkheimer, Lotz trades in Kant's idealism for a materialist approach (2014, p. 5), advocating a social standpoint rather than a psychological one.

The grounds for a Kantian Marx may be associated with Marx's observation that '[t]he categories of bourgeois economy consist precisely of...objective forms of thought' (Marx, quoted in Lotz 2014, p. 51). But this association pertains more to the situation of both the Kantian schema and bourgeois thought within a specified historical juncture. The affinities are in fact deeper, Lotz contends. Lotz suggests that Marx transfers the structure of Kant's First Critique into a 'materialist framework within which money is determined as *thinghood*, since it determines the frame under which individuals can establish and refer to entities' (2014, p. 46). Only by seeing things in their connection to money can we see them as things at all.

From the perspective of a Kantian philosophical tradition, 'everything we think and do is. . .filtered through a schema'. This 'structures every reference and makes the relation between subject and object possible' (2014, p. 5). Where Lotz breaks with Kant's psychological explanation is in his social-materialist approach. Suggesting that Marx is 'closer to Kant than to Hegel', on account of 'his rejection of the logic of being and. . .that social reality is logical' (2014, n. 2, pp. xxi–xxii), Lotz cites a passage in the *Grundrisse*. Here, Marx contends that money in capitalism performs the same function as the rational schematism performed in Kant's idealist philosophy. This schematism 'makes it possible for a rational being to access and represent objects *for* the subject'. Through it, reason establishes 'a framework under which all objects. . .make sense and can exist' (p. xvi).

Lotz's is the most sophisticated and extensive development of the link between the law of value and the Kantian schematism yet given in the NRM tradition. Adopting critical distance from the early Frankfurt School, it represents an advancement of the theoretical project begun by Sohn-Rethel, building in turn on the work of Adorno and Horkheimer. Tracing the roots of this line of inquiry, we will first assess Sohn-Rethel's conceptualisation of the link between money and exchange in the law of value and the Kantian schema, and then Adorno and Horkheimer's work on the topic. In partial dialogue, they suggested a social basis for the schematism in place of the psychological explanation offered by Kant. Crucially, they allow us to situate what at first seems abstract and non-empirical – the value-form, expressed in money – in concrete human practice and social relations, a relationship we will go on to consider in greater detail in the next two chapters.

3.5   The Social Synthesis

For Sohn-Rethel, the social and historical status of the Kantian schematism relates to the exchange abstraction that coheres through the buying and selling of commodities for money, but proceeds also in a practical way in the sphere of production where these commodities are produced – a contradictory unity between two seemingly separate processes we explore further in the rest of Part 1.

Sohn-Rethel's innovation – later picked up by Lotz – is to agree with Kant that 'the basic constituents of our form of cognition are preformed and issue from a prior origin', but go further, in that Kant 'was wrong in

attributing this preformation to the mind itself', to a transcendental synthesis 'locatable neither in time nor in place' (1978, pp. 6–7). Rather, the
'transcendental subject' (or something quite like it) exists very much in time
and space in the shape of money. For Sohn-Rethel, the transcendental
subject exists nowhere other than in the 'innermost core of the commodity
structure' (1978, p. xiii). Preformation is not founded in some transcendental realm outside space and time, but is spatio-temporally circumscribed
in the form of the abstraction that stems from the social practice of
exchange. The exchange abstraction, rather than being purely one of
thought, is one of practice, a practical abstraction. This leads Sohn-Rethel
to the contention that it is necessary to 'dispose of the age-old idea that
abstraction is the exclusive privilege of thought' (1978, p. 7). Rather than
Kant's categorical preformation of concepts persisting solely internally to
the mind, this conceptual activity is forged from the activities that take place
outside the mind, in the interactions between human agents. Hence, as
opposed to Kant's mental and a priori 'transcendental synthesis', Sohn-
Rethel instead posits a 'social synthesis' (1978, p. 37). This allows us to
tread the fine balance in the NRM theory of value between value as a
subjective category and an objective category rooted in social and material
relations – an aspect we will go on to explore further.

Sohn-Rethel, along with work in a similar vein by Horkheimer and
Adorno, retains the understanding of how the synthetic a priori orders
experience, but locates this process in the social structure of commodity
exchange rather than in some transcendental context which otherwise
applies itself to the life of the mind. Whereas Kant thought that the concepts
that we use to understand the world and nature could not possibly have
sprung from that nature, and as such human experience is structured by the
concepts gifted to us by pure understanding, Sohn-Rethel searches for just
these very natural and 'spatio-temporal' roots for the ordering of experience
in conceptual thinking (1978, p. 74). The spatio-temporal explanation that
Sohn-Rethel finds is that of the practice of commodity exchange.

Contemporaneously, Horkheimer also took forward Kant's
conceptualisation of how the mind works, whilst disputing the origins and
location of the cognition and perception conceived of. As Connerton asserts
(1978, p. 21), Horkheimer posited that the faculties Kant associated with
the 'consciousness of the transcendental subject' in fact lie within human
society itself, immanently rather than transcendentally. Exceeding the
explicit link with commodity society that Sohn-Rethel would make in his
work, Horkheimer associates the social origins of cognition not only with

formally commodity producing and exchanging societies, but with other earlier, more communal forms:

> As man reflectively records reality, he separates and rejoins pieces of it, and concentrates on some particulars while failing to notice others. *This process is just as much a result of the modern mode of production, as the perception of a man in a tribe of primitive hunters and fishers is the result of the conditions of his existence (as well, of course, as of the object of perception).* (Horkheimer 1976 (1937), p. 214, emphasis added)

Here it is clear that the social determination of consciousness is an ever-present principle, replacing exactly Kant's idea of some kind of eternal, essential transcendental subject with a similarly all-pervasive immanent social 'subject'. Against Kant's 'idealist' understanding, Horkheimer offers a materialist analysis based on the theorisation of 'reality as a product of society's work', rather than stemming from any 'intellectual source' per se (Horkheimer 1976 [1937], pp. 215–16). In moving consciousness from the mind to human social activity, Horkheimer proposes that it is society itself that cognates and perceives, and therefore cognition and perception are left open to a historical analysis that situates them in the concrete social context in which they take place. Horkheimer writes that

> The classificatory thinking of each individual is one of those social reactions by which men try to adapt to reality in a way that *best meets their needs*. But *[t]he world which is given to the individual and which he must accept and take into account is, in its present and continuing form, a product of the activity of society as a whole.* The objects we perceive in our surroundings – cities, villages, fields and woods – bear the mark of having been worked on by man. It is not only in clothing and appearance, in outward form and emotional make-up that men are the product of history. *Even the way they see and hear is inseparable from the social life-process as it has evolved over the millennia. The facts which our senses present to us are socially performed in two ways: through the historical character of the object perceived and through the historical character of the perceiving organ. Both are not simply natural; they are shaped by human activity, and yet the individual perceives himself as receptive and passive in the act of perception...* The individual sees himself as passive and dependent, but society, though made up of individuals, is an active subject.... (Horkheimer 1976 [1937], p. 213, emphasis added)

Therefore, due to the sedimentation of socially circumscribed forms in the objects and phenomena perceived by human agents, the 'perceived fact' can be seen to be the result of 'human ideas and concepts' well in advance of its being subjected to further ideas and concepts in its 'theoretical elaboration by the knowing individual' (Horkheimer 1976 [1937], p. 214). This makes clear Horkheimer's replacement of the transcendental subject with society itself. As Sohn-Rethel also indicates, this is not just the case in capitalism, but can be extrapolated to earlier societies. Although fully 'synthetic society' can only be found in systems of commodity production, the 'social synthesis' is 'a general and basic condition of human existence, with no historical limits' (1978, p. 37).

In line with this, Sohn-Rethel suggests that 'the socially necessary forms of thinking of an epoch are those in conformity with the socially synthetic functions of that epoch'. In this he retains fidelity to Marx's approach to the relationship between consciousness and social being, with the synthesis corresponding to the latter category. Significantly, Sohn-Rethel extends the category of consciousness away from those essentially ideological aspects Marx identifies – the legal, the political, the religious, the philosophical and so forth – towards 'the conceptual foundations of the cognitive faculty' itself (1978, pp. 5–6). Therefore, we may say that the social synthesis – or rather, the need or requirement for a social synthesis in a society marked by a division of labour – determines the structure of the cognitive faculties. This insight rests on an appropriation of the Kantian schematism from a social and historical rather than transcendental standpoint.

Although Adorno and Horkheimer made claims as to the specificity of the culture industry in bringing about the capitalist schematism – something Lotz picks up and we consider further at the commencement of the final chapter of this book – it was Sohn-Rethel who most comprehensively unfolded the specific development of such a 'social synthesis' in a society based on commodity exchange by means, most importantly, of *money* as the expression of abstract labour.

As we saw in the last chapter, the abstraction of human labour is not a feature of labour itself but of exchange. Money is central to this. Sohn-Rethel contends that in a commodity-exchanging society, the 'social synthesis', the set of relationships and collective mental constructions through which society coheres, is itself constituted by the function of money as a universal equivalent which expresses the abstraction from individual human labours in the process of exchange. Sohn-Rethel claims that the social synthesis of any given time conditions its 'conceptual basis of cognition' (1978, p. 6). The development of coinage and the use of money as the universal equivalent brings about the capacity to think in 'abstract univer-sals' (1978, p. 60), which makes possible conceptual thinking *tout court.*

Against the division between 'intellectual' and 'manual' labour upon which abstract thought is founded, Sohn-Rethel argues that abstraction is not the 'exclusive privilege of thought', but is subject to concrete human activity (1978, p. 6). It is the example of the exchange abstraction which is corralled to confirm this. The abstraction from different concrete labours in the service of the equal, undifferentiated abstract labour of exchange is nothing other than a mental abstraction, yet originates from outside the mind in the actions of those involved in the process of production and exchange. Rather than the 'exclusive property of mind', then, abstraction 'arises in commodity exchange' (1978, p. 19). To put it crudely, the commodity abstraction is the creation not of the head, but the hand. Yet it exists only in the head. As Sohn-Rethel writes, '[i]t exists nowhere other than in the human mind but it does not spring from it'. It is, rather, a *'real abstraction* resulting from spatio-temporal activity' (1978, p. 20). This understanding of 'real abstraction' therefore privileges the practical and not the mental as the principal explanatory element of how concepts like value come to rule social interaction. We will explore the ramifications of this for the understanding of labour in the next chapter, and how it allows us to relate wider social processes of dispossession and coercion associated with class antagonism in Chap. 5.

3.6   Non-empirical Reality

As well as allowing us a window on the cognitive and conceptual through which society becomes structured by the abstract quantitative relationship of money – a relation of measure, as we will see in Part 2, that is increasingly in question among the postoperaist strand of revisionist Marxism – Sohn-Rethel also helps delineate the 'non-empirical' character of value, and its elusiveness as an object of knowledge and critique. In so doing, he also roots it in a set of practical relations that, in the next two chapters on labour and class respectively, allow us to ground what until now seems abstract in identifiable concrete processes of dispossession, exploitation, struggle and human crisis.

The exchange abstraction, despite giving rise to cognitive forms, is not 'thought-induced', originating in the mind. Rather, it originates in practical activity – the act of exchanging two different things. It originates from activity but eventually rests in the mind. The concept of value that the exchange abstraction depends upon 'exists nowhere other than in the human mind but it does not spring from it' (Sohn-Rethel 1978, p. 20). The exchange abstraction therefore has a dual quality. Against the familiar mental portrayal of abstraction, it is 'a real historical occurrence in time and space'. Yet, in the mental character that it assumes following its origins in action, it is also 'an abstraction in the strict sense acknowledged in epistemology' (Sohn-Rethel 1978, p. 22). This retrospective nature is best described here:

> the abstractness of [the act of exchange] cannot be noted when it happens, since it only happens because the consciousness of its agents is taken up with their business and with the empirical appearance of things which pertains to their use. One could say that the abstractness of their action is beyond realisation by the actors because their very consciousness stands in the way. Were the abstractness to catch their minds their action would cease to be exchange and the abstraction would not arise. Nevertheless the abstractness of exchange *does* enter their minds, but only after the event, when they are faced with the completed result of the circulation of the commodities. (Sohn-Rethel 1978, p. 27)

The position of money as a universal equivalent rests on the exchange abstraction, which establishes money as a 'pure abstract form arising from the *disregard* of the use-value of the commodities operated by the act of exchange equating the commodities as values' (1978, p. 6, emphasis added). We might think here of Nietzsche's contention that the practice of quantification relies on the *forgetting* of difference and dissimilarity (see Porter 1994).

Preoccupied with the *use* of commodities, Sohn-Rethel suggests, the minds of those involved in exchange cannot have attributed to them the exchange abstraction. Rather, this abstraction is attributed to the action that they conduct in the process of their preoccupation to acquire an item of use. In exchange, therefore, 'consciousness and action. . .part company' (1978, p. 26). This is a curious presentation in light of Sohn-Rethel's earlier statement that the abstract form of exchange arises from the 'disregard' of the particular use-value of the counterpart commodities. This is explainable by means of the action–consciousness distinction drawn by Sohn-Rethel. Rather than the disregarding of use-value being a *conscious* operation, it should instead be seen as an *active* operation, and non-conscious. The *remembrance* of use-value *is* conscious – in the mind rather than in action. Sohn-Rethel writes that commodity exchange is abstract because it excludes use; that is to say, the action of exchange excludes the action of use. But while exchange banishes use from the actions of people, it does not banish it from their minds. The minds of the exchanging agents must be occupied with the purposes which prompt them to perform the deal of exchange. Therefore whilst it is necessary that their action of exchange should be abstract from use, there is also necessity that their minds should not be. *The action alone is abstract.* (1978, p. 28, emphasis added)

Furthermore, '[i]n exchange, *the action is social, the minds are private*' (1978, p. 29). Thus, exchange is therefore of the realm of social action and use of private consciousness, against more typically materialist presentations of this differentiation. Use is both remembered and forgotten. Exchange relies on the two, in that it is founded on the basis of the dialectic between difference (the remembering of specific use-value) and identity (the forgetting of specific use-value) through which both desirability (the desire for a specific use-value) and commensurability (the ignoring of reconciliation of specific use-values) are made possible. As Sohn-Rethel notes, commodities are not 'equal in the evaluation of the exchanging agents', for if they were, to 'not see an advantage to themselves in performing it' would 'reduce their action to an absurdity'. However, the 'postulate of equality' that is necessary for exchange to take place takes hold in spite of this specific experience of difference that motivates the individuals involved. The evaluations of the difference or specificity of a given commodity are isolatable only to individual consciousness: appreciations of difference or specific use-value between persons are 'incomparable' and do not constitute a uniform principle in the manner in which equality can be said to do so. The postulate of equality, in fact, 'cuts across the gap of experience that separates the exchanging owners', and relies not on experience at all, but the practical activity of exchanging two distinct items. This exchange is the condition of the same postulate of equality upon which it depends. In a circuitous way, the very act of exchange establishes its own basis in equality: 'They are equated by virtue of being exchanged, they are not exchanged by virtue of any equality which they possess' (1978, p. 46).

The obliviousness of those involved to the abstraction they actively perform is secured through the reduction of these actions to 'strict uniformity, eliminating the differences of people, commodities, locality and date', and the establishment of money as a 'uniform denominator' which allows the relations of exchange to express themselves purely as a framework of 'quantitative differences. . .as different "prices"'. These elements help 'create a system of social communication of actions performed by individuals in complete independence of one another and oblivious to the socialising effect involved' (1978, p. 30).

What are the implications of this inscrutable non-empiricality for thinking through and resisting the nexus of value and labour? How do we grasp it in thought and practice? In the development of conceptuality from commodity exchange, the real abstraction of the latter is converted into the ideal abstraction of the former, through which the social synthetic function of exchange is manifested through the solidification of social forms of thinking as 'second nature' – something unnoticed to those involved. However, according to Sohn-Rethel, the conversion holds a mysterious and intangible status:

> Thinking of the conversion as a performance in people's minds, it can, of course, never be either demonstrated or denied because it cannot be witnessed. The concepts in question being *non-empirical*, their mental presence cannot be testified by observable objects or facts. To try to ask the people themselves is equally non-availing since we have ourselves made out that the conversion must be blotted out from the minds engaged in it. All we can argue is the problem at issue in the conversion and how to make it recognisable. In real life, the ideal abstraction blots out the real abstraction so as to make it irrecognisable. (1978, p. 62, emphasis added)

Furthermore, as well as being 'non-empirical', the abstraction is also 'non-factual'. The exchange abstraction itself operates around a series of 'social postulates' that guarantee exchangeability, equality, incommensurability, private property and so forth. However, these are conceptual in nature and resolutely non-factual. They can be said to exist by virtue of the deduction of the necessity of these rules to the 'social synthesis' of commodity society. Without the 'rules of reification', 'anarchical society' would not survive (1978, p. 68). However, it still remains that the forms of thinking that govern this are non-empirical and non-factual.

The non-empirical reality of the forms of conceptual thinking conducive to a system of exchange poses a direct problem. The conceptuality of exchange is not completely unconscious, but relies upon forgetfulness and concealment of the aspects that disrupt the postulate of equality: irreconcilable difference, contingency, change and so forth. *The real abstraction is social, whereas the minds of those involved in it are private.* The real abstraction is not represented in its full abstractness to the workings of the mind, because it is abstract in action rather than upon reflection. In fact, rather than merely not being reflected, '[t]he action of exchange stands in *antithetic polarity* to the sense-reality of things in the private minds of the individuals in their social life' (emphasis added). The non-empirical concepts that pass from the exchange abstraction into second nature – 'abstract time and space, abstract matter, quantity as a mathematical abstraction, abstract motion, etc.' – attain an obviousness that discourages any further reflection once they made this transition. They come to describe, when utilised, the action of the exchange abstraction 'reduced to bare-bone physical reality', shorn of all abstractness in keeping with the 'sense-reality of things in the private minds' of those participating (Sohn-Rethel 1978, pp. 72–3). Passing into second nature, there comes to be nothing in the universe to which these concepts cannot be applied.

By virtue of their springing from abstraction, these non-empirical concepts cannot be explained accurately in 'materialistic ways', Sohn-Rethel suggests. They cannot be directly reflected upon. Therefore, idealism, in spite of its 'blatant absurdities', possesses an 'epistemological premium' in their study (1978, p. 73). However, Sohn-Rethel suggests that a historical-materialistic explanation can be applied which situates the conceptuality of the real abstraction within a concrete social context (1978, pp. 74–5). What might open up to scrutiny the non-empirical reality of the exchange abstraction and the ideal forms it assumes may be those junctures when the postulates that govern the socially synthetic smooth functioning of the exchange abstraction – those of equality, commensurability and so forth – are confronted with the awkwardness of social circumstances, marked by struggle, failure and crisis. By conceptualising the breaches and ruptures that open up when systems of quantification break down, and the experiences of those subject to these breaches and ruptures, this non-empirical reality is brought into some kind of relief against the backdrop of concrete practices from which it springs in its social existence, outside of the private minds of the individuals involved. With and against Kant, Sohn-Rethel suggested that we could seek the origins of non-empirical conceptual frameworks in historical conditions, in some kind of spatio-temporal basis (1978, p. 74). In the next chapter, we will evaluate the methods by which it is possible to grasp, in thought and practice, this basis undergirding the non-empirical reality of value, and the dynamic relationship between non-empirical reality and the real social relations in which it is grounded.

3.7 CONCLUSION

This chapter has examined, through the terms if not the letter of the Kantian schema, the ways in which money as a means of exchange structures our experience of and interaction with the world. What this shows is that, although a non-empirical reality between things rather than of them, value has a basis in real concrete life, even though it exists as a real abstraction. The innovative approaches of NRM thinkers and forerunners like Lotz, Horkheimer and Sohn-Rethel, resituating central Kantian problematics on the plane of spatially and temporally bound social, historical and material human activity, gives us a springboard to interrogate more fully how what humans do day by day – work for a wage, exist as labour power consumed by the capitalist, buy and sell the things they need to live by means of money – relate to the specific system of abstract rule – the social synthesis – to which they are subject. From the most abstract level this analysis links the circulationist account of value charted in Chap. 2 with the practical and political lived experience of labour and the social constitution of capitalist society in the class antagonism that we will go on to assess in Chaps. 4 and 5. As we will see, value may be a non-empirical reality, but it is one that is posited and codified in the labour process and outside, and takes on a practical human effect in and through the dispossession and domination inherent to class society. This is just as the critical theory covered in this chapter would have it: an abstraction rooted in human practice.

BIBLIOGRAPHY

Bellofiore, R. 2009. A Ghost Turning into a Vampire: The Concept of Capital and Living Labour. In *Re-reading Marx: New Perspectives After the Critical Edition*, ed. R. Bellofiore and R. Fineschi, 178–194. London: Palgrave Macmillan.

Bowie, A. 2010. *German Philosophy*. Oxford: University Press.

Horkheimer, M. 1976 [1937]. Traditional and Critical Theory. In *Critical Sociology*, ed. P. Connerton, 206–224. London: Penguin.

Kant, I. 2007. *Critique of Pure Reason*. London: Penguin.

Lotz, C. 2014. *The Capitalist Schema: Time, Money, and the Culture of Abstraction*. Lanham: Lexington Books.

Porter, T.M. 1994. Making Things Quantitative. *Science in Context 7* (3): 389–407.

Scruton, R. 2001. *Kant*. Oxford: Oxford University Press.

Sohn-Rethel, A. 1978. *Intellectual and Manual Labour: A Critique of Epistemology*. London: Macmillan Press.

CHAPTER 4

Labour in the Valorisation Process

4.1 INTRODUCTION

We ended the last chapter with the insight that value is a non-empirical reality with a practical dimension. How then do we relate what goes on in the workplace to what goes on in exchange? This chapter seeks to answer this question by taking a detour through the issue of how, in research and practice, we can grasp the abstract, totalising social relation of the value form in and through the study of labour and, more simply, what goes on day by day in the workplace. I will first set out some theoretical conceptualisations of why this is so difficult, and why it has not formed the focus of any considerable or engaged tradition of value-form-oriented social research. This will focus on one hand on the differentiation between the labour process and the valorisation process of which it is the carrier – a point picked up again at the end of the chapter – and the conceptualisation of the 'modes of existence' assumed by value in capitalist society, which, following Richard Gunn, are forever fleeting, fugitive and unfixed in form and content. This makes for an elusive object of inquiry that cannot easily be mapped onto the everyday conditions of workplace life, just as labour effort cannot simply be projected outwards to its eventual realisation in the market.

We then go on to assess two very different approaches to capturing the totality of capitalist social relations and social forms inside and outside the workplace. The Italian workers inquiry tradition, of which some of the same theorists critiqued in Part 2 of this book were notable practitioners, takes a

F.H. Pitts, *Critiquing Capitalism Today*, Marx, Engels, and Marxisms,
DOI 10.1007/978-3-319-62633-8_4

revolutionary rereading of Marx's class analysis to inquire into the changing composition and character of workplace life as Western capitalism pivoted from Fordism to post-Fordism. In its original form, I suggest, it attempts unsuccessfully to wring the universe of capitalist society from the grain of sand that is the immediate form assumed by labour in the workplace. Later strands of 'social inquiry' launched by Antonio Negri, among others, more successfully capture work in its wider imbrication in capitalist social relations and the social forms of value. However – and as we will see in much greater detail in Part 2 – the study of immediate forms of productive activity richly rewards the operaist and postoperaist fixation on change and endless novelty, diminishing any appreciation of how things stay much the same under the continued rule of value as a category of social mediation. There is more to say about this than is possible in this chapter, and we will pick it up again in due course in the second half of the book.

The second approach we consider is the 'life trajectory of the commodity' approach found in feminist approaches to ethnographic social research concerned with economic life. By charting the different dimensions and interactions taken by commodities as they course through the circuit of capital, this method proves far more capable of providing a basis for the operationalisation of value as a category of applied inquiry. However, recognising the distance this predominantly circulationist approach travels from the contradictory unity between production and consumption central to the understanding of value in the NRM tradition, in a final movement to the chapter I place the conceptualisation of what can be said about value from the perspective of labour on a surer theoretical footing by means of the work of I.I. Rubin and Chris Arthur on the relationship between the labour process and the valorisation process, and, within this, concrete labour and its market-mediated expression in abstract labour.

4.2   Researching Value in and Beyond Labour

Marx writes in *Capital* that the 'production process' is composed of 'two aspects', the 'labour process' and the 'valorisation process' (1976, p. 304). The former is the carrier of the latter. This has implications for how we approach the workplace, epistemologically and ontologically, and how value is 'posited' (Arthur 2013) in the relation between it and its outside. In a 1981 paper on value theory and social research, Erik Olin Wright identifies the relative isolation of Marxian value theory from the 'concrete investigation...of social life'. The two meet only implicitly in the wide body of Marxist-influenced workplace studies. The issue of how the two might be reconciled is the central problem of this chapter. Wright contends that

> Debates on the LTOV are usually waged at the most abstract levels of theoretical discourse. Frequently these debates are preoccupied with questions of the appropriate methodological stance toward social analysis, epistemological disputes about what it means to 'explain' a social process, and mathematical arguments about the merits of competing ways of formally deriving certain categories from others. Rarely are the issues posed in terms of their implications for the concrete investigations of social life in which social scientists would engage. (1981a, p. 36)

According to Wright, the Marxist analysis of labour and value provokes researchers to look closely at the labour process, due to the central role played by the 'socio-technical conditions of production' in determining the value conferred upon the commodity. In this way, a simple picture of the inputs and outputs of production is inadequate; rather, what happens in-between becomes central (Wright 1981a, p. 63). The LTOV 'systematically direct[s] research towards questions of the labour process and its relationship to classes' by situating the 'conceptualisation of classes in terms of exploitation based in the relations of production' (Wright 1981b, pp. 130–1). This could be used as an explanatory factor for both class-struggle and labour-process streams of empirical research. In the seminal workplace ethnographies published in the UK over the 1970s and 1980s, examples such as Ruth Cavendish's *Women on the Line* (1982) and Huw Benyon's *Working for Ford* (1984) focused on the everyday conditions of work and the struggles between workers and management. The former possessed the virtue of linking what happens in the workplace to wider set of social positions and practices constituted on the basis of gender. Its author, otherwise known as Miriam Glucksmann, is central to a body of literature on the study of work and economic life we will consider in due course as an alternative to complement prevailing Marxist modes of analysis.

The most notable among attempts at fully fledged social research within the Marxist tradition are those carried out in Italy over the course of the 1960s and 1970s under the banner of the 'inquiry', of which some of the theorists critiqued in Part 2 of this book were practitioners. We will consider these in due course, suggesting that such approaches are deficient where the study of the theory of value is concerned. Whilst providing valuable insights into the quotidian conditions of work in contemporary capitalism, and compelling evidence as to the veracity of the Marxist concept of exploitation, such examples bear only the slightest proximity to the conceptual framework of the theory of value, with its explanation of how individual labours are rendered social by the system of commodity exchange, a mistake, incidentally, that largely owes to the specific theoretical assumptions of those involved with the development of the inquiry method. I will critique these assumptions in Part 2.

These examples suggest that instances of class conflict and domination provide a far more observable set of phenomena for research than do the categories of Marx's theory of value. The theory of value and its attendant categories (such as abstract labour) are only ever at best *implicit* in such research, but 'rarely is it explicitly incorporated into the *conceptualisation of the problem*' (Wright 1981a, p. 65, emphasis added). It is in light of this that this chapter explores how the theory of value can be *conceptualised as a problem* for social research to investigate. We will first outline in brief the conception of value theory henceforth utilised, with an emphasis on the latency and process of becoming behind the non-empirical ephemerality that makes value such a difficult topic to research with an empirical study.

As we have seen, the only labour that takes place is concrete, and, by extension, the study of concrete labour in and of itself offers little in the way of understanding of the true function of labour in the production of value, which relates to abstract labour. This inhibits the ability to interpret what is specific and notable about the existence of capitalist labour itself. Rather than constituting a set of observable and researchable practices that allow us to get to the bottom of value-producing labour, concrete labour comes to take a role in the production of value only by means of its mediation through the immaterial process whereby value is assigned to a quantity of abstract labour.

Thus, research geared solely towards concrete labour, its conditions and the experience of it, can touch upon only part of the reality of labour under capital. Research must instead be geared towards the social totality in which abstract labour is brought into existence. The 'commodity moment' marks only the resolution of a process of abstraction that begins with the inception of the production process. The expectation of monetary return which guides business activity already gives a tentative, latent form to abstract labour, and lays the foundation for its social validation over the whole course of the circuit of value creation. It is the crystallisation of abstract social labour-time in the form of money that marks the endpoint in what is in effect a *process* of social validation that begins in an ideal form as soon as bank finance sets the ball rolling. Whilst one can accept that the material paraphernalia of working life – wages, timesheets, performance indicators, targets, commission and, perhaps most of all, the clock – can all be seen as agents of this process of abstraction that are actively lived and experienced by workers, there remains a sphere of determination which exceeds these easily experienced and observed manifestations of social validation, taking on both empirical and non-empirical reality in the social totality at large, in money, commodities, circulation and consumption – namely, in the circuit of capital as a whole. This will be a recurring theme in the second part of this book.

Beginning from the basis that the exchange abstraction that synthesises capitalist society is a real abstraction (Sohn-Rethel 1978), here I set out some foundations for a way forward for research agendas around the value-form. The latter is a conceptuality with a material, practical existence in antagonistic social relations. This is sublated (Arthur 2013) in the value form. But as Bonefeld writes, 'reality contains within itself what it denies' (2014, p. 64). Critiquing economic categories reveals the materiality of concepts and the conceptuality of the material world. Thus, the coin in one's pocket 'carries the bond with society', a bond that concerns 'the struggle for access to the means of subsistence' (Bonefeld 2016b, p. 240; see also Marx 1993, pp. 156–7). The coin expresses and is concerned with this bond. But it also expresses a concept – value – inseparable from its constitution in the actual relations of life. The struggle for subsistence is as conceptual as it is material. But through its rootedness in subsistence the concept attains a real materiality. Reality, in this way, is socially constituted through human practice. As Horkheimer (quoted in Bonefeld 2016a, p. 60) writes, '[h]uman beings produce, through their own labour, a reality that increasingly enslaves them'. This link with practice defines value as a possible object of knowledge.

4.3   Modes of Existence

The idea of value as being the product of a social validation of labour enacted through exchange but present in a pre-emptory way in production conceives value as an abstraction which is essentially *emergent*, reliant upon a dialectic of potentiality and actuality. It is therefore hard to grasp, in theory and practice, academically and politically.

Bellofiore follows Lucio Colletti (1973, 1989) and Claudio Napoleoni (1975) in suggesting that the abstraction of labour is a mystical, metaphysical, mental abstraction that takes the form of a *real hypostatisation* taking place *in reality*. The abstraction that takes place in exchange is merely 'the end-point of a *process* of real hypostatization' that involves the whole capitalist cycle, including production (Bellofiore 2009, p. 180 [emphasis added]). At its most basic and earliest level, this can be exhibited in the fact that '*on the labour market*, the *worker* has to be seen *as an appendix of the commodity he[/she] sells*, labour power'. This leads Bellofiore to posit that 'abstract labour is not a mental generalization but a *real abstraction*. It goes on daily in the 'final' *commodity market*, but also in the *labour market* and *immediate production*' (2009, p. 183).

Such a perspective holds abstraction to be a process rather than an instance. As the *Endnotes* collective suggests (2010), value is a process which takes different forms at different times – money, labour-power, commodities, and then money again. This process-oriented conception of value is a central element of circuitist positions on value, and provides a useful counterguard against theorisations which present the production of value in a static, reductive way. Bellofiore and Finelli (1998) associate the theoretical foundations of Marx's conceptualisation of value in the nexus of possibility, potentiality and actuality presented in Aristotle's *Metaphysics* (1998, Book *Theta*, pp. 251–83). In Aristotle's schema, *possibility* is only the conceivable 'capacity to be', *potentiality* achieves 'being' in the sense that it is 'the unfolding of a form already implicit', and *actuality* is the result of potentiality's full unfolding. According to Bellofiore and Finelli, labour and value can be read along these lines, with labour power as 'the potentiality for labour', of which living labour is the actuality. At the same time, this actuality of labour is *potential* value, of which money is the actuality. Money then stands as 'potential capital', which can attain actuality through the valorisation of the labour process by means of exchange (Bellofiore and Finelli 1998, pp. 55–6).

As such, rather than the simultaneous 'performance' of concrete and abstract labour, it is perhaps better to see the latter as merely *latent* in the former, a mere possibility or potentiality awaiting actualisation. As Marx writes, '[s]ocial labour-time exists in...commodities in a latent state,...and becomes evident only in the course of their exchange'. Therefore, writes Marx, '[u]niversal social labour is consequently not a ready-made prerequisite but an emerging result' (1859). It is this latency that constitutes the conceptual thread which situates value at a point of articulation *between* both production and circulation. Rubin saw Marx as situating the exchange abstraction not merely post-production, but as a process which has its traces at every stage of the capitalist circuit (Bellofiore 2009, pp. 183–4). Following Rubin, Bellofiore discusses money and abstract labour as '*diachronic* concepts 'in motion', perpetually *in becoming*' (2009, p. 188). Rubin's belief in the latency of abstract labour is best summed up where he writes that abstract labour is 'not something to which form adheres from the outside. Rather, through its development, the content itself gives birth to the form which was already latent in the content' (Rubin 1972, p. 117). Bellofiore sees labour as inhabiting two characteristics in the very same activity. It is both concrete in that it possesses specific properties and '*latently abstract*' in that it possesses the 'tentative' promise of producing money (Bellofiore 2009, p. 189).

In contrast to productionist and circulationist variants of value theory, this perhaps is a more moderate way of placing abstract labour at the point of exchange – to say that it is only *latent* in production, a dual character of labour that is only half 'there' at any one time. In the same way that labour-power is not labour but the potential to be so, so too is abstract labour *not* labour but its residual aggregation. The first 'non-labour' is introduced before the labour process, the second arises afterwards. The belief in abstract labour as a 'type' of labour incites the expectation that this labour should be responsible for producing something, a misguided expectation that Marx does nothing to discourage with his representation of abstract labour as that element which gives rise to value and acts as its 'substance' (Elson 1979, p. 148) Marx himself does confuse matters somewhat when he writes of abstract labour that it is at once 'quantities of homogeneous human labour' (1976, p. 128) and 'human labour pure and simple, the expenditure of human labour in general' (1976, p. 135). The two accounts are marked by differing temporal perspectives, the first conveying abstraction as a retrospective summation of the labour that has taken place, the second suggesting that this abstraction functions through the expenditure of general human labour on the job. The first places an emphasis upon abstract labour as the aggregation of abstract labour-time *ex post*, whereas the second places an emphasis upon abstract labour as something with a concrete, active existence. It is the former, *ex post* appreciation – henceforth referred to as one of 'social validation' – which proves adequate to a conception of abstract labour as latent.

This latency is evinced in the means by which abstract labour is measured, as an average established after production has taken place. Abstract labour cannot be counted on the clock, like the hours expended in acts of concrete labour. Rather, abstract labour is not expended at all. Instead, as

Heinrich asserts, abstract labour is a '*relation of social validation* that is constituted in exchange'. In this process, 'privately expended concrete labor' is validated as 'a particular quantum of value-constituting abstract labor' (Heinrich 2012, pp. 50–1). Therefore, as charted in Chap. 2, the determination of value is considered to be subject to a process located within the entire circuit of production and circulation.

In foregrounding the process of social validation by which labour is rendered productive of value, the theory of value given here has placed an emphasis upon abstract labour rather than concrete as the key guise in which labour attains significance in the capitalist mode of production. The content of labour may be much the same in other kinds of society. What renders this one specific is the *form* labour assumes. In this conceptualisation, what is most important is that once a product of labour is confirmed as a commodity possessed of value and exchangeability, the *concrete* specificity of individual labours is *abstracted from* in order to smooth out the former's differences and constitute pure, undifferentiated homogeneous labour expressed in exchangeable commodities. By means of this process, the labour which went into a commodity's production is *validated* as a portion of the total abstract labour of society, as *productive* labour which has helped bestow value upon a good or service so that it can stand as a commodity in a relationship of equivalence and commensurability with the other commodities of the market by means of money.

Hence, abstract labour does not take place at all, but is an invention of the process of abstraction that stems from the concrete, private nature of the labour that takes place in capitalist society. It becomes social and abstract only after it has occurred.

Part of the problem with extracting from this nexus a suitable object of study and knowledge is the appearance of value in various modes of existence hard to capture with a conventional research approach. We will begin sketching a conception of an adequate object of research by establishing some theoretical foundations. Richard Gunn differentiates two modes of theorising, *determinate* and *empiricist* abstraction (1992, p. 23). The simplest way to sum up what Gunn means when he poses empiricist abstraction against determinate abstraction is that the former refers to a mental category, such as 'production', which abstracts from and irons out the differences between all the different modes of production to create one which functions as a synonym for all, whereas the latter refers to an abstraction that has a real existence, such as the abstraction 'labour', which may well function as an empiricist abstraction, taking all the different kinds of work and abstracting from them for ease of presentation, but also has a social form that arrives with the development of the exchange relation, in which different and multifarious labours are abstracted from in the shape of value (Gunn 1989, pp. 19–21). Whereas empiricist abstraction relies upon a set of *external* relations, determinate abstraction describes a situation of *internal* relatedness strung together by the totalising modes of existence of social phenomena. In this internal relatedness, A might be B's mode of existence (or 'form'), with B also as A's mode of existence. Furthermore, C might be B's mode of existence, and D the mode of existence of C whilst also having a separate mode of existence as A. This 'criss-crossing field of mediations' constitutes a totality, no part of which persists on its own (Gunn 1992, p. 24).

The internal relatedness described by Gunn is not defined by mere *relations* between things, nor *equivalences*. Rather, what faces us are actual *samenesses*, complete *identicalities*, in which things stand as modes of existence of one another (1992, p. 24), but in which is implied an irreducible non-identity. This has implications for apprehending value and its appearances in programmes of social research. One that may be inferred from this explanation of determinate abstraction is that research objects are essentially *elusive*, present only in the totality of relations, appearances and modes of existence itself. The mode of existence, for Gunn, conforms precisely to that Aristotelian notion of process which we earlier attributed to the production of value. For Gunn, 'actuality and activity are the same thing', and to *be* is to *do* (1992, p. 38, n. 14). The mode of existence, then, must not be seen as a passive or static 'being', but an active 'doing', in which 'existence' is read as exsistence or ek-stasis or ecstasy, that is, in an active way, in which 'nothing static…inheres' (1992, p. 21).

For Gunn, such 'existence-in-practice' is the hallmark of determinate abstraction, and 'mode of existence' the true object of the study of 'form' (1992, p. 23). As such, a clear link can be drawn between the study of value as a social form and the idea of value as a process of possibility, potentiality and actuality – a mode of active *existence*. Furthermore, such a form is not only marked by its active existence as a process, but through its constitution as 'an internally related 'field'', in which 'anything can be the mode of existence of anything else'. In these two aspects – what Gunn calls 'unfixity of form' (1992, p. 32) and internal relatedness – is presented the real problem which faces researchers who venture into the study of value theory and its categories: the mode of existence.

Thus, in the course of its becoming, value can be seen as subject to a constant procession of such 'modes of existence', of which internal relatedness and unfixity of form are the chief features. In the first, *internal relatedness*, all things appear as everything else. In the second, *unfixity of form*, each manifestation of form is fleeting, fugitive and elusive. These issues present obvious problems for social research geared to the investigation of the value form. The conceptualisation offered by Gunn would seem to suggest that what is needed is a social research which rather than avoiding or attempting to reduce the internal relatedness and unfixity of the phenomena which it studies, is geared towards the investigation of modes of existence as an object of investigation.

We might phrase the sequence of these modes of existence in the following way. Labour is significant in capitalism by virtue of its abstraction and validation as value-producing. Hence, to investigate labour under capital, one must look to value. Value and its categories are elusive, and its investigation always points towards another place. For instance, value theory might direct inquiry towards the other commodity in which the value of a given commodity is represented. Furthermore, the social labour-time necessary for a commodity's reproduction of course pertains to that amount of labour time necessary to expend in order to be able to create the means by which the commodity may be purchased or exchanged for. This implies that in order to judge SNLT, one must look at another commodity, and for that, another, and so on and on endlessly. The commodity only possesses value insofar as it is drawn into a relation of equivalence with other commodities – or indeed the universal equivalent of money. In order to research labour-time, for instance, we must first look not at the commodity produced in that labour-time, but another commodity, or, indeed, money itself. This demands a holistic approach to research which encapsulates both production and circulation. This means that it cannot follow previous Marxist social research in limiting itself to the workplace, instead situating itself in the whole totality of capitalist social relations, pushing against the constraints that confront any attempt to capture the totality of social form in an applied research context.

As the description of the different stages that value takes in the process of production and circulation which forms its central movement displays, value is an elusive category to research, constantly withdrawing from quick and easy observation. A social, all-encompassing investigation of the totality of relations is needed in order to capture some impression of the 'modes of existence' that value assumes in society. The law of value cannot be researched without consideration of exchange, abstraction and circulation. What is needed is a research approach which does not limit itself to the labour-process or the realm of production, but can appreciate the capitalist circuit in the round. In the following, I will consider two alternatives in the study of capitalist social relations – the workers inquiry tradition stemming from Italian operaismo, and the 'life trajectory of the commodity' method found in feminist approaches. Each has its merits, and each its flaws. But, in assessing the two methods, we can probe the possibilities of grasping in practice the relationship between labour and value suggested by the NRM in theory.

4.4   THE WORKERS' INQUIRY TRADITION

Many examples of Marxian research into work and the labour-process are deficient for the purposes of an inquiry into value and its categories. Often this is attributable to the simple fact that their object is typically class struggle and its transparent, observable instances. Turning our attention towards the Italian worker's inquiry tradition we find many such problems. Whilst providing a useful case study for delineating some of the problems faced by a social research approach to value theory, however, the history of 'workers' inquiry' in Italy also points us towards a potential way out.

The 'workers' inquiry' is perhaps the most notable strand of Marxian social research, specifically for the fact that it originates with Marx himself (2013). However, it was the Italian autonomists who provided the necessary update to the inquiry template, and, in the process, its popularisation. Scholars and activists grouped around the journal *Quaderni Rossi* eschewed the remote engagement of the questionnaire in order to insert themselves within industrial workplaces (often as workers) and perform research from *within* and in conjunction with the object of their research, the workers themselves (Brown and Quan-Hase 2012, p. 489).

These attempts to infiltrate the factories and their workers had historical foundations in Mao's clarion call 'No investigation, no right to speak!', which inspired Maoists in the West to send 'moles' into factories in their home countries. At the same time, they rubbed shoulders with militant Leninists who had entered workplaces in order to whip up revolt under their exclusive leadership (Aufheben 2004). Within these two earlier instances, Maoist and Leninist, can be traced the basis for a split between two tendencies in the *Quaderni Rossi* group.

On the one hand, the *Quaderni Rossi* grouping arose from young elements of the Italian socialist and communist parties who, Wright tells us, sought to 'apply Marx's critique of political economy…to unravel the fundamental power relationships of modern class society… In the process, they sought to confront *Capital* with "the *real* study of a *real* factory", in pursuit of a clearer understanding of the new instances of independent working-class action' (Wright 2002, p. 3). This gave rise to what is referred to as a 'sociological-objectivist' current who wished to simply understand and analyse working conditions employing interview techniques inspired by industrial sociology (Aufheben 2004). This understanding and analysis could then be turned towards the effective political activity of the organisations pitched in on the side of the workers (Thorne 2011). Panzieri (1965), a key representative of the current, suggests that such research provides an empirical bulwark against over-optimistic portraits of class power at any one time. In this way, it mirrors the Maoist invocation of investigation before action.

Whereas the sociological-objectivist current characterised the workers only as an *object* of research, the second 'political-interventionist' current saw the worker as constituting a joint subject-object who effectively participates in the performance of the research. The political-interventionist tendency also displayed scepticism about the sociological-objectivist current's use of industrial sociology, which was seen as a bourgeois tool of the capitalist academy and of utility only in so far as it provided a first step in researching the field before the jointly constituted co-research of worker and researcher could begin (Aufheben 2004). Rather than merely understanding or analysing the situation, research in the political-interventionist vein was conducted from a strategic and tactical standpoint of encouraging workers to come to (correct) consciousness and participate in the class struggle through their own self-activity and self-understanding as co-researchers (Thorne 2011; de Molina 2004). As such, it compares to the earlier militant interventions carried out by Leninists who inserted themselves artificially in potential sites of workplace revolt.

As Brown and Quan-Hase suggest, the one similarity that persisted between Marx's inquiry and that of the autonomists was the strict location of such studies within the 'factory as the central site of study', not only sociologically but physically. Whilst principally a matter of convenience in that factories concentrated workers 'in geographically specific locations…working en masse at regular and predictable hours, and on jobs that could be observed or described first hand' (not to mentioned compared), it could be claimed that the narrow focus upon such workplaces is also attributable in part to the 'workerist' ideology popular on the Italian left at the time, and exhibits many of the pratfalls of Marxian research I have highlighted in the preceding discussion of the role played by labour in the production of value – which, in the Italian case, provide the material with which the critique presented in Part 2 works.

However, an alternative trend to that of the workerist tendency in the inquiry tradition provides valuable pointers for potential ways forward. By the end of the 1960s, many of the representatives of this workerist tendency ended up in the organisation *Potere Operaio*, which took the political-interventionist current to its logical conclusion by dispensing with inquiry entirely in favour of struggle and intervention in the factories through rank-and-file committees. However, inquiry was rejuvenated at the end of the 1970s with publications such as *Primo Maggio*. The new spirit of inquiry developed partly in reaction to workerism. Negri had posited the new *operaio sociale*, 'a new proletariat disseminated through society' through capitalist restructuring and the 'massification of abstract labour'. The study of this new class subjectivity, defined by its activity in the social fabric at large rather than the traditional workplace, necessitated an inquiry 'obliged to follow the workers outside the factory' (Aufheben 2004) in their roles as agents of consumption and circulation as well as of production. The necessity to turn outside the workplace into society is one that still confronts Marxian research today – although not, as shown in Part 2, in such a way as that suggested by the likes of Negri, which, as we shall see, still rests upon a fairly traditional understanding of how work and society relate, in spite of its claims to a radical and revolutionary revisionism.

In the investigation of the *operaio sociale*, co-research came to play a central role. This co-research is described by Negri as 'involving building a description of the productive cycle and identifying each worker's function within that cycle; but at the same time it also involves assessing the levels of exploitation which each of them undergoes' (Negri 2008, pp. 162–3). As such, co-research retains a focus on exploitation within the realm of production whilst seeking to situate this experience in the overall processes of capitalist valorisation. It resembles what today is known as participatory action research, expanding 'the scope of research locales' into other areas of society such as the school and the community.

As Brown and Quan-Hase suggest, this expansion, like earlier developments in inquiry method from Marx to the *Quaderni Rossi*, demonstrates the way in which 'it is the problems presented by the contemporary labouring context that force us to once again change our strategies' (2012, pp. 490–1). Furthermore, new understandings of value, forged through the immanent critique of work on the topic in the Marxist tradition, should also provoke us to consider new strategies for research. Not least among the novelties of any new strategy must be an approach that does not reduce all Marxian research to a study of the workers who bear the brunt of capitalist production as has the workers' inquiry tradition, but rather opens a window upon the system of commodity exchange to which capitalist production stands in service. This latter aim requires a radically new conception of the object of such research, the broader social context of which is only hinted at by the developments in autonomist inquiry achieved by *Primo Maggio* and their investigation of the *operaio sociale*.

Within this more outward-facing conception of the inquiry is contained an attempt to embed work and those who perform it within the wider totality of production, circulation, consumption and the circuit of capital. Hence, one can see within the inquiry tradition a potentially convergent path from that of a study simply of the conditions and subjectivities of production, which, rather than limiting itself to the workplace, extends its reach into a more *social* path of investigation – a *social* inquiry. This potential is foreshortened, ultimately, by a residual productivism that ascribes orthodox assessments of the primacy of production to fields of activity formally outside it. We will consider this further in the second part of the book.

Whilst there is a clear chronological development that leads from the workers' to the social inquiry, there is no simple fixed point at which the 'factory went social' and the inquiry adequate to it became social in turn. Even in the new kinds of work to which the moniker 'immaterial' has attached itself, fairly traditional techniques of inquiry remain. A notable example is that of Kolinko's call centre inquiry (2002). Despite the stated recognition that '[w]e cannot only focus on call centres because these – like any sector – can only be understood by looking at capitalist cooperation', in *Hotlines*, the isolated workplace is the singular focus of the inquiry. Rather than the inquiry building into a wider conceptualisation of the position of call centres in the circuit of capital, the external context in which call centre work is situated is largely considered only as preliminary preparation for the real business of the research itself. In spite of paying lip-service to a theorisation of the broken boundaries between the formal realm of production and the valorising forces found in society outside the workplace (2002, p. 193), Kolinko's inquiry stays squarely within a traditionally workerist paradigm.

Elsewhere, contemporary inquiry has become endowed with a more 'social' quality in response to the perceived development of 'cognitive capitalism' and the hegemonic position assumed by immaterial labour in capitalist society. De Molina (2004) suggests that the eminence of knowledge and the exploitation of the common in new immaterial forms of production require a mode of inquiry geared towards the mapping of 'cartographies' of the manifestations of valorisation in society. This largely corresponds to the argument made here, albeit for the weight of the emphasis placed upon the novelty of the present condition. The theorisation of the law of value given above privileges an explanation oriented around the social validation of abstract labour rather than the expenditure of concrete labour. Put simply, any and all labour may be reconciled with the former, whatever the distinct guise or form taken by the latter. Therefore, against accounts such as that of Hardt and Negri (2001, p. 292), which would suggest that any proper theory of value is compromised by the immateriality and immeasurability of the new forms of production, the alleged advent of immaterial labour does not compromise or render dated the theory of value given above, a point expanded on at length in Part 2 of this book. What this suggests is that the insistence of de Molina and others upon the imperativeness of social inquiry in the context of specifically contemporary conditions of capitalist production is misleading. No 'new facts' are needed to guide us from the traditional workers' inquiry to that of the social. A fully 'social' inquiry has always been necessary, because capitalism is and has always been subject to a process of immaterial social abstraction, of which cognitive capitalism is as much a piece as any other previous appearance of the same system, and which can be better, if not fully, appreciated by means of a perspective that treats all society as a factory in which valorisation is achieved.

What is needed is a research approach which does not limit itself to the labour process or the realm of production, but can appreciate the capitalist circuit in the round. This entails a research which has as its object the totality of capitalist social relations. In the next part of the chapter, I will sketch out an example of the research practice that this necessitates, reflecting upon some of the ways in which the initial threads of such an approach are promised in existing research programmes derived from feminist approaches which follow the 'life trajectory of the commodity' through society, as a medium through which the social relations that constitute the value-form – production, circulation, consumption – can be captured as an object of social research which gives over to its essential unfixity and endless interrelationality rather than coming up against these qualities as obstacles.

4.5   THE LIFE TRAJECTORY OF THE COMMODITY

By way of illustration, there is one body of literature in social research which seems to be able to grasp production as a process unlimited to the workplace and to appreciate the internal relatedness of the totality of social relations, to the extent that working tasks cannot be considered in and of themselves without reference to the commodities they create and the way in which they fit into to the total labour of society. This body of literature is associated with a feminist understanding of social phenomena as criss-crossed with relations of gender and social reproduction. The gender-oriented approaches detailed here illustrate a broad, all-encompassing and essentially *processual* understanding which incorporates commodities, labour and economic relations as parts of a totality. Whilst this tendency, exemplified here by the theoretical contributions of Miriam Glucksmann on the 'total social organisation of labour' and the empirical research of Cynthia Cockburn and Susan Ormrod, does not possess or provide all the answers we are seeking, it can be seen to point us in a number of worthwhile directions.

In her understanding of the organisation of production, Glucksmann is interested in the way in which interconnections exist within different types of work activity, and between work and non-work activities outside the formal confines of the workplace. In an attempt to provide the necessary 'equipment' for a 'new sociology of work' adequate to contemporary capitalism, her 'total social organisation of labour' schema defines four dimensions. The first is 'across the processes of production, distribution, exchange and consumption'. The second is 'across the boundaries between paid and unpaid work, market and non-market, formal and informal sectors'. The third is 'the articulation of work activities and relations with non-work activities and relations'. The fourth is 'differing temporalities of work and the significance of temporality across the other three interconnections' (2005, p. 19). Glucksmann suggests that temporality is the 'golden thread' that connects the first three dimensions, 'denot[ing] the organisation of time in durations, cycles, synchronies, sequences and rhythms, and their articulation' (2005, p. 33).

Glucksmann emphasises the 'overlapping and inseparable' quality of these linkages (2005, p. 19). Rejecting the notion of a 'circuit' of production and consumption for its implied linearity, Glucksmann suggests instead that we adopt a conception of *overall process* as the means by which the interlocking mechanisms are expressed (2005, p. 25). As examples of the way in which the internal relatedness of economic processes can be appreciated with an overall approach, Glucksmann writes of the complex ways in which the 'provision' of ready-made food is intricately linked to the productive role of women in society and the way in which commodities such as washing machines were turned from industrial use in laundrettes to instruments of female reproductive labour in the home. She suggests that 'ever-extendable' examples such as these demonstrate the way that they cohere only through a process consisting of 'a particular configuration of production, distribution, exchange and consumption', from which no element 'can be properly appreciated on its own' (2005, p. 28).

Having, as mentioned, carried out a seminal workplace study under the *nom de plume* Ruth Cavendish, Glucksmann's earlier study *Women Assemble* (1990) attempted to put these principles into action. With a focus upon the role of technology as a factor in a social process encompassing production, circulation and consumption, the study focused upon assembly-line production and the way in which it not only positioned women as the users of technology as part of the production process but also the purchasers and users of the commodities produced when they reached the realm of circulation. It is such a perspective, with its object as commodity production and consumption considered *in the round*, as a totalising social process, which might be most adequate for research into the theory of value.

Cockburn and Ormrod cite Glucksmann's earlier work as an influence upon their own inquiry into the social interaction between, and dual constitution of, gender and technology (1993). In this piece of research, Cockburn and Ormrod studied the path a specific commodity takes through society, in this case the microwave oven. From design, through production, distribution, marketing, selling, consumption, use and obsolescence, Cockburn and Ormrod analyse the different dimensions of the way gender is inscribed within and constituted in conjunction with the commodity. Although, as the authors acknowledge, this treatment might seem to unduly reify the commodity itself, the analysis of this commodity as the product of a complex system of social relations insures against such a pratfall. Further, unlike other studies that reify not so much the commodity itself but a specific, isolated *aspect* of the commodity's production – such as research which confines itself solely to the labour-process in a formal workplace with no consideration of the wider economic apparatus in which such a labour-process is situated – Cockburn and Ormrod's study of the microwave oven, through the conduit of the conceptualisation of a commodity as subject to a process which encapsulates multiple different social modes and activities, is distinguished by its emphasis 'not on any one moment in the life of a technology (design, diffusion etc.) but rather to trace the whole life trajectory of an artefact' (1993, p. 3). The motivation for this overall view of production and circulation consisted in the fact that extant approaches to the social study of technology had emphasised only the initiation of technology in production, where the engineers and scientists participating were overwhelmingly male. By extending 'the scope of the technology world' beyond 'the initiatory moment' and into consumption and use, the study could account for women's engagement with technology in a more explicit way (1993, pp. 9–10).

Cockburn and Ormrod criticise approaches focused only on one or the other aspect of the 'innovation' and 'impact' of technology. Where a focus on 'innovation' ignores the way in which the social role of technology is partly constituted after its production, one occupied only with 'impact' reifies the particular technology in question as something that appears entirely unproblematically as somehow 'given' in society (1993, p. 11). Research into value is faced with a similar conundrum. A focus purely on the labour that takes place in the production of a commodity misses the important way in which this labour is only rendered a productive component of the total labour of society by means of an abstraction located in exchange and merely latent during production. Meanwhile, a focus only on the 'commodity-moment' in which the instantaneous validation of concrete labour as abstract takes place misses the parts of the process which necessitate and presuppose this occurrence. Cockburn and Ormrod's emphasis of the 'life trajectory' of the microwave oven provides a possible template for a circuitist, processual research approach aimed holistically at both production and circulation which might circumvent these dilemmas.

Cockburn and Ormrod perform this analysis of the 'life trajectory' of the microwave oven by exploiting the commodity's ability to 'provide…a rationale for, and [give] coherence to, a sequence of contacts and case studies'. These 'linked case studies' thus give a picture of a series of interlaced 'phases in the life trajectory of the artefact, involving an overview of a wide network of actors and agencies' (1993, pp. 3–4). This meets the two criteria implied by the preceding critique of value and the possibilities of social research. On the one hand, the processual nature of the research is susceptible to an understanding of *unfixity*, the movement of possibility, potentiality and actuality which defines commodity production and exchange, and an appreciation of the fleeting and fugitive nature of economic categories within the constant transition and overhaul which marks this process. On the other, the incorporation through the medium of the commodity of a wide network of social relations represented in a range of case studies encourages recognition of the radical *internal relatedness* of the capitalist totality.

Any such programme of research which uses the commodity as its basis poses a number of serious difficulties. The study of the commodity can be problematic – not least for the fact that a commodity is only a commodity in relation to the wider world of commodities, and only has value in so far as this value is expressed in an equivalent commodity, inviting an endless inquisition into a seemingly infinite procession of 'modes of existence'. It is by virtue of its lack of an explicit commodity-analysis that Cockburn and Ormrod's study of the microwave oven leaves only *pointers* towards possible directions rather than a template. Whilst a research approach geared towards unfixity and internal relatedness can *open up upon* modes of existence as an object of research, these modes of existence are nowhere more profound, mysterious and *real* as with the world of the commodity and the production of value of which it is the agent.

One of the chief problems of the more myopic treatment of the commodity circuit that may follow from a life-trajectory approach is that it may unduly reify the commodity and its social position. In the same way that a myopically labourist study of valorisation would simply reflect the fetishisation of labour in capitalist society, an approach inspired by the life-trajectory method might perform the same mirroring of capitalist social relations. Cleaver (2000, pp. 76–7) asserts how the strands of post-operaist thought and workers' inquiry inspired by conceptualisations of the social factory sought to undermine such fetishisations by compromising the clean separation of productive work from non-productive leisure, of commodities from the underlying class struggle from which they are forged. The 'social' inquiry provides a basis for both the recognition of the importance of the whole circuit of capital in the process of valorisation – and the way that this can be traced through the travel of the commodity through society – whilst endowing any study of this movement with an understanding of class and social reproduction and the struggles that pertain to them.

Looking for evidence of this mode of research and analysis in the inquiry tradition, perhaps the closest recent parallel we might identify with reference to this radicalised 'life trajectory of the commodity' approach is that exhibited in the Uninomade Collective's inquiry into the logistics sector (2013). The study of logistics is the study not only of an isolated sector, but also the study of commodities and their valorisation in a much wider sense. An inquiry into logistics invites scrutiny of the movement of commodities in society, and the unfolding of their valorisation at the different stages of this movement. The example of logistics provides an exemplary focus for such a study, bringing into perspective one of the chief means by which the valorisation of commodities is made possible, namely via the lubrication of the structures which bring goods to people and people to goods. We will return to this aspect in Chap. 9.

What this excursion through method has shown is that the position of work and workers in capitalist society – and by extension its link with value, that key principal towards which all critique of capitalism must direct itself – cannot be understood solely on the basis of work, workers and workplaces, without consideration of the process of exchange, abstraction and circulation which truly renders work and those who perform it socially significant, by means of the role played in the determination of value and, thus, the forms of appearance value assumes.

The workers' inquiry tradition has tended to fall short of this model of social research, subject to a narrow preoccupation with the workplace, even where extrapolated to society as a whole, as we shall see in the discussion of Negri's thought in Part 2. However, later strands inspired by the theorisation of the 'social factory' can be seen as providing the initial germ of a basis for future research into value, calling into dispute the reification of the formal workplace in favour of an outward-facing position that encompasses the process of valorisation in the domestic, cultural and educational realms. Alongside such contributions, inquiries into certain key areas of capitalist activity, such as that by the Uninomade Collective into the logistics sector, also provide the basis for a deeper and more extensive exploration of the interrelational and unfixed procedures of valorisation. The later trends in the Italian inquiry tradition point towards the kind of social, all-encompassing research of the totality of capitalist social relations that is needed in order to capture some impression of the 'modes of existence' that value assumes in society, even if they ultimately fail.

Equally, this non-empirical reality is rooted in a non-conceptual sphere of material relations that can be accessed more easily at the level of social research. The theorisation of value given up to this point may seem, in emphasising the abstract unfolding of the value relation through exchange, somewhat ephemeral and uprooted from concrete circumstance. But, as critical complements to the NRM tradition make clear, we cannot forget that what happens in exchange also depends upon the existence of certain social relations of production and 'actual conditions of life' that make abstract labour practically possible (Bonefeld 2014, see Chap. 5).

4.6   THE LABOUR PROCESS AS CARRIER OF THE VALORISATION PROCESS

Capturing this in method hinges on the relationship between what goes on in the workplace and the forms it assumes and is determined in and by virtue of the market. In order to research how what goes in the workplace relates to what goes on outside in the market and commodity exchange, it is necessary to take a perspective whereby value cannot be seen only as an abstract unfolding uprooted from concrete circumstances, but rather an abstract unfolding rooted in a contradictory relationship with the concrete conditions of its existence – conditions it at one and the same time thrives on and denies. Here I will explore how this relates to the concept of 'practical abstraction', and, in the next section, how this implies what Chris Arthur calls the 'sublation' (2013) of the social relations of production within the value-form which any inquiry must retrieve.

A good starting point is Rubin, who sets out to 'reveal how people's productive relations find their expression in value' (1978). This approach does not 'take the concept of value as the starting point of the investigation', but rather the concept of *labour*. However, this does not mean that the concept of labour is either given or unchanged in its encounter with that of value. Rather, writes Rubin, 'we define the concept of labour in such a way that the concept of value also follows from it'. We begin from labour only to read it through the prism of value, examining labour via an understanding of its imbrication in capitalist valorisation and the social relations of production that support it.

The key concept for how I understand labour through value is abstract labour. This embeds an appreciation of abstract labour into a wider account of how we work and what work is like for those who do it, so that the concept of abstract labour runs through our understanding of the buying of selling of labour power, the wage, exploitation, time discipline, measurement and workplace control and resistance like the lettering runs through a stick of rock. This, I consider, is what Rubin means when he writes that we should look at labour only insofar as we do so with a conception of value that flows directly from it. Abstract labour, here, can be taken as what Geert Reuten (2005) describes as a 'placeholder' for value and money, bringing those concepts into the study of work. It is, as previously defined in sect. 4.3, a mode of existence of something wider.

Abstract labour is distinct from the concrete labour practically expended in the sphere of production. It is the outcome of the commensuration and equalisation of diverse labours by means of the meeting of the commodities they produce via exchange in the sphere of circulation. But labour takes on an abstract dimension earlier, both before and during its expenditure in the sphere of production. In this section, I use the work of Chris Arthur to explore how. His conceptualisation of labour's 'practical abstraction' equates roughly with Gunn's understanding of 'empiricist abstraction', covered at the head of this chapter, and captures the feasibility of a study of value through the study of labour. Whilst the abstraction of labour culminates in the exchange of commodities by means of money in exchange, Arthur gives an account of how this abstraction is practically formed in a preliminary sense in the realm of production.

Arthur contrasts the presentation of abstract labour in *Capital* with the earlier presentation given in Marx's notebooks for the latter, the *Grundrisse*. In the former, abstract labour is derived logically from simple circulation, reasoned from the chain exchange–value–labour–abstract labour. But in the *Grundrisse*, abstract labour as a category is derived from the relations of capitalist production. This chimes with the historical reading offered by Bonefeld, which, as we will see more clearly in the next chapter, poses against the 'logical' understanding of value's abstract unfolding given in the NRM a story of the 'social constitution' of value in a continuing process of primitive accumulation. As Arthur writes, 'the *determinateness* of the category of "abstract labour" is the outcome of specific historical conditions and retains its validity only within these conditions' (2013, p. 102). We will hear more of these conditions in Chap. 5.

Whilst *Capital* in many ways gives a more sophisticated rendering of Marx's theory of value – and, as Marx himself suggests, we must analyse the ape from the vantage point of the human, treating his most final complete work as the most definitive – Arthur contends that Marx leaves behind certain insights present in the *Grundrisse* that flesh out our understanding of precisely how concrete labour is reduced to abstract in and by means of the value-form.

For Arthur, what Marx regrettably leaves behind in the transition from the notebooks to the end product is any idea that abstract labour possesses a 'practical truth' situated *within* capitalist production itself, rather than only in the exchange of commodities that follows in the sphere of circulation. In *Capital*, therefore, we find abstract labour at the beginning, but seldom thereafter. But, following Rubin's instruction to read labour in such a way that value follows seamlessly from it, Arthur uses Marx's work in the *Grundrisse* to explore the initial buying and selling of labour-power as centring upon a foundational abstraction that makes possible the positing of value in the first place.

Arthur reads Marx as suggesting in the *Grundrisse* that 'it is *capitalist* production which imposes on labour its determination as abstract (not simply commodity exchange)'. This is because the whole process proceeds from the aim to produce 'wealth in its abstract form': value, measured by money (2013, p. 103). Accordingly, the inputs are priced in this form of abstract wealth and this enables them to be 'posited' as value-bearing and value-producing. Thus labour, for Arthur, is already potentially practically abstract before production proper commences. This is for three principal reasons. First, labour power is sold as the sheer potential to labour, rather than labour itself. It thus carries from the beginning a mentally abstract character. Second, money changes hands in order to bring this labour power – this potential to labour – under the ownership of the capitalist. This, as with other commodities, renders it a commensurate component of the abstract social relation between things that we call value. The link between these first two points, as Arthur has it, is that whilst wage labour might appear as 'an array of specific jobs', as 'a source of value' it 'confronts capital as an abstract totality' to which the framework of SNLT relates as 'the time taken' by production at its average (2013, p. 106).

There is also a third respect in which we can say that labour is abstract in advance of the exchange of the commodities it produces. Arthur writes that 'abstraction is not merely the conceptual result of a concrete totality of labours, but it is a reality when individuals pass easily from one labour to another indifferently' (2013, p. 103). Workers move between jobs – within and without skilled trades and industries. The wage form through which the worker subsists, and through the capitalist acquires the worker's labour power, pays for the reproduction of a commodity – labour-power – via human existence regardless of specific application. The wage abstracts already from all concrete activity, and thus the range of jobs a worker has over the course of a lifetime, and the movement of workers as a whole between and within roles and industries, exerts an abstracting effect already, in advance of production and circulation normally conceived. In this way, unemployment is most abstract condition of all, tied as it is to the requirement to live through the wage form yet free of any specific sale or expenditure of labour power. In Chap. 8, we will complicate this position with reference to the apparently resonant reading of the relationship between contemporary work and abstraction given in the work of Negri.

Situating labour's practical abstraction at the inception of capitalist production may seem to diverge from a reading of value as arbitrated ultimately in exchange. But rather, employing Rubin's call to interpret labour in such a way as value follows from it, what it shows is that labour power is engaged in production through a process of exchange, and from this initial exchange, of the worker's potential to labour for a wage, it gains a preliminarily abstract character. For labour to contribute towards creating something that eventually bears value, it must be bought and sold as a commodity, and itself validated as part of value's abstract social whole which holds in the equivalence of all things with all other things. The validation of labour power as a commodity confers it a monetary status. It becomes practically abstract. This is key to its measurement and manipulation in the process of production. It is the precursor to workplace processes of measurement, and guarantees the continuing conditions of measurability on which the theoretical dispute with the postoperaists surveyed in Part 2 centres. Its validation as monetary and practically abstract creates the conditions whereby labour can be usefully engaged in the generation of a product that can, as a commodity, act as the bearer of the value relation.

The key concept here, for Arthur, is 'positing'. Arthur describes value-positing as 'the truth of the labour process', with respect to the status of the latter as the 'carrier of the valorisation process'. In this sense, 'the labour process is 'subsumed' under the valorisation process' (2013, p. 104). This conforms with our reading of labour as continuous with the conceptualisation of value. One cannot confront labour without value, as the process of the former carries the process of the latter.

The whole endeavour begins with the positing of value. Value is not simply the result, but the intention. By validating labour-power as a commodity, its price – the wage – monetarily posits labour as an activity that carries with it a certain potential value. Arthur suggests that capital must 'posit' labour's status as such, positing labour as both value-bearing with the conferral of a wage on the commodity labour-power, and value-producing by positing its result – the product of labour – as a potential commodity that too bears value. Money is the means through which this abstraction is 'imposed'. And, thereafter, labour is calculable, workable and commensurable. Arthur writes that 'the concrete labour-process carries a distinct set of abstract determinations that posit value' (2013, p. 104). What this gives us is a way of conceptualising how value takes on a real existence in the workplace, despite its formally non-empirical status. For instance, the material world of timesheets, time-tracking software and other such devices act as value-positing 'abstract determinations'. As we will see in Chap. 8, contrary to the claims of a 'crisis of measurability' made by the postoperaists, measure continues in spite of any immediate change in what it measures.

What makes the relationship between labour and value difficult – but also *possible* – to grasp as a topic of inquiry is how the value-form denies and sublates the antagonistic social relations on which it is based. In his theorisation of the practical abstraction by which valorisation proceeds in production and through which it is possible to comprehend the 'non-empirical' reality of value's modes of existence in production, Arthur conceptualises how the concrete practice and experience of work disappear, in a denied but resistant way, into the social form of abstract labour in process.

As we will discuss further in the next chapter on class antagonism, value and the role of abstract labour-time in production are presupposed on a set of social conditions whereby workers must sell their labour power to live. In the first place, workers must objectify their labour power to subsist, exchanging it for money – the wage – with which to acquire the commodities necessary to live. For this objectified labour power to be validated as part of the social necessary labour time of society as a whole, they must engage in production processes, the result of which is 'posited' as, and subsequently validated as, value-bearing.

Labour power, as the foundational commodity, has its value 'posited' at the inception of the labour process through its buying and selling. In a way, the positing of its value is the positing of the value of all that follows, although this is subject to the capitalist's initial expectation of accruing wealth in its abstract form – value, measured in money – upon the sale of a given good or service.

Thus, engaged in the labour process, workers produce not value itself – as has commonly been stated in vulgar accounts of Marx's theory of value – but rather that which bears or carries value – some useful or desirable thing to which value is attached first by positing it as valuable and eventually through its exchange for money in the market.

Two things happen here. On one hand, the very thing through which the worker subsists contradictorily impoverishes them, subject to social relations of inequality and domination. Second, the concrete labour in which they engage is *denied* in the abstract form of labour specific to value. This is how they live: subsisting through impoverishment, doing what is denied.

The labour process sees concrete labour eventually 'enter into' the value-form, Arthur writes, 'not *as* abstract labour but as abstracted *from*' (2013, p. 109). This is an important distinction. It suggests, as Arthur asserts, the 'sublation' of concrete labour 'in the movement of positing value'. 'Sublation' here indicates the disappearance of the concrete labour workers engage in, and the denial of their experience of it, into the value-form, but with the retention of a moment of 'negativity' that offers the possibility of resistance. Lived experience and human 'doing' (Holloway 2010) are sublated but never entirely successfully suppressed. This negativity persists because '[t]he value-form is *imposed* on labours as an alien universal identifying them *against* their reality as concrete' (Arthur 2013, p. 109). Processes of measurement abstract from the work workers do and the way they experience it, structuring both in a manner that denies and negates the very impulses and spontaneity in which they are personally and vocationally invested. As we shall see in Part 2, this ultimately negative assessment conflicts with the untrammelled and spontaneous creativity ascribed to contemporary labour by thinkers in the postoperaist tradition.

Thus, as Arthur contends, 'living labour realises itself in the mode of denial when reified in value' (2013, p. 106). Labour attains the practical abstraction necessary to value 'only in its negation'. We are supposed to forget its specificity, its concrete character, in the exchange of commodities that depends on the commensuration of one with another. And, indeed, its specificity – the eccentricities, desires and particularities that make it what it is – must also be forgotten in the process of its quantification by means of timesheets, performance indicators and targets.

But this negation is a determinate one, to return to the terminology of Gunn with which we began this chapter. It preserves, Arthur writes, 'in sublated form', that which is denied: value's positing in and through the labour process and the buying and selling of labour power as wage labour, with all the violence, coercion and dispossession that this relationship implies. 'Sublation' here indicates the simultaneous denial and preservation of this background (2013, pp. 106–7). In capital, 'the concrete character of labour is thoroughly sublated'. Only the specificity of the particular useful form in which the commodity arrives preserves the specific character of the labour performed.

However, what Arthur does not emphasise clearly enough in his account of sublation is that this value-bearing product is posited much earlier in the labour process itself by measures and practices of abstraction. Despite writing of 'practical abstraction', there is little consideration given to what this may mean for workers themselves in terms of the practice and experience of work and how they can effectively resist against the sublation and denial of their activity. But labour's sublation is always in process and up-for-grabs, around which struggles and conflicts arise. This suggests the direct political and practical relevance of the theoretical issues assayed in this chapter.

4.7   WHY WORK?

The central issue with which we set out to engage in this chapter was how the theory of value could be conceptualised as a problem for social research to investigate. This conceptualisation theorises the determination of the value-form as subject to an 'internal relatedness' whereby the various different parts and components appear as the 'modes of existence' of one another, and by an 'unfixity' whereby these modes of existence persist on a perpetual continuum of becoming. As such, the value-form is defined as a fugitive, fleeting and elusive object of research which withdraws from easy analysis. This conceptualisation of the value-form constitutes the theoretical foundation of our reflections upon how social research into value theory might function in practice. I would suggest that it is these 'modes of existence' which are ultimately revealed to be the correct object of research for investigations into the theory of value. Focus on these brings us to the concrete core contained and sublated within the value abstraction in the pre-emptory 'practical' guise it assumes within the workplace.

It is recommended that the difficulties presented by the fugitive, fleeting and elusive nature of the mode of existence can be overcome by a programme of research inspired by feminist approaches, which rather than focusing on either production or circulation as the locus of capitalist economic processes, seek instead to appreciate the entire circuit as an *overall process* from which no one part can be isolated. This provides a tentative template for enquiry geared towards a positive understanding of the internal relatedness and unfixity that characterise the modes of existence through which the value-form appears in society. It is in such a way that the theory of value can be conceptualised as a problem for social research to investigate.

Even so, what this chapter has shown is that, despite impediments, the study of concrete labour *can* give us a vantage point on abstract labour and value, conceiving labour not as something leading up to value eventually, but as something through which value *moves* right from the start. It is this relationship that programmes of research based upon the immediate form of labour, but with no conception of the social form that labour assumes, miss. Concrete labour for these agendas is a self-sufficient subject of study with no reference to the role that it comes to take in capitalist social relations vis-à-vis abstract labour and value. The leap is not made from looking at labour to looking at value, both through and beyond the concrete activity that takes place in the sphere of production.

By conceptualising labour and labour power in such a way that value flows from them, we can glimpse the latency of value whereby value cannot be said to fully exist before commodity exchange but persists earlier in production as a potential quantity, stemming from the initial exchange of labour-power for a wage. This introduces the practical abstraction that makes the comparison, commensuration and exchange of commodities in the market possible. The latency of value – at first glance an ephemeral and non-empirical concept to grasp – thus can be seen to consist in the most brutal and material of circumstances: that a worker must live only by selling the one commodity they can call their own, their labour-power. Thus we associate the real appearance of value and the relations between commodities with the social relations of production and the 'actual conditions of life' (Bonefeld 2016a). This embeds the spectral forms of value in human practice, subsistence and experience.

So, first, we have the historical circumstance that we cannot subsist except through the wage, on account of the continued state of dispossession of the vast majority of the world's inhabitants from the individual and collective means to independently reproduce the conditions of life. The things we need and want are accessible only as commodities acquired with money. From this circumstance flows the positing of labour as monetary, practically abstract and potentially value-producing. Value reduces, then, to hunger, but is no less abstract and non-empirical for it. We subsist through abstractions. Thus just as one cannot research labour without value, one cannot research value without looking at labour and the social relations of production that compel it to occur. We will explore this further through the work of Bonefeld in the next chapter.

As we will see, the understanding of the latency of value vis-à-vis the initial buying and selling of labour power conforms to the theoretical framework developed thus far. Where the NRM stresses the importance of exchange to the understanding of value, Open Marxism reinstates a focus on separation, coercion and hunger as the historical basis for the abstract unfolding of the value-form. Concurrently, the study of labour opens out, in a complementary rather than antagonistic way, upon the study of value as a social form. Although Arthur errs more towards the NRM theoretical tradition, he too steps away from the purely logical application of its central ideas as critiqued by Bonefeld in the next chapter. Arthur upends the characterisation of commodity production and exchange as something that, in its simple form, can be considered in isolation from capitalist social relations. What Arthur's focus on labour-power communicates is that one cannot divorce value from its actual historical context in a set of concrete events and processes – namely, primitive accumulation, and the situation whereby we must sell our labour-power to eat, but also, as we see in Chap. 9, spatially and temporally distinct economic conditions of commodity circulation and exchange.

Arthur thus challenges the simplistic account of value whereby the latter arises solely in exchange with no prior existence, latent or otherwise. Arthur asserts that seeing the form of value as the logical extension of a certain mode of producing things, naturalises production and restricts all change and social determination to the spheres of exchange and circulation. In this way, fully circulationist accounts prohibit the critique of work, the wage, and the social relations of production that are responsible for most of the immediate misery of capitalist existence. It is cast as an untouchable sun around which we orbit, regardless of the stress one places on the moment of exchange as an explanatory principle. But by reading labour through value, as Rubin recommends, we can critique work, the wage and the social relations of production through, and not in spite of, a form-analysis of the abstract social rule of value. This addresses the question: why, if we are interested in value, it is still worthwhile to build a political and investigatory platform around labour, when the determination of the former ultimately rests in a process of abstraction of which concrete labour is only a carrier? The answer, in Arthur's words, is that '[p]roduction is form-determined when located in the circuit of capital' (2013, p. 105). This is because 'new value arises in production under the impulse of capital to valorise itself', an abstract economic compulsion in the face of which capitalists, their functionaries and workers are equally helpless to resist. 'In this perspective', Arthur writes, 'the capitalist production process is from the start considered as value-formed insofar as all inputs including labour-power are commodities purchased with money-capital'. By emphasising what Arthur terms 'the unity of production and consumption', such a circuitist perspective attains what the circulationist approach does not: theoretical resources with which to critique drudgery and exploitation, via the understanding of labour-power as a foundational commodity, with which value is initially posited. This challenges the circulationist derivation of value from a static account of how goods are produced and ways of exchanging them arise as if by magic. Along with critiques such as that of Bonefeld – which we will encounter in more detail in the next chapter – Arthur reinstates history into the study of the abstract unfolding of value. It is history onto which we hold in research and struggle around and against the value-form.

What is important for my analysis here is that Arthur stresses the role of labour-power within rather than against the theory of the social validation of abstract labour. In line with Rubin's methodological prescription to inter-pret labour in such a way that value follows from it, Arthur views labour-power's relationship with the monetary abstraction as precisely the kind of social validation of a value-bearing commodity as value-form theory would see in any other exchange of a product for money. The difference is, as noted, a matter of where emphasis falls. One can give a rendition of value-form theory that elides labour and labour power altogether. But Arthur – in a way that complements both Heinrich and Bonefeld – here stresses the status of labour power as the foundational commodity of them all, without which commodity exchange cannot be considered. Without the buying and selling of labour power – of an inequality between parties consummated in a formally free and equal contractual relationship – no value could be posited to begin with. This rules out any characterisation of value's existence in pre-capitalist 'simple commodity exchange'. It is, as we will see in the next chapter, what Bonefeld emphasises in his critique of the abstract unfolding of value conceptualised in the NRM: a historically grounded category embedded in continually reproduced antagonistic social relations of pro-duction. Expressing the value-form in layman's terms through the well-worn comparison of the value and perceived workmanship of a nearby chair or table does not therefore quite capture what value is, without reference to the specific historical circumstance of capitalist society. It would be better to begin from the necessity to eat.

When we say that capitalist social relations of production – that one must sell one's labour and submit to employer domination over one's time in order to eat – are essential to the value-form, this is an essence that *must appear* (Adorno 1974). The sphere of exchange is not a false appearance that needs to be 'got behind' in the sense of an illusion that must be overcome, but a real appearance in which the essence of things really appears. Against its fearsome non-empiricality, this fidelity makes value an approachable object of research. The veneer of measure obscures and contains social relations of domination and subordination we will explore in more depth in the next chapter, but these relations are knowable none-theless – an emancipatory perspective that extends theoretical knowledge beyond the enlightened purveyors of correct consciousness. The material relations of life are not here hidden in the forms of quantitative abstraction that take hold, but are expressed in a distorted fashion, that, as I will go on to discuss in Chap. 5, a 'negative dialectical' method can help unpick.

4.8   CONCLUSION

This chapter has taken us from the disempowering insight that value is a non-empirical reality, the modes of existence of which are elusive, fleeting and fugitive, to a conceptualisation of labour that allows us to wager claims about this non-empirical reality by means of the study of the empirical circumstances we find at the level of everyday life. Against the criticism of the NRM as too circulationist in its inclination towards an exchange-focused perspective on the law of value, there is sufficient analytical room within its forgiving and theoretically explosive rereading of Marx to allow, at the other end, with a serious critical engagement with the contradictions and conditions of class society as it is lived and experienced in labour and in our intercourse with the world. This meeting proceeds principally by means of what we will go on to consider in the next chapter: the coin in our pocket, a conceptuality that contains within it dialectically the non-conceptuality of the class antagonism. As we will see, Bonefeld, a leading theorist from within the NRM, advances a critique of certain strands of the tradition within which he sits in order to delineate a negative dialectical approach that unfolds from the conceptuality of the value relation the non-conceptuality of material human life lived against itself and the 'social constitution' of capitalist society in and through class antagonism.

BIBLIOGRAPHY

Adorno, T.W. 1974. Commitment. *New Left Review* I/87-88: 75–89.

Aristotle. 1998. *The Metaphysics*. London: Penguin.

Arthur, C. 2013. The Practical Truth of Abstract Labour. In *Marx's Laboratory: Critical Interpretations of the Grundrisse*, ed. R. Bellofiore, G. Starosta, and P. Thomas, 101–120. Leiden: Brill.

Aufheben. 2004. We Have Ways of Making You Talk! *Aufheben #12*. http://libcom.org/library/we-have-ways-making-you-talk. Accessed 12 June 2012.

Bellofiore, R. 2009. A Ghost Turning into a Vampire: The Concept of Capital and Living Labour. In *Re-reading Marx: New Perspectives After the Critical Edition*, ed. R. Bellofiore and R. Fineschi, 178–194. London: Palgrave Macmillan.

Bellofiore, R., and R. Finelli. 1998. Capital, Labour and Time: The Marxian Monetary Theory of Value as a Theory of Exploitation. In *Marxian Economics: A Reappraisal: Essays on Volume 1 of Capital: Method, Value and Money*, ed. R. Bellofiore, 48–74. London: Macmillan.

Benyon, H. 1984. *Working for Ford*. London: Penguin.

Bonefeld, W. 2014. *Critical Theory and the Critique of Political Economy: On Subversion and Negative Reason*. London: Bloomsbury.

———. 2016a. Negative Dialectics and Critique of Economic Objectivity. *History of the Human Sciences* 29 (2): 60–76.

———. 2016b. Bringing Critical Theory Back in at a Time of Misery: Three Beginnings Without Conclusion. *Capital & Class* 40 (2): 233–244.

Brown, B.A., and A. Quan-Hase. 2012. "A Workers' Inquiry 2.0": An Ethnographic Method for the Study of Produsage in Social Media Contexts. *tripleC* 10 (2): 488–508.

Cavendish, R. 1982. *Women on the Line*. London: Routledge.

Cleaver, H. 2000. *Reading* Capital *Politically*. Edinburgh: AK Press.

Cockburn, C., and S. Ormrod. 1993. *Gender and Technology in the Making*. London: Sage.

Colletti, L. 1973. *Marxism and Hegel*. London: Verso.

———. 1989. *From Rousseau to Lenin: Studies in Ideology and Society*. New York: Monthly Review Press.

de Molina, M.M. 2004. Common Notions, Part 1: Workers-Inquiry, Co-research, Consciousness-Raising. Trans. M. Casas-Cortés and S. Cobarrubias. http://eipcp.net/transversal/0406/malo/en. Accessed 12 June 2012.

Elson, D. 1979. The Value Theory of Labour. In *Value: The Representation of Labour in Capitalism*, ed. D. Elson, 115–180. London: CSE Books.

Endnotes. 2010. Communisation and Value-Form Theory. *Endnotes #2: Misery and the Value-Form*. https://endnotes.org.uk/issues/2/en/endnotes-communisation-and-value-form-theory. Accessed 29 Oct 2016.

Glucksmann, M. 1990. *Women Assemble: Women Workers and the New Industries in Inter-war Britain*. London: Routledge.

———. 2005. Shifting Boundaries and Interconnections: Extending the 'Total Social Organisation of Labour'. In *A New Sociology of Work?* ed. L. Pettinger et al. Oxford: Blackwell.

Gunn, R. 1989. Marxism and Philosophy: A Critique of Critical Realism. *Capital and Class* 13: 1–30.

———. 1992. Against Historical Materialism: Marxism as First-Order Discourse. In *Open Marxism Volume II: Theory and Practice*, ed. W. Bonefeld, R. Gunn, and K. Psychopedis, 1–45. London: Pluto Press.

Hardt, M., and A. Negri. 2001. *Empire*. Cambridge, MA: Harvard University Press.

Heinrich, M. 2012. *An Introduction to the Three Volumes of Karl Marx's* Capital. New York: Monthly Review Press.

Holloway, J. 2010. *Crack Capitalism*. London: Pluto Press.

Kolinko. 2002. *Hotlines: Call Centre. Inquiry. Communism*. Oberhausen: Kolinko.

Marx, K. 1859. *A Contribution to the Critique of Political Economy*. http://www.marxists.org/archive/marx/works/1859/critique-pol-economy. Accessed 15 July 2012.

———. 1976. *Capital*. Vol. I. London: Penguin.

———. 1993. *Grundrisse*. London: Penguin.

———. 2013. Workers' Inquiry. In *A Workers' Inquiry Reader*. Assembled to Accompany. The Politics of Workers' Inquiry Conference, ed. S. Shukaitis, J. Figiel and A. Walker, 8–15. Wivenhoe: Ephemera.

Napoleoni, C. 1975. *Smith, Ricardo, Marx*. Oxford: Blackwell.

Negri, A. 2008. *Reflections on Empire*. Trans. E. Emery. Cambridge: Polity Press.

Panzieri, R. 1965. *Socialist Uses of Workers' Inquiry*. Trans. A. Bove. http://eipcp.net/transversal/0406/panzieri/en. Accessed 14 June 2012.

Reuten, G. 2005. Money as Constituent of Value; The Ideal Introversive Substance and the Ideal Extroversive Form of Value in *Capital*. In *Marx's Theory of Money: Modern Appraisals*, ed. F. Moseley, 78–92. London: Palgrave Macmillan.

Rubin, I.I. 1972. *Essays on Marx's Theory of Value*. Detroit: Black and Red.

———. 1978. Abstract Labour and Value in Marx's System. *Capital & Class* 5: 107–140.

Sohn-Rethel, A. 1978. *Intellectual and Manual Labour: A Critique of Epistemology*. London: Macmillan Press.

Thorne, J. 2011. The Workers' Inquiry: What's the Point? *The commune*. May 16. http://thecommune.co.uk/2011/05/16/the-workers%E2%80%99-inquiry-what%E2%2%.

Uninomade Collective. 2013. *The Logistics of Struggles. Notes on the Italian Case*. Trans. I. Bonnin. http://www.uninomade.org/the-logistics-of-struggles. Accessed 26 Dec 2013.

Wright, E.O. 1981a. The Value Controversy and Social Research. In *The Value Controversy*, ed. I. Steedman. London: Verso.

———. 1981b. Reconsiderations. In *The Value Controversy*, ed. I. Steedman. London: Verso.

Wright, S. 2002. *Storming Heaven: Class Composition and Struggle in Italian Autonomist Marxism*. London: Pluto Press.

CHAPTER 5

Class, Critique and Capitalist Crisis

5.1 Introduction

This chapter reunifies the abstract and concrete levels of analysis of value and labour and their relationship found in the last two chapters. It does so through an interpretation of what it means to subsist in a society constituted in the class antagonism. In so doing, I draw upon the work of Werner Bonefeld. His 'critique of political economy as a critical theory of society' (hereafter CPECTS) has at its core an Adornian 'negative dialectics of economic objectivity'. The first part of the chapter surveys how this method decodes, through an analysis of the conceptuality of the value-form that we charted in Chap. 3, the 'non-conceptuality' of the 'actual conditions of life' that lurk dialectically within it. In this way, it works with appearances to extract the essence that, as we saw at the end of the last chapter, must appear. This relates specifically to how we subsist through the movement of monetary quantities which, as we saw in previous chapters, is a key focus of the NRM reconstruction of Marx's value theory.

As we see in the second part of the chapter, Bonefeld diverges from some elements of the NRM in important respects, via an Open Marxist critique of the tendency to present value as a purely abstract unfolding uprooted from its violent roots in the primitive accumulation that lies at the source of class society. It derives logically what for Bonefeld – as, arguably, for Marx – should really be derived historically. In a third section, I will consider how this resonates with Marx's original work on the commodity fetish, and how the 'real appearance' of the value-form in its various expressions is not an

© The Author(s) 2018
F.H. Pitts, *Critiquing Capitalism Today*, Marx, Engels, and Marxisms,
DOI 10.1007/978-3-319-62633-8_5

illusion to be stripped away by those of privileged consciousness, but rather contains, dialectically and in negation, its own blood-soaked essence, expressing social relations precisely as they are.

   The account of class antagonism presented in this chapter conflicts in significant ways with presently popular modes of talking and thinking about class, in academia and outside. This is something I consider in the penultimate section. Finally, I explore the significance of a class-centred account of value for Marxian conceptualisations of the causes and conditions of capitalist crisis. In so doing, I draw on the accounts of Simon Clarke and Michael Heinrich in setting out what they saw, following Marx, as the 'central contradiction' confronting capitalism in its attempts to stave off crisis: in short, the constrained consumption of one class and the tendency to overproduce above and beyond this narrow social basis on the part of the other. I chart the contention that ensued around Heinrich's forthright dismissal of the false legitimacy the so-called 'Law of the Tendency of the Rate of Profit to Fall' has accrued as the Marxist left's go-to explanation of crises always around the corner. From this critical perspective the latter overlooks the class contradiction – rooted as much in social form, social reproduction and social relations as in anything inherent to labour or production itself – that Marx himself considered most important in determining crisis and, this aside, more foundational contradictions rooted in the very dispossession that guarantees a society of wage labour and commodity exchange to begin with. It is the constitution of this society that the concepts covered in this chapter help us better understand. We return to the specific crisis-proportions of these contradictions in further detail in the discussion of creative industries in Chap. 9.

5.2   THE NEGATIVE DIALECTICS OF ECONOMIC OBJECTIVITY

What Werner Bonefeld calls the 'critique of political economy as the critical theory of society' (2014) recasts Marx's critique of political economy not as an alternative economic theory, but a demystifying explosion of the objective economic forms specific to capitalism. It focuses, methodologically, on 'the negative dialectics of economic objectivity' (2016a). According to Adorno, dialectics is the 'ontology of the wrong state of things' (1973, p. 11). It decodes a world of real appearance, wherein things exist as themselves and something else all at once. It is, as Bonefeld (2016a, p. 66) writes, 'the cunning of reason in a bewitched society'. Negative dialectics is the critical application of dialectics. It extends its cunning to the active 'presentation of the wrong state of things'. It demystifies a reality in which the results of human practice pose themselves above and against its performers. It explodes the economic abstractions through which humans subsist in capitalist society. It takes 'thing-like concealed relationships' and 'render[s] their immediacy transparent – as socially constituted things'. This helps us critically decode, in Part 2 of the book, the changes in immediate labour content on which postoperaists base their prognoses.

The means by which we can render immediacy transparent in this way is through an '*ad hominem* critique of political economy' (2016a, p. 65). It is 'ad hominem' in that it deals in the dirt of life, the 'muck of ages', as Marx (1845) puts it. It contends that our access to the means of life is mediated through the conceptual apparatus of economic categories. The ad hominem critique assesses these categories with reference to that which they sublate and deny. It suggests that this conceptual apparatus rests in our relationship with 'sensuous things'. This relationship, however, proceeds through 'supersensible' things. But, for Bonefeld (2016a, p. 72, n. 11), it remains the case that '[t]he actual relations of life are the non-conceptual premise of the economic categories' that constitute this 'supersensibility'.

We have seen already the tricky non-empirical character of value as an object. But we have seen also how it rests in human practice in such a way as to afford the ability to research it. Bonefeld gives us a basis to understand how to grasp the conceptual and empirical world this engages with. In a world of abstract economic forms, the subject disappears into the object. Bonefeld's theorisation of how non-conceptualities are implied in conceptualities, and how the subject vanishes in economic objectivity, gives us a basis to understand the processes of sublation and denial covered in the previous chapter, embedded within the central constitutive feature of capitalist society: the class antagonism.

The basis on which we can do this is by means of the 'negative dialectics of economic objectivity'. This permits us to access the non-conceptualities that undergird the non-empirical conceptualities of capitalist society via a critique of the objective economic forms through which they are expressed and governed. The conceptual forms through which live and subsist rule over the non-conceptual, most of all our needs and our humanity. As Marx writes, 'the individual carries his social power, as well as his *bond with society*, in his *pocket*' (*Marx* 1993, pp. 156–7). The coin carries a concept, but also a material relationship of subsistence. The subject 'vanishes' in the conceptuality of objective economic categories. This is a particular situation, specific to our social conditions – a specific 'enchantment of the subject in its own world' (Adorno, quoted in Bonefeld 2016a, p. 65) dependent on the circumstances of that world of the subject's own making, but which, just as the results of labour take an alien existence over and above the control of the labourer, escape their own making to take on a dominating social form.

The object is the mode of existence of the subject, into which the subject dissolves. But this 'vanishing subject' disappears only to reappear as constituted and living through money in order to live and subsist. As Bonefeld suggests (2016b, p. 24), if the coin carries our relationship with society, it carries also our own reproduction as living labour, in a world where the reproduction of labour power is the mode through which life itself proceeds. This is why, and how, the value-form can be explored through an attention to work, the wage, and the social relations of production. This latter is the non-conceptuality upon which the conceptuality bases itself, over which the conceptuality rules and, at the same time, through which the conceptuality expresses itself, whilst expressing the relations of the non-conceptuality at one and the same time. Economic objectivity 'entails the definite social relations between individuals as the vanished premise of its economic force' (Bonefeld 2016a, p. 64). This duality is decoded by negative dialectics.

Where the subject disappears into the object – with the latter standing in as the mode of existence of the former – only a dialectical theory can grasp this and adequately capture the subject by means of an analysis of the object into which it disappears. This requires a grasp of contradiction only dialectics can offer. Contradiction, taken negatively, is the mode through which dialectics analyses the world. It appreciates that things may be one thing and another at once. And, in yet another sense, thinking through contradictions puts the mode of thought at odds with the world. But, at one and the same time, it too thinks against those contradictions, treating them critically as a part of the same false and wrong world of which they are a part. What a negative-dialectical approach does, therefore, is suspect, refuse and problematise all identity whatsoever, all positing of things as being of one kind, commensurable and in common (see Bonefeld 2014, p. 69). Only in such a refusal to accept things at face value can it get to the world's rotten core. In this way, bolstered by a critical historical materialism, negative dialectics restores the vanished subject – and, what is denied in the objective economic categories that mark the procession of the value-form through society.

The relation between conceptuality and the non-conceptuality behind it – the actual conditions of life – is accessed, Bonefeld contends, by means of a critical historical materialism, which turns the crude determinism of orthodox historical materialism on its head to 'open. . .up the non-conceptual with the aid of the concept, without reducing it to the concept' (Adorno 1990, p. 65). This 'strips the blindfold from our eyes' – but, as Adorno notes, the 'concept is a concept even when dealing with things in being' – albeit one that 'is *contained within a non-conceptual whole*' (1990, p. 12, my italics), in continuing modes of concrete practice and coercion. As I will assert in Chaps. 6 and 7, this proves a radical counterpoint to the postoperaist fixation on change. Changes in the immediate form of labour do not imply changes in forms of abstract social mediation like value. Equally, changes in the value relation do not disclose changes in the fact we must work to live. Only dialectics – specifically in its negative guise – can grasp this.

The critique of postoperaismo presented in Part 2 of this book, therefore, rests on a critique of economic categories, and not merely their passive acceptance or approval. The 'critique of economic categories' is, for Bonefeld, the aim of Marx's work. The latter reveals the origin of these categories in the social relations of production – in, for example, antagonism, hunger and violence. In so doing, it reveals the materiality of concepts and the conceptuality of the material world. For Bonefeld, the coin in one's pocket represents this relationship between economic categories and the actual conditions of life they express and to which they relate. The coin expresses and is concerned with this bond. But it also expresses a concept – the real abstraction of value – that cannot be separated from its constitution in the actual relations of life. The struggle for subsistence is as conceptual as it is material. The reality of life, in this way, is socially constituted through human practice.

Because the selling of our labour power, and our living through and by the value-form, is our link to the means of subsistence, the abstract economic categories that dominate us exist through human practice, and not apart from it. The negative dialectics of economic objectivity suggests that the 'incomprehensible economic forces' that rule over subjects in capitalist society, as Bonefeld (2014, p. 66) suggests, rest in human practice and can be explained through human practice. The 'relations of economic objectivity' abstract from lived experience. But they are also a mode of existence of the latter. Existing this way, economic categories represent an 'inverted and perverted world of definite social relations' rooted in everyday life. As touched on in Chap. 4, this practical and experiential aspect gives us our basis to investigate value's non-empirical reality. In decoding this, Bonefeld (2014, p 71) writes, citing Horkheimer, negative dialectics casts a 'judgement on existence'. It opens out upon political questions about the delineation of the good and right life in a wrong world. Far from mere theory, it constitutes what Alfred Schmidt (quoted in Bonefeld 2016a, p. 65) calls a 'conceptualised praxis', some implications of which I draw out in the next three chapters on postoperaismo.

It thereby provides not the 'impoverished praxis' popularly associated with critical theory (Bonefeld 2016b, p. 237), but poses precisely the key 'question' of praxis: 'what really does it mean to say "no" in a society that is governed by the movement of economic abstractions?' This praxis consists in a method that critiques and negates what is, rather than seeking to prove anything about that world only so as to reflect that world back upon itself. But, in negating the world, by passing judgement, it also describes the way that world really is. If dialectics is the ontology of the wrong world, the 'cunning of reason' in that world, then *negative* dialectics is the presentation of this world in a critical light. And this negative-dialectical method is also a 'conceptualised praxis' that represents an intervention in that world on the basis that the conceptual is real and reality conceptual.

This, as we shall see in Chap. 6, differentiates it from Negri's postoperaist approach. The latter's immanentist conceptualisation sees all things as one. In so doing, it selectively affirms parts of the capitalist totality in such a way so as to ultimately affirm the whole. It reflects the world back upon itself, where critical theory breaks the mirror. In negating the world, by passing judgement, critical theory also describes the way that world really is.

This criticality rests in the refusal to accept at face value the economic objective forms taken by congealed social relations in capitalist society, whilst at once working within this face value insofar as it is the thing refused. This distinguishes it from traditional and quantitative approaches to social phenomena, that reflect the world back at itself by working not with, but *within*, the same objectified economic and social forms that dominate us. Rather than sociology or political economy, this stands outside disciplinarity. What distinguishes this is its ability to ask questions across supposed disciplinary boundaries and grasp the totalising tendencies of capitalist social relations.

Neither sociology nor economics ask why society reproduces itself through the economic categories it does. The division between the two 'sets aside the really central interests of both disciplines' (Adorno, in Bonefeld 2016a, p 62). This is because, as Bonefeld (2016a, p. 70) puts it, '[e]conomic reproduction is social reproduction'. On one hand, economics seeks to calculate the world 'with mathematical precision', whilst sociology 'fails to recognise' its reproduction through precisely such an economic objectivity (2016a, p. 62). This is because it is detached from its object, unlike critical theory, which thinks 'in and through society' (2016a, p. 70).

However, the exchange abstraction that the negative dialectics of economic objectivity presents 'lies therefore not [only] in the abstracting mode of thought by the sociologist, but in society itself' (Adorno 2000, p. 32). Thus the 'conceptualised praxis' of the negative dialectician bests the separation between thought, practice and reality implicit in the vocation of the sociologist. In line with Marx's 8th Thesis on Feuerbach, 'all social life is essentially practical', thinking included. As Bonefeld notes of Marx's thesis, '[t]hinking is part of social life and all social life is essentially practical' (2014, p. 60). This is an emancipatory stance squarely against the ascriptions of 'false consciousness' to unthinking laymen for which Marxist groupuscules are famed.

Moreover, in this, the negative dialectics of economic objectivity also denies the divide between the theoretical and empirical implicit in much sociological research, merging as they do on the terrain of the practical and experiential existence of the abstract categories with which we work conceptually, and the real social and political existence, and material efficacy, of those concepts in turn. As such, conceptual processes and theoretical categories such as those outlined in Chap. 3 are not apart from the reality that each seeks to capture or describe, but part of it. Ideas are a material fact – the coin in our pocket, for instance, by means of an abstraction, arbitrates our access to food, to the means of survival. The idea that governs this – of the universal commensurability of diverse use-value by means of monetary exchange value – is as real and material as the hunger it mediates. This is what Adorno refers to when he describes the role of a *critical* historical materialism in negative dialectics. One moves through the concept to the non-conceptual, as each implies the other.

The conceptual abstraction surveyed in Chap. 3 is not confined to the individual minds of humans, but 'holds sway in reality', as Bonefeld (2016a, p. 68) puts it. The 'actual social relations' that persist at one level are not 'defied' by the 'independent economic forces' of capitalist society. The latter do not give the lie to the former, but are the *form of appearance* they assume. There are not two realities, but one, and it exists through appearances in which 'essence must appear' (Bonefeld 2014, p. 63).

The appearances of the social relations of production in objective economic forms do not distract us from reality, but rather take on a real efficacy in reality. Our experience and access to the world really is mediated through a monetary schema composed of abstract economic forms. As Bonefeld writes (2014, p. 59, my italics), individuals are governed by abstractions, and their life-circumstances *really are dependent* on the movement of economic quantities'.

Value is a 'real appearance' – a 'constituted social nature' (2016a, p. 66). What this shows is that we can only work with the appearances available to us. But these appearances are both appearance and essence. The latter must appear through the former. The objective economic forms through which we live: value, money, price, labour, labour-time and so forth – imply the social relations through which they arise and hold. So, whilst refusing to take the concrete forms assumed by the abstract world of economic objectivity at face value, the CPECTS simultaneously permits us to take them at face value – but *critically* so.

5.3   The Historical and Logical Premise of the Value-Form

These social relations centre on the class antagonism. Class, for the tradition of critical theory, is not a positive status, subjective position or conscious category, but a negative and objective relation between the buyers and sellers of labour-power (Bonefeld 2014, p. 102). It is, in the words of Simon Clarke, the 'logical and historical presupposition for the existence of individual capitalists and workers, and the basis on which the labour of one section of society is appropriated without equivalent by another' (1991, p. 95). It is, thus, 'constitutive' (Bonefeld 2014, p. 105). In this sense, for critical theory, the social constitution of capitalist society and the issue of class cannot be considered separately. Society as we know it is the form taken by the contradictory unity of the class antagonism. This antagonism is not something bourgeois society confronts as a problem, but rather implies as the condition of its being. Contra functionalist accounts, the contradiction is here productive and reproductive. As Adorno writes, capitalist society 'maintains itself only through antagonism' (Adorno 1941, quoted in Bonefeld 2014, p. 60). In turn, class antagonism persists in and through forms of abstract economic compulsion that themselves rest upon the primitive accumulation through which the class antagonism is established to begin with, with class struggle 'the fundamental premise' of class itself (Gunn 1987, p. 16).

This circularity is captured by Clarke, who writes that the class relation is not only capitalism's presupposition, but also its *result* (1991, p. 95). Critical theory climbs inside this circularity to see society as at once the contradictory unity of two disunited sides who not only war with but depend upon each other for their social reproduction. Critical theory is imperative when, as here, 'the concept of reality is divided within itself', mutual dependency appearing as antagonism, unity as disunity. Only a negative dialectics of social constitution can decode a reality that 'contains within itself what it denies' (Bonefeld 2014, pp. 64–5). In this tradition stand Marx, Adorno and today, most notably, Bonefeld, who unites the former two in his account of 'the critique of political economy as a critical social theory'.

Highlighting Marx's insistence on referring to economic categories as 'sensuous-supersensible things' (Marx 1976b, p. 74), Bonefeld characterises this critique as 'a theory of the social constitution of economic categories' (2014, p. 21). The critique springs from the character of the world it confronts, a world characterised by capital. Capital is 'not a thing', but a 'social relationship between persons expressed as a thing' (2014, p 54). This 'entails' the critique of political economy as a critical social theory. As a 'social theory' theory is not a theory *of* society, as Gunn (1992, pp. 4, 25) describes it – one that assumes a distance from its reified object – but a *social* theory, a theory embroiled within its object, deconstructing its social constitution from within. Or, as Bonefeld puts it, it is 'critical on the condition that it conceives of society from within its mode of subsistence'. This requires, as we shall see, a critical acceptance of the 'real appearance' of social constitution in the coined 'movement of incomprehensible economic quantities' (2014, pp. 55–6), insofar as the latter, like all conceptualities, 'refer[s] to non-conceptualities' (Adorno 1990, p. 11) such as class antagonism, subsistence and social reproduction, upon which we depend to survive, and insofar as those non-conceptualities themselves move through and are expressed in conceptualities themselves. Thus, the coin in one's pocket 'carries the bond with society', a bond that is at once an abstract social mediation and the concrete arbiter of 'the struggle for access to the means of subsistence' (Bonefeld 2016b, p. 240; see also Marx 1993, pp. 156–7). Moreover, the wealth this coin represents has its foundation in an ongoing process of primitive accumulation on which class antagonism centres, and the value posited to it contains within it the pursuit of profit by means of the extraction of surplus-value by the buyer of the seller of labour-power. It is with dialectical reference to this contradictory unity that the critical understanding of social constitution and class unfolds.

This approach radically differs from the classical political economy that Marx assailed, to mainstream economics, to traditional 'worldview' Marxism. All are 'haunted by the spectre of social constitution', of the 'uneconomic' roots of that which they speak (2014, p. 21). To the economists, Horkheimer writes, '[s]ociety appears "as a thing"' (Horkheimer 1992; cited in Bonefeld 2014, p. 24) to which apparently natural economic laws and categories apply. In this, '[e]conomics is the standpoint of economic matter in abstraction from society'. It does not recognise that not only are the economic categories around which it theorises the result of social constitution, but their 'validity is fundamentally social' in turn (Bonefeld 2014, pp. 24–5).

Here the theory of social constitution segues with the NRM focus on the social validation' of labour-time as abstract and socially necessary (Heinrich 2012, pp. 50–1; Bonefeld 2010). For Bonefeld, the NRM does not do enough to embed its analyses of the social validation of economic categories in an analysis of the social *constitution* of these categories in antagonistic class relations. Whilst it 'introduced a Marxism stripped of dogmatic certainties and naturalistic conceptions of society' (2014, pp. 41–42), for Bonefeld the NRM's 'critical focus' is thereby 'blinkered'. The NRM rightly undermines 'the orthodox instrumentalization of the categories of class and labour'. But it goes too far in substituting these categories with the value-form. This leads to a general neglect of labour, class, surplus-value and the separation of the worker from the means of subsistence. Where Bonefeld sees these as integral to the value-form, other proponents of the NRM display a tendency to underplay or ignore them.

On surface inspection, Bonefeld is of a piece with NRM theorists. He arrives from a similar Marxian tendency of reinterpretation and revisionism. He has a background of published interaction and collaboration with many of its key names (see contributions to the edited collections Bonefeld et al. 1992 and Bonefeld and Psychopedis 2005; see also Heinrich and Bonefeld 2011). Both Bonefeld and the other thinkers associated with the New Reading take a Frankfurt School-inflected approach to Marx. This recasts the critique of political economy as a social theory (see Bellofiore and Riva 2015). In his value theory, Bonefeld shares with the NRM an anti-substantialist emphasis on abstraction and social validation.

As discussed, Bonefeld recasts the 'critique of political economy as a critical social theory' (Bonefeld 2014, p. 3). The critique centres upon economic objectivity and the political form of capitalist society. It exposes their imbrication in the relationship of class antagonism upon which capitalism rests. Exploring the social constitution of economic categories in antagonistic social relations that sustain the law of value, Bonefeld highlights their absence in the NRM. He attributes this to the NRM interpretation of the 'logical' rather than historical exposition Marx employs in *Capital* (1976a). Bonefeld stresses instead the importance of the real historical separation of workers from their means of subsistence in the development of capitalism. Bonefeld's critique of the NRM rests on the salience of these 'historically stamped relations' to its otherwise sound interpretation of value as a form of social mediation

(Bonefeld 2014, p. 82). Class is therefore a key element of the capitalist form of wealth. There is a relationship between classed labour and its expression as abstract labour in exchange, historically and logically:

> ...class is the historical and logical premise of the value form. It entails the force of law-making violence within its concept. This force of law-making violence is the divorce of labour from the means of subsistence, which appears in the law of value in the form of economic compulsion. (Bonefeld 2014, p. 79)

For Bonefeld, the study of the value-form does not exclude class relations, but presupposes them. Valorisation is presupposed upon the pursuit of profit. Profit cannot occur from the exchange of equivalents. Someone must lose out. Thus surplus value cannot be absent from the conceptualisation of the value-form, but immanent within it. The motivation for equivalence and commensuration is the pursuit of profit from the appropriation of surplus labour. This is because it is upon the exchange abstraction that the validation of this appropriated surplus labour depends. Capital seeks to 'validate in exchange in the form of value' the 'appropriation of the surplus labour that capital is able to extract' (2014, p. 87). It is only insofar as this happens that one can identify surplus-value. But, equally, '[l]abour has to produce surplus value for money to maintain value validity' (2014, p. 66). So the two sides are implicated in each other. The value relation and the exchange abstraction are 'premised' on surplus value (2014, p. 43).

Because of the centrality of surplus value to the value form, class is the 'critical category of the entire system of capitalist wealth'. It 'appears in the form of an equivalent exchange...between unequal values'. Expressed in this 'real' appearance is the 'surplus value that has been "pumped out of the workers"', in Marx's words. Thus, Adorno can make his claim that, as Bonefeld puts it, 'the mysterious character of the value form' lies 'in the concept of surplus value' (2014, p. 102). Class is central to this in that profit 'entails the class relationship between the buyer of labour power and the producer of surplus value as seller of labour power' (2014, p. 43). This in turn implies the pre-existence of labour power as a commodity. The condition of this is primitive accumulation, the forceful and continued separation of workers from the means of subsistence. This sets them to market with only their potential to labour to sell.

For Bonefeld, this story is seldom told in the work of the NRM. Bonefeld states that '[t]he conceptuality of the law of value is antagonistic from the outset' (2014, p. 82). According to Bonefeld, the NRM's oversight relates to two broader imperatives. The first is the interpretation of Marx's presentational progression in *Capital*. For the NRM, this is chiefly a *logical* exposition. For Bonefeld, this reading irons out the specific historical context of the establishment of commodity exchange and the value relation. It elides the centrality of property relations and the commodification of labour power. The value-form cannot be considered in abstraction from the continued unfolding of a historical process: the separation of one class from the means of subsistence, through enclosure, dispossession and coercion; the creation of a class of workers, with another class purchasing their only means of survival, the commodified potential to labour; the continuing contemporary role of state and capital in reproducing and enforcing this separation. From each other, from nature, from property, from independent means, this division proliferates on a daily, national and global basis. For Bonefeld, *Capital's* exposition 'is in reverse order to the actual, historical sequence in which the social relations underlying [its] categories developed' (2014, pp. 90–1). One understands the ape from the vantage point of man, rather than man from the vantage point of the ape (Marx 1993, p. 105).

This history is not something of the distant past, but a continuing state of affairs that must be reproduced. A second imperative compounds the NRM's neglect of this antagonistic constancy. According to Bonefeld, the NRM holds the value-form to be an 'abstractly self-moving essence of wealth'. This conceptualisation of the law of value as an abstract compulsion elides its antagonistic undertow. Rather than deriving from this abstract compulsion, class antagonism is rather its 'constitutive premise' (2014, p. 9). The equivalence of exchange that theories of the value-form explore has its basis in the pursuit of profit by way of *unequal* exchange. This unequal exchange is predicated on a classed society. To ignore this is to adopt exactly the 'logical' stance discussed previously. It sees the value-form 'as some secularized thing that is valid in-itself, as if value posits more value just like that, without certificate of birth' (2014, p. 42).

Thus, Bonefeld has a dual critique of the NRM key to his conceptualisation of class and social constitution. It focuses first on the account of Marx's purportedly 'logical' exposition. It then moves to the ascription of a 'dull compulsion of economic need' (2014, p. 175). In both respects, the critique of the NRM flow into radical political implications. This has two features. First, by following Adorno in understanding society as 'antagonistic from the outset', Bonefeld shifts the focus of the critique of political economy from economic form to political (2014, pp. 10–11). The second point relates to Bonefeld's sensitivity to the 'fire and blood' that sustains the value-form (2014, p. 90). Understood like this, it is clear that the value-form does not 'come about. . .and maintain itself just like that'. Its 'reality is neither given nor assured' (2014, p. 175), a point more suggestive for projects of political change than Bonefeld's pessimistic position would appear to permit. Hence, class is contained within the concept and approach of social constitution – a factor a one-sided focus on abstract labour's 'social validation' (Heinrich 2012, pp. 50–1) alone leaves intact, centring social validity analytically without considering how that validity is based in concrete social relations and social reproduction.

It is this negativity, and the concrete social relations it implies, that makes possible practical programmes of inquiry and political action around the topic. It opens out upon class struggle, the struggle to subsist, and the everyday lived experience of the violence of abstraction in the workplace. Thus, combining the classical NRM with the Open Marxist critique of value's abstract unfolding gives us a guide to the real abstraction of social form as it is undergirded in a set of identifiable practices and processes, and provides a steer not only to thought but to action.

5.4   Class and the Commodity Fetish

In short, much must happen to make the world such that our lives are mediated by spectral forms of value that spring from our actions but take an alien power above and beyond our capacity to control them. The theory of social constitution, as we have seen, turns its attention to the antagonistic class character of capitalist society to explain this. While '[i]t is only by being exchanged that the products of labour acquire a socially uniform objectivity as values' (Marx 1976c, p. 75), value 'does not have its description branded on its forehead; it rather transforms every product of labour into a social hieroglyphic'. Thus what Marx called the 'social hieroglyphic' of the commodity fetish (1976c, p. 77) 'requires explanation from within the actual social relations' of capitalist society (Bonefeld 2014, pp. 36–7). Thus, the commodity fetish is decoded not only at the level of exchange relations, but owes, for example, in the first instance to a division of labour where some make one thing and others another. Where goods are privately produced they must exchange for money expressing a value – the price of the alienability of a good from the private ownership of one individual to that of another.

Thus Marx writes that 'as soon as men start to work for each other in any way, their labour also assumes a social form. [The] fetishism of the world of commodities arises from the peculiar social character of the labour which produces them' (1976c, p. 74). The commodity fetish, while seemingly spectral, has a basis in real social relations. Not only does the positing of value between things contain within it the presupposition of 'the profitable extraction of surplus value' by the buyers of the sellers of labour power, but it is this extraction on which the latter depend to live (Bonefeld 2014, p. 59; Adorno 1941, p. 320). 'The world of economic rationality is a perverted world', Bonefeld writes – but real nonetheless.

By seeing the social as concrete and rooted in real social relations, here the theory of social constitution continues the work commenced by Marx not only in his section on the commodity fetish, but from the inception of his critique of Hegel. Viewing Marx through Adorno, the NRM in particular has focused on the Hegelian concepts latent in Marx's presentation of his critique of political economy: contradiction, doubling, semblance, phenomenal manifestation (Bellofiore and Riva 2015, p. 25). This has allowed a critique of the social constitution of objective economic categories at both the level of their real appearance and the essence this expresses in the antagonistic social relations of capitalist society.

This picks up where Marx left off. What results in the theory of the commodity fetish that is today couched as that of social constitution begins with Marx's engagement with Hegel's *Phenomenology of Mind*. In the *Phenomenology*, Hegel writes that 'Self-consciousness exists in itself and for itself, in that, and by the fact that, it exists for another self-consciousness; that is to say, it *is* only by being acknowledged or "recognised"' (1976, p. 41). The subject here can only realise itself in some outside object. Marx, however, sought to, on one hand, historicise the absolute, eternal and ideal subject Hegel presented, rooting this process of 'recognition' in a set of historical and collective relations, and, on the other, introduce an element of negativity, whereby the realisation of the subject in the object came back to haunt the subject through its domination, so that

> [t]he *real, active* relation of man to himself as a. . .human being, is only possible if he really employs all his *species-powers* – which again is only possible through the co-operation of mankind and as a result of history treats them as objects, which is at first only possible in the form of estrangement. (Marx 1976b, p. 56)

Marx thereby 'stood Hegel on his head' by inverting this idealist dialectic for a *materialist* dialectic whereby this process is embedded in our metabolism with nature, our work to eat and subsist and live. Here, the self-consciousness of 'imaginary subjects' was eschewed in favour of a historically grounded account of the estrangement of humans in objective reality and forms of abstract thought, inspired by Feuerbach's critique of relation as a creation of human activity come back in alien form to control it. In his critique of Hegel, Marx writes that

> *sensuous* consciousness is not *abstractly* sensuous consciousness, but *humanly* sensuous consciousness. . .religion, wealth, etc., are only the estranged reality of *human* objectification, of *human* essential powers born into work, and therefore only the *way* to true *human* reality. (1976b, p. 55)

But in turning Hegel on his head, Marx also placed him on his feet, taking forward the core of the theory in a critical sense. Although, he wrote, the *Phenomenology* is 'concealed and mystifying criticism', in grasping the 'estrangement of man' in a world of his own creation, behind its idealistic presentation of 'mind' lurks '*all* the elements of criticism' fit for the reality of the situation (Marx 1976b, p. 55). This realisation represents a golden thread through Marx's work that links estrangement, alienation and the commodity fetish at different times and phases of his work: the contradiction whereby 'there can be no subject without objectification' (Bonefeld 2014, p. 62), in its 'reified mode', what Adorno labelled 'the enchantment of the subject in its own world' (quoted in Bonefeld 2014, p. 63).

More orthodox strands of Marxism have tended to separate out Marx's early work from his later work. The NRM breaks with this by suggesting that the theory of the commodity fetish is central to the theory of the value-form in *Capital*, and this, in turn, marks a continuation of Marx's Hegelianism, the subject–object dialectic, and the concept of estrangement (which appears elsewhere as alienation, alienability etc.). The theory of social constitution, therefore, is another manifestation of this conceptual thread based on the subject–object dialectic. As Backhaus suggests (quoted in Bellofiore and Riva 2015, p. 25), society is 'objective' since it is an 'abstract universality which subsumes and dominates particulars'. At the same time, society is subjective 'because it only exists and reproduces itself by virtue of human beings'. This duality is socially constituted in that it mediates our practical life through social forms beyond our control that spring in turn from our human practice. This is the fateful contradiction whereby, as Marx writes, our 'own movement within society has. . .the form of a movement by things, and these things, far from being under [our] control, in fact control [us]' (1976c, p. 77). This, for Reichelt (quoted in Bellofiore and Riva 2015, p. 25), is the 'core problematic' of Marx's whole edifice: 'how is it possible to understand the circumstance that human social practice is constitutive at the same time as when the individuals are ruled by really existing abstractions'?

Here the dialectical relationship between abstract and concrete, objective and illusory is made clear. Economic abstractions are not a layer of untruth to be stripped away, but rather objective illusions (Bonefeld 2014, p. 63) through which, as classed subjects, we find ourselves in the strange situation of subsisting. The critique of social constitution, therefore, does not centre on a crusade to shake others from false consciousness. Any 'demystification' of the distorted fashion in which human practice appears in the commodity form only reveals to us the 'constituted untruth of a world...which asserts itself independently from the social individuals that constitute, comprise and sustain it through their own social practice' (Bonefeld 2014, p. 40), and without being aware of it' (Adorno 1990, p. 5).

The appearance of these relations other than in their blood-soaked verisimilitude is not a 'false' appearance to be stripped from either the world or its beholder, but rather an 'objective illusion' produced in the fetish form itself which expresses within it the truth of the situation, 'the objective appearance of the social characteristics of labour' (1976c, p. 86). As Adorno states (1997; quoted in Bellofiore and Riva 2015, p. 26) 'on the one hand, commodity fetishism is a semblance; on the other hand, it is ultimate reality'. To use Marx's analogy, the positing of a relationship between coats, boots and linen by means of money might seem 'absurd', but it expresses a real constituted relationship between 'private labour and the collective labour of society' (1976c, p. 79). Similarly, at the level of production, to workers, 'the social relations between their private labours appear as what they are, i.e., they do not appear as direct social relations between persons in their work, but rather as material relations between persons and social relations between things' (Marx 1976c, p. 75). The critical theory of social constitution thus accepts the appearances of things in society. As Adorno suggests, to not do so would be 'pure idealism', in recognition that 'appearance is always the appearance of reality, never pure illusion' (1976 [1962], p. 255). Thus critical theory is marked by a critical acceptance of appearances, only to condemn them.

Springing from our creation but beyond our control, the world of economic abstractions consists of real appearances that are both true and false at once. What is abstract implies within it the concrete, and the concrete is expressed in and through the abstract. Money both expresses a socially mediated relationship between two commodities, whilst also allowing us to acquire, via commodities, the things that we need to materially reproduce ourselves as humans. It is this power that affords it the socially synthetic and schematic character covered in Chap. 3.

It is from this basis in Marx's critique of the commodity fetish that the contemporary critical-theoretical engagement with the subject of social constitution sets out. In challenging their naturalisation in mainstream economics, the theory of the social constitution of economic categories sees society as not an abstract thing but 'concrete society', the sum of human practice, of 'the social individual in her social relations' (Bonefeld 2014, p. 27) or, as Horkheimer puts it, bringing the class antagonism to the fore:

> ...a definite individual in his real relation to other individuals and groups, in his conflict with a particular class, and, finally, in the resultant web of relationships with the social totality and nature. (1976 [1937], p. 221)

So, where traditional theory takes a standpoint outside its object, the 'starting point' of critical theory is not, say, 'man' in general, but definite social relations. This immanence has an impact on how we consider the limits of the critique of social constitution and the class antagonism. In critical theory, 'there is always, on the one hand, the conceptually formulated knowledge and, on the other, the facts to be subsumed under it' (Horkheimer 1976 [1937], p. 210). But, as we saw in Chap. 3, in adapting the Kantian schema not as an ideal structure but as socially preformed, the first-generation Frankfurt School was able to show that theory is already practical and practical life already conceptual. As Horkheimer puts it, 'facts' are 'co-determined by human ideas and concepts', prior to 'theorisation'. On one hand, this indicates that abstract reifications of human practice in objective economic categories also themselves rest in practice, in the 'actual conditions of life' which are the 'non-conceptual premise of the economic categories' (Bonefeld 2016a, p. 76, n. 11; see also Marx 1976a, pp. 493–4, n. 4), so that the coin in our pocket carries both a concept, but also our ability to subsist. On the other hand, it reveals the implication of our own theorisation of social constitution within its object. The relationship between theory and the facts is not an external one but internal – critical theory moves within this. The contradictions and antagonisms uncovered are not only a matter of presentation, but a real and constitutive part of the world, of which critical theory, too, is part. There is no 'external' standpoint to take (Gunn 1992, p. 25). This is immanent critique, which achieves, through the exposition of the system, the explosion of the system, and of that which is natural as socially constituted.

The critique of political economy as a critical social theory contests the eternal naturalness economics ascribes to economic categories, because their social validation can only ever be socially and historically grounded in a set of antagonistic relations. In 'dissolv[ing] the economic categories on a social basis' and 'arguing that definite forms of social relations manifest themselves in mysterious economic forms', the theory of the social constitution of economic categories therefore centres on class antagonism, 'the critical concept of a capitalist society' (Bonefeld 2014, p. 22). Class, rooted in historical and ongoing primitive accumulation, renders individuals, 'on pain of ruin', dependent on the movement of economic abstractions in order to subsist. Bonefeld writes that

> Economic laws impose themselves behind the backs of the acting subjects that sustain society, and society is governed by the movement of real economic abstractions, which akin to the mythical idea of fate impose themselves on the social individuals with devastating force, cutting them off from the means of subsistence at the blink of an eye. (2014, p. 24)

The key question for the social constitution of this situation is 'why does this content of human social reproduction take that fateful economic form?' Hence 'social constitution' here relates both to how human practice takes on a social form, but how human practice itself moves through socially mediated abstractions. And the compulsions placed upon individuals to subsist through these abstractions are structured by the class antagonism whereby one group is rendered dependent on the selling of their capacity to labour in order to subsist materially through the mystical, money-mediated exchange of commodities for the price their labour-power is paid in the form of the wage. This relationship between abstract social forms and concrete social relations the theory of the social constitution of economic categories sets out to decode. Its critical acceptance of appearances does away with the idea that the class struggle is to be waged through finding the right level of informed consciousness. The critical acceptance of appearance is here its condemnation.

5.5   Contemporary Confusions

In this, the critical theory of social constitution and class given by scholars in the NRM offers an alternative to presently popular ways of talking and thinking about class. This is because it grasps in theory what others claim to do with reference only to the facts, which, as Adorno asserts, 'may well contribute to the critique but may also, according to Critical Theory, obscure social structures' that are objective, in relating ultimately to 'the ownership of the means of production' and not subjective indices like income or lifestyle (2003b, p. 112). Today, the academic and popular critical imaginary of class society thrives on competing, but equally con-fused, narratives that claim to assimilate the 'facts' of the situation at the expense of theory. Critical theory furnishes us with the intellectual resources to combat these confusions, of which the 'multitude', covered in the next chapter, is just one.

Mobilised to create ever more complex stratifications of different social groups, bourgeois sociological chatter over 'class situations' begs the question of how the class situation develops to begin with. As Clarke (1991, p. 211) notes, the sociology of, say, Weber, saw classes as interested groups united by a 'class situation'. The use of 'ideal types' (Adorno 2003a, p. 101) re-asks the question of class as one of methodology. The search to construct schema of different class strata indicates how sociological conceptualisations of class seek to 'fit tidily into groups' that will not conform so easily to clean-cut distinctions of lower or upper 'middle' class, for instance (Gunn 1987). This is because, as Gunn (1987) suggests, the class relation central to critical accounts sees the relation as 'structuring the lives of different individuals in different ways' that cut through and across individuals and groups. In this, the class reductionism and dogmatism (Adorno 2003b, p. 112) often attributed to Marxian analyses actually reaches full fruition in bourgeois sociology, which attempts to classify in fixed ways that which it cannot conceptualise, by assuming that which needs to be explained.

As in Weber, voguish Bourdieusian notions of class focus on the way in which a given set of workers 'achieve…a favourable market situation', however, 'not as traders of their own labour power', but via diverse types of so-called 'capital' (Bonefeld 2014, p. 119, n. 45). This situation is seen as uncompromised and unproblematic. For Weber, class collectivities form around shared lifestyles, ethics and a sense of 'status honour' (Weininger 2005, pp. 120–1, p. 132). Class is seen here as somehow *positive*.

The problem with this perspective is that it sees class – and the process of being classed, of being classified, with the social rule that this entails – as something that struggled *for* rather than struggled *against*. The aspirations of the actors involved reduce to a given status within class society rather than pushing against, outside or beyond it. The Bourdieusian-Weberian approach does not permit consideration of the contradictory or antagonistic character of the situation. Its hegemony in the academy and outside rules out questions about antagonism, struggle and change, with class is seen as a status' attained, rather than as an unfortunate allocation subject to capitalist social relations of property ownership and waged labour.

These theories of social stratification – and not *class* in any substantive sense – positively identify individuals 'according to economic positions, levels and sources of income, social status and labour market situation', not to mention so-called 'social' and 'cultural' capital (Bonefeld 2014, p. 103). This neuters the 'critical function' of the concept 'class', 'by claiming that [its] negative aspect simply does not exist', as Adorno puts it (2008, p. 139). Moreover, it sees capital; as a "thing beyond critique", an "economic mechanism that can be made to work for this class interest or that class interest", as opposed to itself existing as a social relation presupposed upon those classes themselves (Bonefeld 2016b, p. 238).

Theories of social stratification, in the hands of bourgeois sociologists, Marxists and other 'critical' scholars, also associate its social groups with particular forms of revenue – the working class with the wage, the capitalist with profit – exhibiting a complete lack of curiosity about the conditions potentiating the situation whereby each secures their social reproduction on the basis of these categories to begin with. In so doing, these bourgeois sociological and traditional Marxist theories of class 'seek...to render intelligible the observable "facts" of life without conceptualising them as forms of definite social relations'. This is because, as Bonefeld suggests, '[t]he concept of social groups does not inform, and is not informed by, the concept of social relations' in the first place (2014, p. 103). The theory of social groups seeks to discover 'facts' treated in abstraction from their 'concrete concept' – as Adorno writes, 'the concept of their relation to the present state of exploitation'. This concept is both 'contained' in the facts and determines them (Adorno 2003a, p. 101). As such the failure of sociologists to confront the concept is not a methodological issue, but a fetish tied to objective illusion.

Had they the concrete concept to hand, bourgeois and Marxist sociologies of class would grasp that '[t]he class relation does not just amount to the wage relation; rather, it subsists through the wage relation' (Bonefeld 2014, p. 107). Any suggestion that the working class should be synonymous with the category of revenue 'wage' does not enquire as to what the relationship of class with the wage is, which is to say it centres on the 'economic compulsion' of a 'daily struggle [to] secur[e] the means of subsistence by means of wage income' in the historical circumstance that all other means have been deprived the worker. And this proceeds in 'competition' with other sellers of labour power 'to achieve and maintain that income' (Bonefeld 2014, p. 107). Hence, even on the basis of wage revenue, the concept of class does not hang together. The creation of new class categories like the 'precariat' (Standing 2011) to capture workers who fall foul of this contradictory unity miss that the reality they seek to define is already contained within the conceptuality of class as its stands. The same can be said for the concept of the 'multitude', covered in the next chapter.

Clarke draws on Marx's critique of the fetishism of the 'Trinity Formula' (Marx 1991, pp. 953–70) to suggest that this revenue-based understanding recites a 'Smithian' concept of class also shared by traditional Marxism (Clarke 1991, pp. 21–8, 97–9). Here, the division of labour bestows different revenue streams – land, labour, capital – to different groups that thus become 'classes' – landowners, wage-labourers and capitalists. But this, for Clarke as for Marx, is simply 'the culmination of the fetishism of commodities' (1991, p. 98), mystifying class by taking things that result from it as its cause. The social constitution of these categories in the class antagonism itself goes unquestioned. That land must be private property, labour-power a commodity, and the historical and ongoing process of primitive accumulation that guarantees this is so is left undisturbed in theory. It presupposes that which it seeks to explain, like Bourdieu and his forms of capital (Bourdieu 1984). The categories on which classes are arbitrated themselves imply the class antagonism they are taken to describe.

Owing partly to its association with a deficient theory of value that treats the latter as an objective economic category as opposed to a social form which is inextricably grounded in the social relations of class society (Clarke 1991, p. 27), this Smithian approach has taken in Marxists as well. It has concerned traditional Marxism with arcane questions – to be charted in Chap. 9 – of which workers do and do not bear what Marx deemed the 'misfortune' of being productive, for instance, based on which form of revenue – capital, state and so forth – they are paid out of (1976a, p. 644; see Gough 1972 for an example). In this wage-based understanding of class, which enquires just as little as non-Marxist theories into the provenance of the circumstance whereby the wage exists at all, the 'social position' theories of class found in mainstream sociology reappear as concerning instead one's *economic* position (Bonefeld 2014, p. 103).

Heretical strands within classical Marxism have defied this characterisation – something at stake, for instance, in E.P. Thompson's assault (1978) on Althusser (2001). But, according to Gunn (1987), both are wrong. Thompson counterposes an 'empiricist' understanding of class that sees it as resiting in a 'group of individuals' with something 'in common' – in this case a culture – where Althusser's 'structuralist' understanding of class emphasises class as a 'place' in the 'social landscape' which individuals occupy. Each in their own way is incorrect: Thompson, because class exists against itself, a 'fracture-line' 'running through' individuals, and Althusser because class is a relation between people and not a standalone position one can occupy.

Endowing this economic 'position' with great positivity, classical Marxism sees the working class, as producers of social wealth, occupying a privileged historical role culminating in its rise to power. But the critical Marxism advocated here thinks otherwise. The 'struggle of the dispossessed sellers of labour power does not express a historical privilege' (Bonefeld 2016b, p. 241). This is because 'it is dictated by hunger' (Adorno 2005, p. 102), a result of a social history of dispossession untold when class is seen as the outcome of active possession of a kind of economic revenue or capital. The struggle of this hungry class, in seeking comfort, aims, crucially, toward its self-abolition, and with it that of class society itself. Class is not a positive category because, from the perspective of critical theory, it exists 'in *and against* its historical practice, and in *and against* its social reality' (Marcuse 1972, p. 90). Mainstream accounts miss this – and, as we shall see in the next chapter, the postoperaist account of class, centring on the concept of 'multitude' misses this conflicted negativity, too.

5.6   CRISIS AND CLASS ANTAGONISM

By emphasising the contradictory unity of production and consumption in a society where one side is dispossessed of independent means to survive, centring the class antagonism within a wider social-form analysis of capitalism gives us pause to radically revise many of the assumptions about crisis found in the Marxist tradition to date. This is a revisionist stance best exhibited in the recent controversy around Heinrich's attack on the legacy of the 'law of the tendency of the rate of profit to fall' which, resonating with the traditional Marxist standpoint on class as a positive category, suggests that the collapse of capitalism will surely come and the working class rise to power on its back – a supposition found in a different but complementary form in the postoperaist thought covered in subsequent chapters.

Where many Marxist accounts obsess over the origin of capitalist crises, Heinrich's theory of crisis explains, in Simon Clarke's neat phrase (1989), their *necessity* rather than their source. He examines the contradictions present within capitalism, their relationship with the class antagonism and their propensity to give rise to failings. His theory of crisis rejects the central position taken by the law of the tendency of the rate of profit to fall (LTRPF) in Marxist analyses of crisis.

In setting out the LTRPF, Marx's treatment of the interrelationship between trends in the organisation of labour and the manifestation or mediation of crises relies upon a series of concepts: constant and variable capital and the organic composition of capital, the contradictions inherent in which lead to the tendency for the rate of profit to fall. For Marx, the inputs into the labour process are divided into constant and variable capital. Constant capital represents all means of production, machinery and raw materials. Variable capital is the human living labour which engages the elements of the former category. For Marx, the ratio between these two elements is of paramount importance in analysing capitalist production. This ratio Marx labelled the organic composition of capital (Marx 1976a, p. 762). The organic composition of capital (OCC), for Marx, presents the moving contradiction in his analysis of the LTRPF. The increased productivity of capitalist production inevitably leads to the influx of new and greater means of production into the labour process. This drive toward improved efficiency necessarily results in the expulsion of labourers from employment, or in workers assuming control individually of an ever-expanding amount of technology. Either way, the proportion of constant capital to variable can be seen to rise, as either the amount of workers or the amount of hours worked decrease. For Marx, this proportional change can impact negatively upon the rate of profit, depriving as it does capital of the human labour to which it owes the creation of specific use-values for sale on the market as commodities (1993, p. 318).

Thus, when we speak of the rising organic composition of capital, we refer to the increase in constant capital (raw materials, machinery, means of production) against variable capital (living labour) as a proportion of the total capital submitted to the production process. It is not hard to see the potential contradiction in the rising OCC. The increase in the 'social productivity of labour' through the influx of new technology at once promises the opening of the full potential of capitalist production whilst simultaneously belying the destruction of the very foundation upon which it is established and maintained. This is an exposition of capitalist development that appears also in the Fragment on Machines, discussed in Chap. 7. The devaluation of labour-power, and the diminishing of variable capital in the OCC starve capital of the one thing upon which it thrives: human labour-time. Constant capital, despite its role in productive growth, bestows no new value through the means of production. Human labour plays an ever lesser role. Whilst this can be masked to an extent by an ever-increasing *mass* of surplus-value and profit, these false glories only serve to obscure an underlying tendency towards falling rates of surplus-value (and, of course, more immediately, rates of exploitation) and profit (Marx 1991, p. 324).

Heinrich's rejection of the LTRPF has two aspects. The first is theoretical. Advocates of the LTRPF stake a great deal on the direction of the organic composition of capital. Heinrich suggests that the OCC is ascertainable. But the *extent* of this direction is not. For instance, historical limits and qualitative factors place constraints on the growth of constant capital. One such limit is itself the reduction in variable capital. Such qualitative eccentricities affect the quantitative magnitude of the direction taken by the OCC. Thus, for Heinrich, 'nothing can be said concerning long-term tendencies of the rate of profit' (2013a, pp. 24–5).

The explanatory burden the OCC assumes in the LTRPF rests upon the understanding that there can only be two ways of increasing the rate of surplus value. The absolute route sees an increase in working hours. The relative option witnesses a reduction in the value of labour power through productivity gains. For Heinrich, this is already a much too narrow outlook that elides the manifold different outcomes that a rise in the rate of surplus value might have upon the rate of profit.

Heinrich highlights the weakness of popular interpretations of how movements in the OCC affect the rate of profit. On one hand, the generation of surplus value through the lengthening of the working day acts as a countervailing tendency to the LTRPF. On the other, the generation of relative surplus value through productivity gains manifests in a rising OCC and thus brings about the development of the law. But to take this view, one has to ignore the dual impact of productivity increases. The ratio of constant to variable capital witnesses a rise in the former relative to the latter. This, advocates suggest, leads to a falling rate of profit. But a rising rate of surplus value to variable capital manifests in a rising rate of profit. The projection of a 'law' here must overlook the second manifestation of the production of relative surplus value through productivity gains. Instead, the lawmaker must place a one-sided emphasis on the former. But a rise in the OCC is decisive in this situation only if the value of labour power falls by a sufficient amount. Yet for proponents of the LTRPF, Heinrich suggests, a rising OCC is sufficient in and of itself to generate a falling rate of profit. As Heinrich writes, '[w]e cannot escape the problem that the capitalist development of productivity has two contradictory effects on the profit rate' (2013b). Thus, the basis for a past, present and future identification of a real tendency in the rate of profit is weak.

The second aspect of Heinrich's critique is exegetical. He uses evidence from Marx to support his theoretical claims. Heinrich notes Marx's own acceptance of the impossibility of cohering a law around these contingencies. In a 'handwritten remark in a personal copy' of *Capital* Volume I, Marx suggests the feasibility of a situation wherein a rising profit rate accompanies a rising OCC (Heinrich 2013a). Friedrich Engels deemed this remark significant enough to include it as a footnote.

The LTRPF issued not from Marx's sense of theoretical completeness, according to Heinrich. Rather, it stems from the manner in which Engels edited, abridged and compiled the scattered material that came to constitute *Capital* Volume III. This enshrined Marx's thoughts into a 'law' within the framework of a total 'theory of crisis' that did not exist ahead of editing (2013a, pp. 25–6).

What Marx *did* consider 'the most general formulation of capitalism's tendency to crisis' is 'completely independent' of the LTRPF (Heinrich 2013a). This is the central contradiction whereby, as Marx writes,

> To express this contradiction in the most general terms, it consists in the fact that the capitalist mode of production tends towards an absolute development of the productive forces irrespective of value and the surplus-value this contains, and even irrespective of the social relations within which capitalist production takes place; while on the other hand its purpose is to maintain the existing capital value and to valorize it to the utmost extent possible (i.e. an ever accelerated increase in this value). In its specific character it is directed towards using the existing capital value as a means for the greatest possible valorization of this value. The methods through which it attains this end involve a decline in the profit rate, the devaluation of the existing capital and the development of the productive forces of labour at the cost of the productive forces already produced. (1991, p. 357)

Here the LTRPF expresses a deeper malaise, rather than being the cause itself. Heinrich suggests that we pay attention to what Marx considered most significant. It soon becomes apparent that the LTRPF is not the central element of his theory of crisis. It actually 'express[es] something more general' (2012, p. 154). This is that, in Marx's words, 'the capitalist mode of production comes up against a barrier to the development of the productive forces which has nothing to do with the production of wealth as such; but this characteristic barrier in fact testifies to the restrictiveness and the solely historical and transitory character of the capitalist mode of production' (1991, p. 350).

Significantly, this relates squarely to class. This barrier, as Heinrich explains (2012, pp. 172–174), is that 'capitalist production and capitalist consumption are differentially determined' and 'downright antagonistic'. Production advances on the basis of an inequality that ensures the restricted capacity of one section of the population to consume. This antagonism is both the precondition of the sale of labour power, and immanent within the structure of the wage form. Heinrich does not apply to this an underconsumptionist analysis suggestive of Keynesian state remedies. Rather, Heinrich emphasises the *overproduction* of commodities in the context of restricted consumption. It is not the insufficient demand that is problematic. This is the basis of capitalist production. It circulates around private property, the separation from the means of subsistence, and the sale of labour power as a commodity to survive. Rather, it is capitalism's ceaseless drive to overproduce and, in turn, overaccumulate, that is problematic. This leaves the commodities overproduced unsold and the capital overaccumulated unvalorised. This is what generates conditions of crisis in capitalist society: its constrained basis in the class antagonism.

Thus, crisis does not issue from the LTRPF. It issues from 'the immediate purpose of capitalist production, surplus-value or rather profit' (Marx 1991, pp. 352–3). It is not an aberration or unsuccessful manifestation of this purpose, but its necessary expression. Crises thus do not arise from the conditions of production, or from the imbalances of the OCC. Rather, crises present themselves principally as crises of realisation. This owes to the separation of the moment of production and exploitation in one sphere and the realisation of the value it generates in another sphere, the market. As Marx writes, '[t]he conditions for immediate exploitation and for the realization of that exploitation are not identical. Not only are they separate in time and space, they are also separate in theory. The former is restricted only by the society's productive forces, the latter by the proportionality between the different branches of production and by the society's power of consumption' (Marx 1991, pp. 352–3).

Thus, according to Heinrich, the 'fundamental contradiction' of capitalism is 'between the tendency towards an unlimited production of surplus value, and the tendency towards a limited realisation of it, based upon the "antagonistic conditions of distribution"' (2013a, pp. 25–6). I return to this in Chap. 9, exploring how creative industries help remedy crises of overproduction.

Heinrich's approach has attracted the ire of Marxists still drawn to the unfolding of the LTRPF as a hook on which to hang one's political aspirations. Kliman and his allies criticise Heinrich and the new reading for their suggestion that Marx's work was incomplete and in need of critical reconstruction. Kliman et al. state that Marx refused to publish the first volume of *Capital* without finalising the complete structure of the subsequent volumes (Kliman et al. 2013, p. 12). But this overlooks the tremendous publisher pressure under which Marx laboured (Wheen 2000, p. 298). He had deadlines to meet, both at the business end and as regards the political necessity of striking whilst the proverbial iron was hot. Numerous revisions, and various international introductions, illustrate Marx's piecemeal undertaking. Heinrich's critics claim that Marx planned to release the first volume only when the whole theory was complete. It follows, they suggest, that its publication proves that Marx's system was complete. But, ironically, this lacks any Marxist appreciation of the material circumstances of its production and existence.

For Kliman et al. (2013, pp. 13–14) Marx's work is complete and beyond modification or dispute. But this changes when the subjective input is that of Engels. Engels's contribution to how *Capital* appeared is, Kliman asserts, merely editorial. Whereas Engels channels the 'true' Marx, Heinrich, or anyone else with which his critics disagree, cannot.

These critiques and others have also asserted that Heinrich- and, by extension, the wider NRM- has no theory of crisis, or neuters Marx of an effective crisis theory. For Fuchs, 'Heinrich ignores the dynamic and crisis-prone character of capitalism' (2014, p. 45). Fuchs follows Robert Kurz, inferring from Heinrich's crisis theory that capitalism always regenerates itself. It faces no eventual terminal breakdown. This claim that Heinrich has no theory of crisis circulates in the recent controversy over the latter's examination of the textual basis for the LTRPF. Heinrich suggests that Marx had no complete theory of crisis resembling that put forward by advocates of a falling rate of profit theory of crisis. In response, Kliman et al. suggest that Heinrich has no 'alternative theory of crisis of his own' (2013, p. 2). But Heinrich does offer an alternative. He charts the necessity underlying how capitalist crises manifest, as discussed above.

But whilst critical assessments such as that of Kliman et al. suggest that Heinrich has no theory of crisis, they simultaneously associate Heinrich with the *Monthly Review* School of crisis theory. This emphasises underconsumption as the cause of capitalist crisis. But they cannot have it both ways. He either has a crisis theory or he does not. Kliman et al. (2013, p. 2) highlight the publication of Heinrich's critical examination of the LTRPF in the pages of the *Monthly Review*. The article, they allege, contributes to the theoretical agenda of underconsumptionist theory. This it does by setting out to discredit advocates of the LTRPF approach. Guglielmo Carchedi and Michael Roberts (2013) write that Heinrich's account 'is really a continuation of the argument by *Monthly Review* that Marx's law of the tendency of the rate of profit to fall…is not the main cause of economic crises'. The 'underconsumptionist' allegation shows that his interlocutors have not read him carefully enough. Heinrich is no ally of underconsumptionist theories of crisis. Indeed, his critique of them is crucial and decisive (see 2012, pp. 172–4). Underconsumptionist accounts centre on the 'constricted power of consumption of the working class'. But that the demand represented in this 'power of consumption' is lower than the supply of goods produced by capitalists cannot be a cause of crisis. This is because it is a permanent condition. Underconsumptionists focus upon low wages. Their recommendations in times of economic turmoil often fall back upon this as the target of government intervention. But it is a necessary characteristic of the capitalist mode of production that 'wages are always lower than the total value of the product'. Wages, whether they are high or low, 'are never sufficient enough to constitute the demand for the total product'. For Heinrich, this continuing contradiction may create crises, but not by itself. Crises of underconsumption are not the proper expression of this contradiction. The contradiction manifests instead in crises of *overproduction*. It is transparent: Heinrich is no ally of the *Monthly Review* School, for whom the constitutive and thus inescapable role of the class contradiction in determining the imbalance between production and consumption is not nearly clear enough.

As we have seen in Chap. 2, Heinrich emphasises 'social validation' as the key principle of capitalist value. Capitalists face a constant struggle to successfully validate products of labour as value-bearing commodities. This occurs in exchange, where value comes to full existence. As we see in Chap. 9, fields such as graphic design, advertising and marketing help make this happen by endowing products with a saleable character. If they are not successful in attaching meaning and significance to a product of labour, it will not sell. It will not exchange for money. It will not be validated as a commodity bearing a value. It will not enter into a relationship, by means of money, with all the other commodities of the market.

A produced good that sits unsold in a warehouse *has no value*. Value is thereby tied to monetary realisation in exchange. It is not intrinsically contained within the commodity itself, whether potentially or actually. Value arises in the *relationship between* commodities, a relationship mediated by and expressed in money. An artwork hanging in a gallery, price tag intact. A car fresh off the production line standing on a factory floor. An unperformed song played by a band in their practice space. What these have in common is that they have no value. There is no value to speak of until the artwork, the car and the song enter into relationship with counterpart commodities through monetary exchange.

Accordingly, this account of crisis circulates around the ability of capitalists to realise value in exchange. Crisis is a failure of social validation. Capitalism's crisis tendencies issue from a central contradiction. This is between the propensity of capitalists to produce and the capacity of society to consume. The antagonistic relations of distribution and property in capitalist society explode this contradiction. The overproduction of potential commodities by capitalists hell-bent on accumulation is an ever-present possibility.

Whilst this sounds like an underconsumptionist account of crisis, it is not. For Heinrich, as for Marx, the worker's capacity to consume can never be in line with production. Capitalist society thrives on an antagonistic relationship that guarantees the precise opposite. A constraint must always be in place to ensure the ready availability of workers willing to sell their labour power to survive. The wage must always be lower than the cost of goods. As Marx writes, 'there must be a constant tension between the restricted dimensions of consumption on the capitalist basis, and a production that is constantly striving to overcome these immanent barriers' (1991, p. 365).

Consequently, appeals to 'insufficient demand' as the cause of crises ring hollow. Instead of demand, focus should be upon the mass of unrealisable commodities. Underconsumption cannot by itself explain crises. This is because the classed contradiction of limited spending power for a great swathe of the population is permanent. It is not a temporary or incidental cause of crisis. It is an unchanging condition immanent within the system itself. Underconsumption is problematic only when seen in the light of its flipside, overproduction. Capitalism has a tendency to produce over and above the capacity to consume implied in its antagonistic class basis. Hence, explanatory weight does not fall not upon the latter objective limit. It falls upon the persistent drive to produce and accumulate pursued by capitalists regardless of that limit. We will return to this in Chap. 9, examining the strategies used by capitalists to overcome this limit, contrary to the claims of the postoperaists that capital has entered a crisis beyond measure.

5.7   CONCLUSION

In this chapter I have drawn on the work Werner Bonefeld to set out a means by which we can decode the material determinations present in the abstract unfolding of the value-form. Bonefeld's critique of the NRM's tendency towards a 'logical' rather than 'historical' reading of the genesis of the rule of value is staged from within the theoretical tradition but augments it with the Open Marxist centring of class struggle and primitive accumulation. This conceptual commitment is reflected in Marx's own presentation of the commodity fetish, where the real antagonistic social relations between human agents are not something submerged beneath the appearances these relations take in the modes of existence of value, but rather something that is expressed in these. This gives us a way to talk about life under capitalism without outsourcing all contentions or commitments to pure speculation as to how things 'really' are or could be. It is there for us to grasp by means of the 'negative dialectics of economic objectivity' Bonefeld presents in his CPECTS.

This has impacts on how we consider the future or present possibilities for any escape from capitalism. It is to this aspect that we now turn our focus in the second part of this book. What the theory of class and crisis given in this chapter emphasises is that there are persistent and contradictory relations of class antagonism at the core of capitalist society which cannot be discounted in considering not so much the *source*, but the *necessity* of crises. As we will see next, such a consideration of these constitutive contradictions is missing in much of the postoperaist-inspired thinking that takes, variously, one of two contested and contentious elements of Marx's *oeuvre* as their basis: the Fragment on Machines, and the passages on the falling rate of profit. By treating each in their place within a wider reading of Marx's work, we can put right what is wrong in many Marxist theories of crisis.

In a time where new theories of capitalist collapse draw on the contested inheritance and overly optimistic political efficacy of the LTROPF, the following analysis works against attempts to recoup it in light of the radical rethinking of Marx's work that has unfolded in the wake of the New Reading. Today we see a reappearance of ideas around the rising organic composition of capital sounding the death-knell of capitalism, mainlined into the mainstream of left thought via the new reception granted Marx's

Fragment on Machines. A new cadre of postcapitalist dreamers contend that so-called 'info-capitalism' exhausts capital's capacity to instigate countervailing measures against the falling rate of profit, in a time of accelerating automation, 'free machines' and endemic unemployment. The second part of the book uses the ideas of the NRM to take these ideas apart.

BIBLIOGRAPHY

Adorno, T.W. 1941. Spengler Today. *Zeitschrift fur Sozialforschung* 9: 305–324.
———. 1973. *Negative Dialectics*. London: A&C Black.
———. 1976 [1962]. Sociology and Empirical Research. In *Critical Sociology*, ed. P. Connerton, 237–57. London: Penguin.
———. 1990. *Negative Dialectics*. Trans. E.B. Ashton. London: Routledge.
———. 1997. Seminar Mitschrift of 1962. Appendix to Backhaus. In *Dialektik der Wertform*, 501–512. Freiburg: Ca Ira.
———. 2000. *Introduction to Sociology*. Cambridge: Polity Press.
———. 2003a. Late Capitalism or Industrial Society? The Fundamental Question of the Present Structure of Society. In *Can One Live After Auschwitz? A Philosophical Reader*, ed. R. Tiedemann, 111–25. Trans. R. Livingstone. Stanford: Stanford University Press.
———. 2003b. Reflections on Class Theory. In *Can One Live After Auschwitz? A Philosophical Reader*, ed. R. Tiedemann, 93–110. Trans. R. Livingstone. Stanford: Stanford University Press.
———. 2005. *Minima Moralia: Reflections from Damaged Life*. London: Verso.
———. 2008. *Lectures on History and Freedom*, ed. R. Tiedemann. Trans. R. Livingstone. Cambridge: Polity Press.
Althusser, L. 2001 [1971]. Preface to Capital Volume One. In *Lenin and Philosophy and Other Essays*, 45–70. New York: Monthly Review Press.
Bellofiore, R., and T.R. Riva. 2015. The Neue Marx-Lekture: Putting the Critique of Political Economy Back into the Critique of Society. *Radical Philosophy* 189: 24–36.
Bonefeld, W. 2010. Abstract Labour: Against Its Nature and on Its Time. *Capital and Class* 34 (2): 257–276.
———. 2014. *Critical Theory and the Critique of Political Economy: On Subversion and Negative Reason*. London: Bloomsbury.
———. 2016a. Negative Dialectics and Critique of Economic Objectivity. *History of the Human Sciences* 29 (2): 60–76.
———. 2016b. Bringing Critical Theory Back in at a Time of Misery: Three Beginnings Without Conclusion. *Capital & Class* 40 (2): 233–244.

Bonefeld, W., and K. Psychopedis, eds. 2005. *Human Dignity: Social Autonomy and the Critique of Capitalism*. Aldershot: Ashgate.

Bonefeld, W., R. Gunn, and K. Psychopedis, eds. 1992. *Open Marxism Volume I: Dialectics and History*. London: Pluto Press.

Bourdieu, P. 1984. *Distinction: A Social Critique of the Judgement of Taste*. Trans. R. Nice. London: Routledge and Kegan Paul.

Carchedi, G., and M. Roberts. 2013. A Critique of Heinrich's, 'Crisis Theory, the Law of the Tendency of the Profit Rate to Fall, and Marx's Studies in the 1870s'. *Monthly Review*. http://monthlyreview.org/commentary/critique-heinrichs-crisis-theory-law-tendency-profit-rate-fall-marxs-studies-1870s/. Accessed 1 Oct 2014.

Clarke, S. 1989. The Marxist Theory of Overaccumulation and Crisis. Presentation Given at Conference of Socialist Economists 1989: Value Crisis and the State Stream. https://homepages.warwick.ac.uk/~syrbe/pubs/CSECONF1989.pdf. Accessed 10 Nov 2014.

———. 1991. *Marx, Marginalism and Modern Sociology*. London: Palgrave.

Fuchs, C. 2014. *Digital Labour and Karl Marx*. New York: Routledge.

Gough, I. 1972. Marx's Theory of Productive and Unproductive Labour. *New Left Review* I/76: 47–72.

Gunn, R. 1987. Notes on Class. *Common Sense* 2: 15–25.

———. 1992. Against Historical Materialism: Marxism as First-Order Discourse. In *Open Marxism Volume II: Theory and Practice*, ed. W. Bonefeld, R. Gunn, and K. Psychopedis, 1–45. London: Pluto Press.

Hegel, G.W.F. 1976 [1807]. Master and Slave. In *Critical Sociology*, ed. P. Connerton, 41–50. London: Penguin.

Heinrich, M. 2012. *An Introduction to the Three Volumes of Karl Marx's* Capital. New York: Monthly Review Press.

———. 2013a. Crisis Theory, the Law of the Tendency of the Profit Rate to Fall, and Marx's Studies in the 1870s. *Monthly Review* 2013: 15–32.

———. 2013b. The 'Fragment on Machines': A Marxian Misconception in the Grundrisse and Its Overcoming in Capital. In *Marx's Laboratory: Critical Interpretations of the Grundrisse*, ed. R. Bellofiore, G. Starosta, and P. Thomas, 197–212. Leiden: Brill.

Heinrich, M., and W. Bonefeld, eds. 2011. *Kapital & Kritik: Nach der 'neuen' Marx-Lektüre*. Hamburg: VSA.

Horkheimer, M. 1976 [1937]. Traditional and Critical Theory. In *Critical Sociology*, ed. P. Connerton, 206–224. London: Penguin.

———. 1992. Nachtrag [Postscript]. In *Kritische und Traditionelle Theorie*, 261–269. Frankfurt: Fischer.

Kliman, Andrew, Alan Freeman, Nick Potts, Alexey Gusev, and Brendan Cooney. 2013. The Unmaking of Marx's Capital: Heinrich's Attempt to Eliminate Marx's Crisis Theory. http://ssrn.com/abstract=2294134. Accessed 1 Oct 2014.

Marcuse, H. 1972. *One Dimensional Man*. London: Abacus.

Marx, K. 1845. *The German Ideology*. https://www.marxists.org/archive/marx/works/1845/german-ideology/. Accessed 29 Oct 2016.

———. 1976a. *Capital*. Vol. I. London: Penguin.

———. 1976b. The Critique of Hegelian Philosophy. In *Critical Sociology*, ed. P. Connerton, 51–72. London: Penguin.

———. 1976c. The Fetishism of Commodities. In *Critical Sociology*, ed. P. Connerton, 73–89. London: Penguin.

———. 1991. *Capital*. Vol. III. London: Penguin.

———. 1993. *Grundrisse*. London: Penguin.

Standing, G. 2011. *The Precariat: The New Dangerous Class*. London: Bloomsbury.

Thompson, E.P. 1978. *The Poverty of Theory*. London: Merlin.

Weininger, E.B. 2005. Foundations of Pierre Bourdieu's Class Analysis. In *Approaches to Class Analysis*, ed. Erik Olin Wright. Cambridge: Cambridge University Press.

Wheen, F. 2000. *Karl Marx*. London: Fourth Estate.

PART II

Postoperaismo

CHAPTER 6

Immanence, Multitude and Empire

6.1 Introduction

This chapter begins our engagement with the ideas of postoperaismo and how the New Reading of Marx can help critique them at a time of their peak uptake in the popular literature on 'postcapitalism'. In it, I introduce the philosophical and theoretical foundations of Antonio Negri's postoperaist assault on the Marxian theory of value, as a central point around which to orient a wider consideration of how this critique has been adopted and developed in the work of his associates and followers. Key to this undertaking will be the setting out of a series of shifts: in the first section, from operaismo to postoperaismo and towards a Spinozist turn in Negri's thought, concomitant with the move from a more conventional proletarian class subject to the all-encompassing figure of the 'multitude'; in the second section, a swing from the more antagonistic refusal of capitalist work to its celebration as an expression of the autonomous creativity of the aforementioned multitude; and, in the third section, the switch, by means of an application of the Marxian concept of subsumption with reference to the so-called 'social factory', from any kind of Marxist dialectics to a Spinozist standpoint of immanence whereby all is as one. This trades in the contradiction, mediation, abstraction and the socio-material transcendence of the value-form for compliance, immediacy, concreteness and immanence, in so doing foreclosing any capacity to get close to the categories critiqued by the reconstruction of Marxian value theory presented in Part 1 of this book.

On this basis, the final section of the chapter critiques the claims associated with Negri's Spinozist turn, focusing centrally on the complete absence of

© The Author(s) 2018
F.H. Pitts, *Critiquing Capitalism Today*, Marx, Engels, and Marxisms,
DOI 10.1007/978-3-319-62633-8_6

conflict, struggle, antagonism and domination in the presentation of a world the development of which is one and the same as that autonomously chosen and made by the spontaneously cooperative and creative multitude. By foregoing the theoretical resources to complicate the possibility of the positivity they ascribe to work and workers in capitalist society, I suggest, Negri and postoperaismo as a whole fall well short of the analytical standard set by critique of political economy as a critical theory of society (CPECTS), a weakness that, as we shall see in subsequent chapters, undermines its assertions as to the irrelevance of the theory of value the NRM has done so much to rescue and resurrect.

6.2   Operaismo to Postoperaismo

The work of Antonio Negri has long been a vector for revolutions in radical thought. Specifically, the progression of his work charts the development of the 'Italian New Left' (Cleaver 2000, p. 64) from operaismo to postoperaismo. And, with it, a wider body of political and theoretical engagement grouped under the epithet 'autonomist Marxism' (Cleaver 2011, p. 51). His work with Michael Hardt, *Empire* (2001), introduced the world to this tradition in its latest stage of sophistication. And, far from a high-water mark, its influence has percolated since, bubbling over in its translation into UK left discourse via the new and voguish 'postcapitalism' literature (Mason 2015a, b, 2016). This follows an initial, earlier uptake of operaismo, the forerunner of postoperaismo – including the early work of Negri – on the UK left via the 'Revolutionary Socialist Feminist organization with a working class orientation' Big Flame (Cleaver 2014), and specifically through the translation work of Ed Emery, who, as Abse (2016) notes, was among a milieu from the group who followed Negri's journey to *autonomia*. But the population of the popular left imaginary with the kinds of thinking present in postoperaismo by public intellectuals like Paul Mason marks a qualitative shift towards the mainstream.

Operaismo was inspired by the proliferation of worker struggles in 1960s and 1970s Italy (see Cleaver 2000, pp. 64–77). Their actions and demands exceeded the narrow parameters of party-sanctioned political praxis. Operaismo's English rendering as 'workerism' misleads (Hardt, cited in Thoburn 2001, p. 92). It is not delimited to workers or workplaces. Operaismo's application extends to other spheres of activity that, as we shall see, it rebrands as work. Empirically, however, the context in which it hatched drew its attention to a specific kind of work and worker. And the factory, more or less, was its location. Its analysis thus hinges on what is most significant at any given time for capitalist development. And, at the time of its inception, this was the factory worker. Specifically of interest was the antagonistic relationship these workers entered into with capital.

Postoperaismo takes this potential theoretical looseness of application to new terrain. New empirical conditions dictate a shift in focus. The 'post' aspect stems from the attention lavished on new forms of work and worker. Through the prism of operaismo, struggles of factory workers were hegemonic. But, in the transition to postoperaismo, the creative activity of new 'immaterial labour' (Lazzarato 1996) comes to the fore. The distinction from operaismo rests not only on empirical insights. After all, operaismo implied the application of its frame of reference to diverse fields of activity. But, crucially, a theoretical and philosophical shift attends the change in empirical focus. Negri's post-1980s output witnesses a move away from Marx, to read and replace the latter through the work of Spinoza. Out goes the working class, in comes the multitude. Out goes antagonism, in comes immanence. The autonomist lexicon pivots on Negri's move from operaismo to postoperaismo. It is this transition I explore here.

In the following, I trace these issues through the development of Negri's work, from his re-evaluation of Marx in his 1978 lectures on the *Grundrisse* (1992) to his later work with Michael Hardt (2001, 2004, 2009). In Negri's work with Hardt culminates a long engagement with Marx, and, latterly, Spinoza. It was Marx who suggested that 'human anatomy contains a key to the anatomy of the ape' (1993, p. 105). And, we can read Marx along similar lines. Thus, 'the most developed is the key for the knowledge of the less developed' (Bellofiore 2009, p. 179). His most mature expositions of the critique of the political decode what went prior. We can approach Negri the same way. In the following I read Negri's development from the vantage point of the triumvirate of texts with Hardt.

This illuminates a series of shifts. First, Negri discovers Spinoza. Initially, Negri maintains a Marxian fidelity to the dialectic (Cleaver 1992b, p. xxi). His reception of Mario Tronti's 'Copernican inversion' (Cleaver 1992a) of class struggle is a hinge point here. This inversion posed the working class as the motor of capitalist development. As it revolts, capital reacts. New technologies, new working practices, follow. Negri finds in Spinoza a philosophical grounding for this that Marx cannot offer. Spinoza's immanentism has radically anti-dialectical implications. Class struggle drives capitalist development not antagonistically but monistically, at one with capital itself. Spinoza is a skeleton key for the reinterpretation of the working class as the 'multitude' that appears in *Empire*. Negri's turn to Spinoza takes place shortly after his 1978 lectures on the *Grundrisse* (1992). It is expressed fully in his 1980 prison writings on Spinoza, published in English as *The Savage Anomaly* (2009). Here I am most concerned with the subsequent stress it places on how Negri theorises social and political change.

Between what became known as *Marx Beyond Marx* and *The Savage Anomaly*, Negri served time in jail. This is the context for a 'radical break' between Negri's early Marxism and later Spinozism (Ryan 1992a). In the former, there is still some concept of social mediation with which to understand the rule of value (1992, p. 162). But the turn to Spinoza is a radical attack on the dialectical understanding of mediation, in the name of pure immediacy. With this comes an unravelling of any idea that capitalism consists in a set of abstract social forms. The roots were there in Negri's reception of Tronti's Copernican Inversion. But whereas the latter emphasised antagonism, Negri elides negativity to see only positivity. For Negri, liberation is possible in the present state of things. Where humans emancipate themselves, the world follows. This is as opposed to a picture whereby humans emancipate themselves by abolishing the present state of things. These theoretical leaps are made only in light of an abandonment of a Marxian critique. The negativity of the latter exposes the limits of the possibility of liberation within the shell of capitalist society, as we shall see.

The rejection of a Marxian critique goes hand-in-hand with another shift in Negri's approach. Negri's background is in the radical autonomist *refusal* of work (Cleaver 1992a, p. 130). This refusal is still voiced clearly in *Marx Beyond Marx*. But by *Empire* we find Negri, with Hardt, celebrating work as immanently creative, cooperative and communicative, and, crucially, productive of an immeasurable plenitude of value. As Noys writes of this shift in emphasis, 'Negri's earlier, violent emphasis on the necessity for the negation of labour through workers' counter-power in the forms of refusal becomes magically recoded as the expression of an unlimited positive power' (2012, p. 116). The discovery of Spinoza is handmaiden to this transformation of Negri's work. Spinoza's philosophy forces focus on the immanent power of human creativity, desire and democracy. This allows Negri to suspend the antagonism with which the operaist tradition typically tarried.

These shifts show how it is possible to separate Negri's later postoperaist output from its operaist origins. In the following, I conduct a critique principally focusing on Negri's work with Hardt. But in so doing I refer back to the transition in how Negri understands value, labour and capitalism. This relates first to his influences in Italian operaismo, and, second, his own work on the *Grundrisse*. Later output diverges from these bases. Looking at his body of work and its inspiration in this way brings into relief the philosophical and empirical shifts. Most importantly, it exposes the political imperatives that undergird this theorisation. And it affords resources for responding to their resonance today.

Negri's Spinozism takes all things as a singular monad. But the negative dialectics set out in previous chapters encounters reality through its contradictions. As we saw in Chaps. 4 and 5, contradiction, alien to Negri, is the mode through which dialectics analyses the world. It appreciates that things may be one thing and another at once. A negative-dialectical approach problematises identity and, against the grain, does not affirm it. It thereby runs against the grain of Negri's Spinozism. It suspects all positing of things as being of one kind, commensurable and in common (Bonefeld 2014, p. 69). This critique of capitalist society is something that, the further from Marx he travels, the less equipped Negri becomes to match. But only in such a refusal to accept identity at face value can theory get to capitalism's rotten core. This consists, for Bonefeld, and crucially for our approach, in one component above all others. Namely, that the results of human practice, of human creativity, come to assume an alien force over us as capital where Negri sees them as immanently within our control.

This irony cannot be appreciated in the confines of postoperaist theory. In the foregoing, I suggest that Negri's embrace of immanentism leads him to see the best in human practice. With immanence disappears any dialectics capable of comprehending the character of the abstractions and contradictions that rule over us and through which life in capitalist society by necessity proceeds. This leads to a political appraisal of the present that celebrates novelty and positivity. It sees the multitude as one with a world created in its image. In so doing, it suggests, affirmatively, that human practice exists for itself in this world and not the next. This dispenses with the dispassionate critique of capitalist society. It assumes the withering away of the abstract rule of capital and the social relations it implies. But these persist along the lines Bonefeld suggests – as the result of human practice that is not for itself. Our creativity, Negri has us believe, is uncomplicatedly positive and liberatory. And so too, this says, is the capitalist development which trails in its wake. But negative dialectics refutes the positing of identity. In a capitalist society, the things and relations we create coerce us, mediated in the value-form. Creativity cannot be uncritically cited as a realised quantity in capitalist society, but always exists in a mode of being denied (Holloway 2010).

Negri's post-prison output lacks any perspective from which to grasp this. A politics follows, conceptually stuck within capitalist social relations and their forms of appearance. The overarching charge Negri faces is what Benjamin Noys labels 'affirmationism'. This Noys defines as that political and theoretical imperative that 'affirms the creation of unashamedly meta-physical ontologies, the inventive potential of the subject, the necessity for the production of novelty, and a concomitant suspicion of the negative and negativity' (2012, p. ix).

This book is a contribution to the recuperation of the negative from the perspective of a peculiarly Negrian political moment. It is the present-day percolation of this politics that makes the critique here important. The same positivity and optimism today instil an undisappointable hopefulness in the left. This celebrates popular power and the potential for a high-tech postcapitalism. It sees in capitalist development always the unfolding of human emancipation. But by mischaracterising capitalism to begin with, it elides emancipation's obstacles. Here I seek the roots of this in Negri's philosophical development, generating resources to rethink these assumptions today and act accordingly.

In this chapter, I will chart the theoretical motivations of Negri's turn to immanence. It occurs over three texts in which Hardt and Negri set out the new global order of 'Empire'. Synonymous with globalisation, Empire witnesses the breaking down of borders and the concentration of power in a single, diffuse locus. In this new social formation Hardt and Negri contend, power is immanent. No more the transcendental power of imperialism (Hardt and Negri 2001). In Empire, power rests in the constituent force of *multitude*, to which Empire reacts. This new revolutionary subject drives capitalist order from one paradigm to another. It does so through its autonomous activity. Capitalist power can only respond to multitude's unencumbered self-valorising creativity (Negri 2008, pp. 32–48), whereas it is in fact capital that structures and stifles it.

Multitude is bound by a productive identity associated with empirical changes in labour. With 'immaterial labour' (Lazzarato 1996; see Chap. 8) – a transformation it impels – multitude comes into its own. But despite this productive identity, Hardt and Negri disavow the traditional Marxist proletarian subject. The multitude lacks a deterministic relationship with the forces of capital. It is an independent and self-sufficient figure, whose own agency effects change within labour. The paradigmatic figure of the white, male manual worker makes way for a multifarious, mobile body of 'singularities' (2001, p. 53). But the connection between change and production remains. Despite protestations to the contrary, Hardt and Negri posit the revolutionary upheavals of our time squarely in production, broadly defined. And this is not unproblematic, as I show in the next chapter.

The development of the multitude propels that of Empire not from without, but from within. The two are synonymous. Empire springs from the reconfiguration of world order around 'proletarian internationalism' (2001, pp. 51–2). Power globalises as the growing mobility and strength of labour leans against the limits of the old order. The multitude's boundlessness thus precipitates an extensified and intensified world market. This account of capitalist change poses resistance as productive. It casts the latter as 'entirely positive', compelling capitalist progress (Noys 2012, p. 106).

Seeing development as springing from the multitude as a positive force affirms that development. Today, this matters politically to how the left approaches the present. Popular power is portrayed as an already-potent and pre-existing principle. The world, it is claimed, can and will change. But the people – read 'multitude' – leads the charge. This induces affirmation of those changes. And bestowing undue influence in the hands of human practice, it affirms the world that springs from it. This undermines criticality of thought vis-à-vis capitalist social relations. And, I will suggest next, it indicates a divergence from Negri's operaist theoretical formation.

6.3   FROM THE REFUSAL TO THE CELEBRATION OF WORK

In some ways, Hardt and Negri's account bears traces of its origin in operaismo. Relating capitalist development to the multitude's desires and mobility, they refract Tronti's 'Copernican reversal'. The latter turned capitalist development 'on its head' (Tronti, quoted in Noys 2012, p. 106), seeing capital following where working-class struggle leads. Contemporaneously, Panzieri sought to articulate how state policy expresses this inverted relation. Schemes like the New Deal were a recurring topic of interest in the operaist tradition (see Cleaver 2000, pp. 65–6). They showed, writes Cleaver, that 'the only unplannable element of capital is the working class', to which capital must always react.

Operaismo championed the working class's revolutionary capacity to act in advance of capital. This was an attack on the legacy of the first-generation Frankfurt School. Operaists saw the latter conceiving only capital's capacity to order society in its image (Cleaver 2000, pp. 65–6). But, as described in the previous chapters and applied throughout, my perspective differs. The legacy of Adorno and his associates is not to ignore human practice in favour of pure domination. Rather it is to illuminate the contradictory situation whereby human practice takes dominating forms. The roots of Negri's postoperaist divergence from this critical orientation thus lie in operaismo, and it is in the space opened up that my own critique operates.

These insights were not only theoretical observations. They opened out upon political and organisational struggle in Italy at the time. For operaists, the 1960s Italian labour movement was implicated in a Keynesian productivity compromise. In return for greater productivity, workers could expect to receive a greater wage. But crucial for the operaist analysis of class struggle was the breakdown of this compromise. Wage demands exceeded productivity at precisely the point a refusal of work threatened its foundations (Cleaver 2000, p. 68). The breakdown of the Keynesian compromise is crucial in the development of autonomist Marxism. It induces Negri to collapse the distinction between economics and politics. Struggles around economic life need no longer be mediated through politics. They become directly political themselves.

This reappears in *Empire* as the capacity of multitude to strike directly at the heart of global order. This is immediate, unmediated by the abstract social forms a critical Marxist perspective identifies. The immediacy of this struggle hinges on new empirical conditions. Immaterial labour undermines all metrics and measures of work, pay and productivity (Hardt and Negri 2001, pp. 113, 402–3; 2009, pp. 135–6). There are no bases on which to arbitrate competing claims over production. On one hand, control and value capture the move from production to the 'immaterial basin' (Lazzarato 1996) of life itself. And, in turn, the location of struggle shifts from production narrowly defined to a broader politics of everything.

These struggles looked slightly different to the early operaist pioneers. They were interpreted as concerning the expansion of the sphere of working-class needs. These expanded to the ultimately destructive extent of exploding capitalism's contradictions. Thus, they theorised the wage not as a means of exploitation, but as an 'expression of working-class power' (Cleaver 1992a, p. 142, n. 54). The wage appears as the 'working-class power to impose its needs'. And, moreover, these needs – and thus the level of the wage – are subject to struggle (Cleaver 1992b, p. xxiv). The working class – later the multitude – exerts an excessive effect on the ability of capital to capture and control. In postoperaist hands, this eventually becomes the catalyst for a 'crisis of measurability' (Hardt and Negri 2001, pp. 113, 402–3; 2009, pp. 135–6). I critique this concept in Chaps. 7 and 8.

As I note in the next chapter, operaist and postoperaist iterations of Marxism reflect empirical changes. The reconceptualisation of Marx advanced according to posited shifts in society. This method is clear in Negri's reading of Marx's *Grundrisse*. From the context of Italian labour struggles, Negri applies the expansion of needs to the LTOV. Negri suggests that as the 'sphere of needs' expands, so too do labour's sociality and abstractness. Thus the secret of abstract labour is that 'work creates its own needs and forces capital to satisfy them' (1992, p. 133).

The theoretical approach I adopt here, outlined in Part 1, sees value theory differently. Abstract labour sublates concrete need and experience. It does not express them in a positive form. The seeds of Negri's positive appreciation of capitalist development are thus already present. Abstract labour is not a dominating force. Rather it expresses the irrepressible desire of workers. Negri's analysis absents itself from the critical negativity crucial to Marxian critique.

In this, Negri also diverges from the operaismo behind the theory of the self-expansion of needs. In Tronti's Copernican Inversion, there still held a negative moment of antagonism and struggle. The working class drives toward the destruction of capitalist rationality and social relations. But, in Negri, this 'destructive character' is discarded. We get, instead, a celebratory treatment of the positivity and productivity of working-class power (Noys 2012, p. 109). This is already there in Negri's 1978 lectures on the *Grundrisse*. And this later appears as the constituent power of the multitude. Rather than negating capitalism, the multitude promises to deliver its resolution from within.

Negri's divergence from, say, Tronti and Panzieri occurs on two axes. The first relates to periodisation. The moment of conflict between working-class needs and capitalist rationality moves. Tronti and Panzieri see this as something in motion. Needs expand outwards. Eventually, the ability of capital to satisfy them becomes so weak as to usher in a kind of communism. The full unfolding of those needs can then be realised and fulfilled. Negri, in his lectures on the *Grundrisse* (1992), largely pays lip service to this reading. But things look different as Negri's work develops with Hardt. The unfolding of these needs seems fully realised in the present. In *Marx Beyond Marx*, Negri enthuses about the prospect of 'the abolition of work' (1992, p. 160). By *Empire*, this is realised already in a 'spontaneous and elementary communism' (2001, p. 294) coexisting within contemporary capitalism itself. Today, leftist dreams pervade of a similar liberation within the confines of the current system. And it is to Negri that at least part of their appeal owes. But even at the precipice of the changes these affirmationist accounts posit, this rosy prospectus is nowhere to be seen.

For Hardt and Negri, the incipient liberation they practice comes courtesy of the multitude's constituent power. This is a recoding of operaismo's
chaotic and 'unplannable' working class beyond command. The key for this
recoding was a radical immanence derived from Spinoza. The antagonism
politically and theoretically at the centre of the Copernican Inversion
recedes. There is no external position from which to antagonise. The
multitude positively pushes against the limits of capital with new needs
and activities. Capital adapts to capture the immeasurable value produced.
There is here no external position, or radical alternative outside the bounds
of the present state of things. This constituent power springs from within
capital. The multitude is immanent within, not transcendental to or in
contravention of, global order. Although spontaneously creative and autonomously organised, it is at one with capitalism (Hardt and Negri 2001,
p. 83). Its development is that of capital. It is the motor, not the halt-cord,
of the present state of things. Things move in singularity, in symbiosis. In
this, Negri's postoperaismo breaks clearly with the struggle-oriented
operaismo of his antecedents.

   The implications of this become clear only with Negri's embrace of
Spinozist immanentism. But there is a thread of continuity in Negri's
thought on this point. Spinozist 'creativity of desire' (Hardt and Negri
2001, pp. 51–2) simply substitutes for Marxian self-valorisation. Earlier,
Negri attributes to the working class – from Tronti and Panzieri's 'inverted'
perspective – the power of self-valorisation (Cleaver 1992a, pp. 128–9). The
working class produces in a 'self-defining, self-determining' way, 'autonomously from capitalist valorization'. As Cleaver writes, Negri suggests that it
surpasses 'mere resistance to capitalist valorization'. It amounts to a 'positive project of self-constitution' instead. It is clear here that Negri is toying
with concepts of the multitude and the crisis of measurability. Perhaps
cognisant of a basic irreconcilability with the letter of Marx's law of value
(see Chaps. 7 and 8), Negri sought new conceptual glue in Spinoza. In
Spinoza, Ryan tells us, Negri found a 'justifi[cation] for his own political and
philosophical position'. The theoretical discourse of potential against power
and 'world-constituting practice' (Ryan 1992b, p. 216) grounded the
re-evaluation of Marx in a political project. And this has implications for
how we think and talk about contemporary labour under capitalism, as we
will see in the next two chapters.

   This theoretical shift saw a change in emphasis from the refusal of work
to its celebration. The analysis of self-valorisation related to the understanding of Italian worker struggles. The wage-productivity compromise was

undermined by work refusal. 'Self-valorisation' stepped in to conceptualise how workers autonomously organised against and beyond labour. But with Hardt, Negri moved on from this. Immaterial labour and the 'creativity of desire' indicated the possibility of a liberation *through* work (Hardt and Negri 2001, p. 395). Once again, this realises a direction of travel projected in Negri's earlier work. As Cleaver asserts (1992a, p. 130), his use of self-valorisation to read the *Grundrisse* already half-displaced work refusal.

Workers, Negri suggested, autonomously expand abstract labour in line with their needs and desires. Thus their development and creativity was tied up with work in an unacknowledged way. Value is not conceived of as an alien force against workers, but expressive of something essential and not socially specific. To refuse it is to refuse the positive essence it expresses. The discovery of immanence facilitates the full realisation of this perspective. Life is one and the same with work. Liberation is wrought only within this singularity. And so, by *Empire*, the break with refusal is complete.

For Hardt and Negri, the multitude produces value autonomously. This might happen within capitalist production. But capital is capable only of capturing the value the multitude creates – not controlling it. The move towards immaterial labour occurs owing to the multitude's creative and communicative drives. Capital trails in its wake. And the multitude's constituent power generates conditions for an incipient communism. The cooperation enacted through work crafts the multitude as a Spinozist singularity (Hardt and Negri 2001, p. 395). And with it, remodels the world. This happens *through* and not against work. Labour, redefined as synonymous with life, is affirmed along with everything else under the sun. But as set out in Part 1, critical theory critiques from a benchmark of truth, and the truth is that capitalist society is negative, not as a matter of opinion, but as really functioning around negation. Illustrating this negativity, creative autonomy is structured and constrained by capital, and not the reverse as suggested by Negri and his followers.

For Negri, work becomes easier to celebrate once reconceptualised as synonymous with life – and vice versa. The concept of self-valorisation makes this possible. But this intersects with another element of the operaist inheritance. This is the theorisation of the 'capitalist tendency to widen its valorization to the entire "social factory"' (Cleaver 1992a, p. 131). The social factory was initially and most notably defined by Tronti. He contended that 'At the highest level of capitalist development social relations become moments of the relations of production, and the whole society becomes an articulation of production. In short, all of society lives as a function of the factory and the factory extends its exclusive domination over all of society' (Tronti, cited in Cleaver 1992a, p. 137).

As Cleaver (2000, p. 70) notes, this reconceptualises work beyond the confines of the four walls of the factory. It situates it instead in society as a whole. This initially related to, for instance, reproductive work that makes labour-power possible. Or, indeed, to the activities of the reserve army of labour that capital depends upon in vital respects. Negri's initial delineation of self-valorisation pointed towards this politically potent context. It chimed with contemporary conflicts around social reproduction, unemployment and the exploitation of women. But in the development of Negri's work with Hardt it gained new resonances. These resonances carried beyond the context of contemporary struggles. Originally, the social factory concept drew an analogy between life outside the factory and the work inside. But, gesturing to the new immaterial labour, Negri goes further. In Tronti, society becomes a factory. Life becomes like work. But in Negri, the factory becomes *social*. Work becomes more like life. The workplace becomes where workers realise a spontaneously cooperative productivity.

Of course, the other aspect is there too. Outside the four walls of the factory, Hardt and Negri see ever further spheres of life put to work. Capital recoups, after a fashion, their autonomous, self-directed creativity in the framework of value. But the social factory concept, in the hands of Tronti, had an antagonism at its heart. The factory signified exploitation, class struggle. But with work under immaterial labour recoded as creative activity, this underbelly disappears. Hardt and Negri steal work from the antagonistic context in which it sits in the theorisation of the social factory. The multitude realises itself within the newly socialised workplace. And this realisation exceeds, rather than conforms to, the capacity of capital to control and capture it. This is because the changes in the workplace are created by the multitude's own momentum. With all things one and the same, how could the world defy the multitude's inherent positivity? Such a search for reasons to be cheerful characterises left thought today.

6.4   IMMANENCE AGAINST DIALECTICS

In Negri's later work, a Marxist hangover remains linking the social factory with immanence. This is the concept of real subsumption. Marx theorises the movement from formal to real subsumption in the 'lost sixth chapter' of *Capital*, 'Results of the Immediate Process of Production' (1976, pp. 948–1084). This movement represents an intensification of capitalist valorisation synonymous with the world market. Once the latter reaches completion, capital cannot extend its power. There are no conditions for expansion such as those presented in imperialism. In Empire, power plumbs deeper into the fabric of life instead (2001, pp. 225, 329). For Negri, this was expressed in the implication of the social within the factory and vice versa. The logic of the factory seeps out of its spatial and social boundaries into society as a whole. Its rule is no longer transcendental but absolutely immanent. And it works within the bodies and brains of the multitude, who in turn are immanent within *it*. Real subsumption realises empirically that which Spinoza's immanence indicates philosophically: one, single, social substance (2001, pp. 255, 329, 403). With real subsumption, Hardt and Negri write, capital 'operates on the plane of *immanence*, through relays and networks of relationships of domination, without reliance on a transcendent centre of power' (2001, p. 326). The basis for this empirical leap are the new forms of 'socialised labour' (Negri 2008, p. 44). Real subsumption proceeds through labour's intensified exploitation on the terrain of human life itself: emotion, cognition, communication, knowledge, language and affect (Hardt and Negri 2004, pp. 107–9). The advent of immaterial labour verifies Negri's philosophical shift to immanence.

Radical immanentism militates against dialectics or contradiction. This restructures the horizon on which struggle is seen to ensue. The dispersal of power across and ever deeper *into* society means that the multitude struggles at all times and in all places. Although social, this struggle still concerns production. Immaterial labour takes place everywhere, and so all struggles mobilise around it. But the immanence of multitude and its activities in a world of real subsumption mean that '[t]here is nothing dialectical or teleological about th[e] anticipation and prefiguration of capitalist development by the mass struggles' of the multitude (2001, pp. 51–2). There is no external or antagonistic principle. Struggles come squarely from within the fabric of immanence.

This has political implications. Under real subsumption, politics is possible only on the field of immanence. It strikes out within the limits of a singularity. There is nothing beyond it. It therefore affirms only what already is. That the theorisation of subsumption and immanence should resolve itself so is of a specific moment. As Noys (2012) notes, Hardt and Negri write *Empire* with 'capitalism rid of even its intra-systemic rival', a capitalism 'unleashed'. With no systemic point of negativity, Noys suggests, a series of 'affirmationist' theories arose, of which postoperaismo is just one. Capitalism free of external challenge, immanence offered itself as a way to see the world, and with this, subjective actors within a single 'ontological fabric'. There is no Other, no antagonistic or utopian perspective from which to meet the present. Negri's Spinozism, therefore, gains succour from the historical circumstance that there seems no alternative. But, rather than facing up to this negativity with a politics of negativity, it pitches instead a politics of unrelenting positivity, out of step with the parlous situation in which we find ourselves.

The theorisation of multitude and the concept of immanence support specific political outcomes. As Hardt and Negri write, 'every liberatory initiative, from wage struggles to political revolutions, proposes the independence of use value against the world of exchange value, against the modalities of capitalist development – but that independence exists only within capitalist development itself' (2001, p. 185). At singularity with multitude and its desires, society is affirmed as is. We can hear this echoing in the hopeful pronouncements of populist postcapitalism today in the accelerationist utopianisms permitted by capital at its current stage of development.

Whilst the claims about self-valorisation, the social factory and subsumption are empirically grounded, the immanence with which Negri eventually binds them implies certain philosophical assumptions. Here, the divergence from Marx becomes clear. In embracing immanence, Negri lashes out against transcendence, mediation and dialectics. Each, in their own way, are crucial to the negative dialectic approach to the critique of political economy outlined at the outset of this chapter. And their rejection forecloses analysis of certain aspects of actually existing capitalism. Without them, Negri can only wish into existence a capitalism that does not exist. This wishful thinking pervades the influential work of Negri's inheritors today.

Their immanentism collides Hardt and Negri with the whole edifice of dialectical thought. Spinozism acts as a political and theoretical benchmark banishing transcendence from the analysis of capitalism. As Ryan writes (1992b, pp. 217–18), 'Spinoza is radically anti-transcendental.' Negri's Spinozism refutes any dialectic that 'mediates difference, conflict and the plurality of modes of being into an abstract resolution which would be the identity of power'. Human practice, for instance, cannot resolve itself dialectically in transcendent real abstractions. Negri uses Spinoza to attack 'the power of dialectical mediation' to 'subsume...the individual into the universal'. A countervailing 'emphasis on potential', on the other hand, 'reverses this transcendental metaphysic'. The particular is unassimilable, always one step ahead. Human practice exists for itself. It cannot, by this standard, turn against itself in socially mediated forms of domination.

In the name of Spinoza, Hardt and Negri bring other witnesses. Against Kant and Hegel, they cite Schopenhauer's critique of the 'Romanticism' of German Idealism (2001, pp. 81–2). This focuses on two forms of transcendence: on one hand, Kant's transcendental overdetermination of immediacy, and second, Hegel's positing of the dialectical resolution in a transcendental state. As concerns the first, Hardt and Negri follow Schopenhauer in critiquing Kant for a 'liquidat[ion of] the humanist revolution'. It is only in the latter that 'forces that tend to truth and light' – for this, read 'multitude' – 'can prosper'. And, in claiming the impossibility of immediacy, Kant offends against this, and with him the schematic and synthetic understanding of money and value presented in Chap. 3. The necessity of mediation complicates the untrammelled potentiality and positivity ascribed to the multitude. This opposition to mediation is presented in terms of the nature of political power in Empire. In earlier imperialism, social conflicts could be resolved through 'mediatory schema'. But, in Empire, conflicting forces 'confront one another directly', without mediation (2001, p. 393).

As concerns the second, they adopt Schopenhauer's critique of Hegel's transcendent state. Hegel, the critique goes, wrongly consolidates transcendence into the ontological fact of the state. This suborns and transforms 'the immanent goal of the multitude' into something else. But the state in Empire is as a result of the multitude. What the transcendence of the state extinguishes is that which 'strives, desires or loves'. This prohibits the grasp of the 'potentiality' present on the 'revolutionary plane of immanence'. Only 'the refusal of transcendence' makes possible 'thinking this immanent power' (2001, pp. 91–2).

What this all rests on, ultimately, is a rejection of dialectics, and, relatedly, totality. This, as Noys notes, is not specific to Negri's 'neo-Spinozism'. It is, rather, uniform across the various 'affirmationist' theories of contemporary capitalism. Noys attributes this to 'a continuing fear of the supposed totalizing effects of dialectical thought' (2012, p. ix). The unmediated 'singularity' of Empire and multitude (2001, p. 73) might superficially sound akin to a totality of relations. But it describes something very different. It rejects entirely the approaches to totality found in critical theory. Adorno stressed the transcendental domination of totalisation. Lukacs, on the other hand, envisaged the revolutionary recouping of totality. But Negri opposes both (Noys 2012, p. 110). From his perspective, each posits the mediation of parts into a transcendentally dominating or liberating whole. Under the logic of immanence, there are no 'parts' to mediate in such a 'totality'. There is *only one thing*, constituent power, without counterparts.

Kant's schema, Hegel's state – both dialectically resolve principles and relations into a totalising concept. Both Negri rejects, in the name of an attack on dialectics. This rejection comes early in Negri's work, albeit in different forms. In his lectures on the *Grundrisse*, Negri suggests that antagonism in capitalist society no longer forms 'part of the dialectic', but rather negates it (1992, p. 188). There is still a negative moment present in Negri's thought at this point. But Negri's adoption of a Spinozist discourse dispenses with all antagonism and negation. With them disappears any sense that the dialectic is there to be negated at all. The 'negation', indeed, is too dialectical itself to survive Negri's Spinozist turn to immanence.

The dismissal of transcendence, mediation and dialectics unite in Negri's method of analysis. '[M]ethod', Negri writes, 'is not a dialectical to-and-fro, and does not need to bring transcendence into method in order to illustrate the transformations of reality' (2008, p. 176). This posits changes in the immediate form of labour as the basis for changes in capitalism as a whole. But capitalism as a whole is a system of social mediations. Immediate productive activity is significant in capitalist society only in its socially mediated forms. An outright refusal to entertain transcendence and mediation preclude its conceptualisation. And a methodological aversion to dialectics compounds this.

Dialectics describes the process of thinking. It entails a movement from abstract to concrete and back again. But for Negri this diverges from immanence. Things are as they are – no essence lurks within appearance. Social constitution is not revealed by study, but is all there is to begin with. The 'sociological, factual and to-the-point analysis of the transformations taking place in labour' hinges on this (2008, p. 22). A dialectic of 'inside and outside' does not capture, for them, the 'play of degrees and intensities, of hybridity and artificiality' the multitude engages in, spontaneously and autonomously, with immaterial labour (2001, pp. 187–8). This is because this activity is world-constituting, and in an uncomplicated way. As human practice, immaterial labour is not mediated in alien, abstract modes of domination. It is what it is. And the world in which it takes place is inseparable from the activity itself. An understanding of contemporary labour, then, is incomplete without a grasp of the mediatory schemes to which it is subject.

Without dialectics, the immediate form of labour is all we need to know to understand its significance for capitalist society as a whole. This forces focus upon immediate changes in productive activity as harbingers of paradigmatic shifts. As I suggest in the next chapter, this emphasises novelty of content at the expense of continuity of form. And, as I will go on to suggest, it induces a kind of candied optimism. It is an affirmation of the present with unfortunate political and theoretical consequences.

Having set out the motivations behind and implications of Negri's immanentist turn, I will now give a critique. As we have seen, Negri holds to a monist ontology inherited from Spinoza. The world is one thing, and just as it seems. The multitude's constituent power creates it, without complication. The development of society – which is, after all, capitalist society and no other – is one and the same as the development of the multitude. And this puts a positive spin on that development. It represents nothing other than a radical version of the liberal narrative of endless progress. Every change in the workplace, every cross-border flow of capital, is a small victory in the name of human liberation. In the closing section of this chapter, and the next, I will unpick the theoretical leaps through which things appear this way. I do so in the name of a critique of political economy that, by means of negative dialectics, suspects the forms of social mediation through which capitalist society reproduces itself. This centres on abstract categories: value, money for instance. But, crucially, it opens out upon concrete social relations of antagonism, domination and coercion. I contend that Negri, in the development of his work towards a Spinozist immanence, discards the resources necessary for this critique. When all things are one thing, the negative moment, the destructive character, of events exits stage left.

6.5   PERVERSION AND PRODUCTIVISM

For Hardt and Negri, there is a single positive social principle: constituent power. They demonstrate this by using a functionalist metaphor from Spinoza. If we 'cut the tyrannical head off the social body', they write, 'we will be left with the deformed corpse of society' (2001, p. 204). This is not presented as a contradictory state of affairs. It passes no comment on the paradox whereby we depend on the same social rule that dominates us to live. Our bond with society is arbitrated by money. What generates it, regenerates us. But it casts no suspicion on this situation, wherein our subsistence and survival rests on an alien, antagonistic power's reproduction.

Rather, the statement permits of no contradiction. It dismisses conflict within the form of the functionalist, metaphorically organic 'social body'. The head and the body cannot be parsed. The 'head', in so far as they recognise one, can only blindly follow where the body leads. Although phrased in a

Spinozist idiom, this relates to Negri's operaist roots. As Cleaver suggests, operaismo has capital ruling always in response to the autonomous activity of the working class. In this sense, 'then capital cannot be understood as an outside force independent of the working class' (2000, p. 66).

With Hardt, Negri recodes Tronti's Copernican Inversion through the Spinozist idea of constituent power. Constituted power – capital/Empire – always follows where constituent power – working class/multitude – leads. For Negri, this serves the purpose of endowing the working class or multitude with a revolutionary power. In a thoroughgoing critique, Bonefeld suggests Negri's pre-Hardt appropriation of the Inversion achieves precisely the opposite. For Bonefeld, Negri conceives capital as a form of power that wields only a reactive potential. The multitude, meanwhile, enacts autonomous creative urges capital satiates. But this conceptualisation elides capital's status as an antagonistic social relation between people. And, in so doing, it, contrary to Negri's intention, 'destroys the insight that labour is a constitutive power' (1994, pp. 44–5). In such an account, Bonefeld writes, capital (or Empire) '"lives" by cajoling labour's self-activity into serving the capitalist cause'. The very fact that there is a reaction undermines the constituting capacity ascribed to labour, or multitude. So, at the most basic level, on the theory's own terms, the inversion it posits is negated by its central means of explaining how capitalism works.

Bonefeld largely refers to Negri's appropriation of the Copernican Inversion in his early 1990s work. But these issues intensify as the Inversion gains a Spinozist stress in Negri's work with Hardt. As Noys notes, Hardt and Negri 'appear' to posit a 'dualism' between constituent and constituted power in the *Empire* trilogy. Here, one is led to assume, struggle occurs, as set out in the Inversion. But, ultimately, things resolve themselves along the lines Noys cites Deleuze ascribing to Bergson. Dualism, this says, is 'only a moment, which must lead to the reformation of a monism' (2012, p. 111). There is, really, only one power – constituent power – around which no negative moment of social conflict can cohere. Empire is one and the same thing as constituent power. It is a world it creates, autonomously, in its image (2012, p. 112). The only negativity here is that which faces constituent power in its inability to 'realise [its] own power'. These are the immanent limits of capital or Empire. But even these spring from the entirely positive development of the multitude's capacities. The limits are built only to be broken down. I will return to this point in the next chapter.

The relationship between constituent and constituted in Negri's work forms a paradoxically monist dualism. An identity is posited between one and the other. But the identity posited does not capture the contradiction between individuals and capitalist society. We live and produce through human practice, the results of which come to dominate us. The creations of human practice appear to us as commodities carrying value expressed in money. And it is through these commodities that we subsist. We have a hard, material dependency on economic abstractions alien to us and our desires and interests. Similarly, the desire to be creative can be fulfilled in commodity society only through waged commercial work, contrary to the pleasurable use of skill and thought the value relation it generates depends on all the same, even while denying and stifling it. There is no simple identity between capitalist power and human practice. It is a broken mirror, full of contradiction. One thrives upon the other, but not through pure reflection. Rather, they relate through the perversion of one by the other.

We produce and live by means of things and relations that exist against us as alien, dominating forces all the same. Bonefeld's critique puts this in the strongest terms possible. Bonefeld permits that human practice has a 'con-stitutive power'. But, to the extent it has it, it exists – 'as itself' – contradic-torily, 'in the mode of being denied' (1994, pp. 50–1). It does not exist for itself in the way Negri suggests. Shorn of a dialectic, Negri has no route through which to see that things are not always as they seem. That things can exist as themselves and something else cannot be grasped through immanence. But the positing of a world free of contradiction invites the ascription of a for-itself positivity to all human activity. Here, postoperaist accounts of the changing world of work, by imbuing contemporary labour with a liberatory positivity, chime with mainstream bourgeois accounts of work in the new economy.

On this, Negri ignores the true contradiction of how human practice wields a constitutive force in the world of capital. Bonefeld characterises this oversight as follows. In every society humans produce. But the specificity of human productive activity in capitalist society consists in the forms its results assume. Centrally, they take an alien, mystical existence above and beyond the capacity of human producers to control them. As commodities, these products in turn transform human production itself. It becomes a relation-ship not between humans but between things, and between objective economic forms. The value-form 'asserts itself over social relations as mere thinghood' (Bonefeld 1994, p. 50). In short, what human productive activity 'constitutes' comes to assume the '"perverted" form of value' (1994, p. 45). The alienation labour undergoes in this regard turns it 'against itself', even while it is every bit as much itself as before (1994,

p. 46). Human subjectivity realises itself in objective forms stacked against it, but through which it cannot but live. Only a dialectical method attuned to the movement between subject and object gets at the negativity of the human under capitalism. Negri, meanwhile, posits only positivity.

As Ryan points out, for Negri, in the positivity his thought grants, Spinoza only 'justifies his own political and philosophical position' (1992b, pp. 216–18). Spinoza only adds light to a conceptual apparatus already out from under the shadow of the critique of political economy. Negri had broken with an understanding of labour as an abstract mediation of human practice proceeding through transcendental forms. What Spinoza gives Negri is an 'emphasis on human production as potential'. And, politically, this 'opposes the subsumption of that activity into a principle of transcendence, of power'. This 'production' is synonymous with 'collective human activity as world-constituting practice'. For Hardt and Negri (2001, p. 73), bourgeois humanist philosophy's discovery of immanence 'brought down to earth' the 'powers of creation that had previously been consigned exclusively to the heavens'.

But I would contend that this fails to capture how human practice under capitalism attains socially mediated forms. Commodity, value, money, capital: these are transcendental, in that they are alien and above and beyond our capacity to control. But what the CPECTS suggests is that they spring from the very 'world-constituting practice' Hardt and Negri eulogise. Creative activity in capitalist society is mediated as labour as a matter of necessity. We cannot live without selling our capacity to perform it. And we cannot live except through buying the commodities labour produces. In this, the things that dominate us are themselves the perverted results of our creative activity. And this contradictory reality is what the immanent perspective elides. It brings powers of creation too far down to earth. In so doing, it fails to look heavenwards to see how those powers of creation manifest in forms of transcendental capitalist power. Human creative activity is not self-sufficient unto itself, but inseparable from its situation in market relations at either end of the process of production.

This is a wider problem relating to the rejection of mediation. Only the most immediate guise of any given activity is taken as theoretically or empirically relevant. From this are extrapolated changes in capitalism as a whole. But the method set out in Chap. 4 does not delude itself with the superficial content of labour itself. Creative, cognitive, communicative it may be, but a critical approach views it within its full social significance within the circuit of capital as a whole, by reading it through the relations of commodity exchange in which it intervenes, as detailed later in Chap. 9. It is the *form* that is crucial, and not the content.

In Negri's account, however, the forms through which that activity attains significance in capitalist society are ignored. To Bonefeld, Negri sees human practice as existing only for itself. Placing a positive spin on the Copernican Inversion, Negri casts capital as the suitor of the working class. The former constantly struggles to 'cajole [the latter] to its ends' (Bonefeld 1994, p. 46). In all this, the autonomous creativity of the multitude leads. Capitalist development expresses its revolutionary subjectivity. And, thus, Negri inaugurates a tendency to eulogise changes in capitalism that we see bear fruit today. Postcapitalist dreaming provides a radical alibi for mainstream scheming around the same themes. New kinds of work, technological shifts, productive paradigms: the multitude propels the world forward.

That productive activity can be seen as self-sufficient chimes with a pervading productivism in Negri's work. Despite disavowing traditionalist productivist Marxism, in both operaismo and postoperaismo a contrary pull remains. Focus falls on struggles in and against labour. The relationship with work is seen as historically decisive. The LTOV is held to be in crisis only on the most reductive reading (see Chaps. 7 and 8). In all this, it follows the Marxist imperative to exalt labour as a matter of political expediency. Workers are endowed with great power to create the world's wealth and change its course. And from this flows a logical and historical pre-eminence in theory. In this, Spinozism affords Negri a philosophical alibi and ally. It 'affirm[s] the productive force of humankind' (Ryan 1992b, p. 218). This provides a route through which Hardt and Negri recruit Marx to their cause. They claim, along the most orthodox of lines, that Marx sees everything beginning with production (2004, p. 143).

But the question for Marx does not begin with production, but why and how its results take the form they do in capitalist society. Production in and of itself tells us less about the role of labour in capitalist society than do the wider social relations in which it is embedded, at both ends of the process. This is why, one might contend, he begins *Capital* with wealth, money and commodities, and not labour. Hardt and Negri shirk the difficult questions Marx was actually interested in asking. Why does productive activity in capitalism result in certain historically specific social forms? Exalting the productive activity itself, Hardt and Negri display no curiosity in the latter. This, plausibly, is because it renders untenable the positive embrace of the possibilities of the present. The constitutive power of human labour does not exist for itself in a positive sense. What the CPECTS shows is that it is imbricated otherwise. It exists through and for a society where its products rule over it negatively. As I demonstrate in the next chapter, Hardt and Negri's narrow productivism helps them look upon the present from the rosy prospectus of novelty and change.

The one-sided perspective on production is supported by the elision of the forms of social mediation through which production gains significance in capitalist society. And this in turn relates to how Hardt and Negri dismiss abstraction and mediation in their philosophical outlook. As we have seen, they distance themselves from Kant on the basis that his philosophy rests in transcendence rather than immediacy (2001, pp. 81–2). They prioritise concrete immediacy over anything abstract, mediated or transcendent. Things exist for themselves, and are not overdetermined or dominated by anything else. This, as we have seen, impacts upon how antagonism is – or rather, is not – conceptualised. The dualism they posit resolves into a monism. Constituted power is subservient to constituent.

But, as Bonefeld asserts, this ascribes a false subjectivity and intentionality to both. Characterising their relationship as immanent, it elides how capital really relates to its subjects. Which is to say, as a perverted social form assumed by the results of human production, it is turned against those producers. What is concrete is abstracted from, and what is immediate is mediated. And the specific forms assumed by this abstraction, this mediation, characterise capitalism. To understand this, it is necessary to leave sufficient analytical room for abstraction and mediation. Hardt and Negri, however, rule it out from the start. Bonefeld aptly captures the contradictions central to this conundrum when he writes that

> The emphasis on 'inversion' does not raise the issue that 'labour' is the producer of perverted forms. Instead, labour tends to be seen as a power which exists external to its own perverted social world: the constitutive power of labour stands external to its own perversion. This perversion is called 'capital'. Labour is seen as a self-determining power at the same time as which capital is a perverted power by virtue of its 'cajoling capacity'. Thus Negri's emphasis on capital as a 'bewitching power'. The emphasis on the struggle component of the relation between structure and struggle cannot overcome their theoretical separation. The question why does human practice exist in the perverted form of capitalist domination is not raised. (1994, pp. 44–5)

The big issue here, suggests Bonefeld, is Negri's 'romantic invocation' of pure immediacy. Negri's romanticism on this point differs from that he and

Hardt critique the German Idealists for. In the latter, we are led to believe, the stance on mediation is overly romantic. But in return, Hardt and Negri champion immediacy not only theoretically but politically. Immediate changes in labour are celebrated as the basis for incipient liberation. With each leap, the immediate activity of the multitude revolutionises life under capital. This optimism is the obverse of the theoretical attachment to immediacy. Exciting changes outweigh boring continuities. And this owes overwhelmingly to Negri's theoretical blindness around forms of social mediation. The rule of value continues, in spite of any change in the immediate phenomena it mediates. Probing the wider web of relations that sit behind this immediacy, and those into which immediacy is mediated accomplishes a critique of the claims of change Negri fixates upon. In this, the prism of pure immediacy inadequately captures the *social form* 'in and through which the constitutive power of labour subsists in a contradictory way' (1994, pp. 44–5). For Hardt and Negri, the inception of immaterial labour centres on the multitude's powers of constitution. The communicative and affective labour they perform is spontaneously and autonomously cooperative. Its networks model the future in the shell of the present. And, moreover, they produce an excess beyond the capacity of capital to valorise.

Hardt and Negri see the multitude's immanent productivity posing a crisis for value. This is because they see value as a question of quantification rather than a social form of mediation, as we saw was the case in Chaps. 2 and 3 and will interrogate further in Chap. 8. And they see the multitude working towards its liberation only by eliding the domination wrought by this form. This owes to their immanentist attack on mediation. And it owes also to the absence of any dialectics capable of comprehending contradiction. Both relate to the rejection of abstraction and transcendence. The latter conceptually unlock how the things we produce take on a social form that rules over us as an alien, impersonal power. No matter how the content of the labour by which this occurs changes, the commodity form remains. Thus we have a kind of productivism. Only immediate changes in labour matter, and not the forms in which they are objectified.

The immanentist philosophical attack on dialectics is the handmaiden of this productivism. Aufheben (2007) relate this to how Hardt and Negri suspend the subject–object dialectic. For the latter, subjects realise themselves without the necessity of objectification. Their Schopenhauerian view of 'history as pure will and subjectivity' casts labour as squarely 'for-itself'. It need bear no reference to objectivity to be realised. But the CPECTS says otherwise. In capitalism, objectification proceeds by necessity through commodification. We must sell our labour power to eat, and acquire its results to live. The world of capital springs from us but becomes indispensable and dominating. Collapsing the subject–object dialectic forecloses a perspective on this. And it induces untoward positivity about the prospects for autonomous human creativity. The objectifications that rule over subjects under capital spring from and suppress human creativity, still.

Turchetto (2003) criticises Hardt and Negri for being *too* dialectical. But I would claim, following Holloway (2002), that Negri, with and without Hardt, is nowhere near dialectical enough. Negri dismisses dialectics only by associating it with synthesis and order. But the dialectics employed in the CPECTS radically differs. It centres on negation, and posits no resolution. Negri misunderstands dialectics as reproducing a kind of stasis. Against this he poses the immanent revolutionary movement of the multitude's singularity. But *negative* dialectics is about sublation and denial via objectification in social forms. No synthesis is posited. It is confrontational, antagonistic. The 'positivisation' of struggle in Negri's theory achieves precisely the opposite, as Holloway contends. It blunts the force of negativity, of non-identity and anti-identity. And these, Holloway suggests, are by necessity antagonisms around which struggle must by definition – and *against* definition – circulate (2002). As Holloway writes, '[i]n a world that dehumanises us, the only way in which we can exist as humans is negatively, by struggling against our dehumanisation' (2002). It is negative, or it is nothing.

Negri's allergy to the dialectic stems from its understanding as a synthetic search for order. In Negri's terms, it lacks the 'destructive character' Benjamin holds to be its core (1999, quoted in Noys 2012). This destructive character, indeed, is largely alien to Negri's wider worldview. His immanentist complicity with the world as it is suggests no attempt to think outside it in the way a negative dialectics makes possible. This lack of negativity only serves to induce unwarranted optimism as to the propitious conditions of crisis novel conditions of contemporary work precipitate. Negative dialectics looks to that which is denied and sublated in the present. It extracts the non-identity, the excess of that which is denied and sublated, and poses it against the present. But Hardt and Negri cast capitalist society as one thing without the possibility of it being any other. There is nothing else to extract and build a politics of upheaval around. Just sit back and enjoy the ride.

Without a negative orientation, Hardt and Negri underestimate the challenge faced in establishing non-capitalist social relations. They take for granted the establishment of liberation by means of relations that already

exist. The hand of labour is overstated against capital, as change is celebrated and continuities ignored. Capitalism's end or overthrow appears not
only immanent but imminent. As Aufheben assert (2007, pp. 30–1), 'being
non-dialectical would not be too bad in itself', were it not for the theoretical
and political problems produced. In the next chapters, we delve more fully
into these problems and their implications.

6.6   CONCLUSION

This chapter has surveyed key principles of the understanding of how society
and the world works in the post-prison output of Antonio Negri. This
provides a vital undergirding for the discussion in the next three chapters
of some of the empirical and theoretical claims about changes in capitalism
that flow from the perspectives we have discussed here. Seeing all things
immanently as one induces an immense positivity about every twist and turn
capitalism takes, synonymous, as they are taken to be, with the creative drive
of the multitude toward what we will characterise in the next chapter as a
'communism of capital' – the possibility of liberation within the present
rather than in a future without the value-form. The political and practical
consequences of these contentions cannot be considered apart from the
faulty theoretical foundations and analytical leaps that undergird them. In
this chapter I have assayed the dismissal of dialectics, mediation, abstraction,
contradiction and transcendence as fatal to any attempt to get to grips with
the negativity of life under capital. As we will see in further chapters, the
uncomplicated way in which the immediate form and content of labour is
conceptualised in the development of postoperaismo overlooks the continuing forms of abstract social mediation to which productive activity is
subject. It remains all too productivist in the procession of paradigm shifts it
posits. In Chap. 8 we will explore the relevance of this oversight for the
claim of a crisis in the law of value and of capitalist measurability. However,
first, we will explore the centrality of a small fragment of Marx's notebooks
to the increasingly contentious empirical assertions the postoperaist tradition extracts from the recent development of capitalist labour and economic
life. Ultimately, as I will show, this comes to rest in the controversial
assessment of capitalism's coming tech-addled collapse, a theory of inevitable breakdown set to be an article of faith as hegemonic for Marxists today
as the falling rate of profit was once before – and just as flawed.

BIBLIOGRAPHY

Abse, T. 2016. Struggle and Postmodern. *Weekly Worker* 1106, May 12, p. 11.

Aufheben. 2007. Keep on Smiling: Questions on Immaterial Labour. *Aufheben* #14: 23–44.

Bellofiore, R. 2009. A Ghost Turning into a Vampire: The Concept of Capital and Living Labour. In *Re-reading Marx: New Perspectives After the Critical Edition*, ed. R. Bellofiore and R. Fineschi, 178–194. London: Palgrave Macmillan.

Benjamin, W. 1999. Theses on the Philosophy of History. In *Illuminations: Essays and Reflections*, ed. H. Arendt, 245–255. London: Pimlico.

Bonefeld, W. 1994. Human Practice and Perversion: Between Autonomy and Structure. *Common Sense* 15: 43–52.

———. 2014. *Critical Theory and the Critique of Political Economy: On Subversion and Negative Reason*. London: Bloomsbury.

Cleaver, H. 1992a. The Inversion of Class Perspective in Marxian Theory: From Valorisation to Self-Valorisation. In *Open Marxism Vol. II: Theory and Practice*, ed. W. Bonefeld, R. Gunn, and K. Psychopedis, 107–144. London: Pluto Press.

———. 1992b. Translators' Introductions, Part I. In *Marx Beyond Marx: Lessons on the Grundrisse*, ed. A. Negri, xix–xxvii. London: Pluto Press.

———. 2000. *Reading* Capital *Politically*. Edinburgh: AK Press.

———. 2011. Work Refusal and Self-Organisation. In *Life Without Money: Building Fair and Sustainable Economies*, ed. A. Nelson and F. Timmerman, 47–69. London: Pluto Press.

———. 2014. Genesis of Zerowork #1. *Zero Work*. http://www.zerowork.org/GenesisZ1.html. Accessed 30 Oct 2016.

Hardt, M., and A. Negri. 2001. *Empire*. Cambridge, MA: Harvard University Press.

———. 2004. *Multitude*. London: Penguin.

———. 2009. *Commonwealth*. Cambridge: Harvard University Press.

Holloway, J. 2002. Going in the Wrong Direction; Or, Mephistopheles – Not Saint Francis of Assisi. *Historical Materialism* 10 (1): 79–91.

———. 2010. *Crack Capitalism*. London: Pluto Press.

Lazzarato, M. 1996. Immaterial Labor. In *Radical Thought in Italy*, ed. P. Virno and M. Hardt, 133–150. Minneapolis: University of Minnesota Press.

Marx, K. 1976. *Capital*. Vol. I. London: Penguin.

———. 1993. *Grundrisse*. London: Penguin.

Mason, P. 2015a. The End of Capitalism Has Begun. *The Guardian*. July 17. https://www.theguardian.com/books/2015/jul/17/postcapitalism-end-of-capitalism-begun. Accessed 29 Oct 2016.

———. 2015b. *Postcapitalism: A Guide to Our Future*. London: Allen Lane.

———. 2016. Corbyn: The Summer of Hierarchical Things. *Mosquito Ridge*. https://medium.com/mosquito-ridge/corbyn-the-summer-of-hierarchical-things-ab1368959b80#.f8e5z4k82. Accessed 29 Oct 2016.

Negri, A. 1992. *Marx Beyond Marx: Lessons on the Grundrisse*. London: Pluto.

Negri, A. 2009. *The Savage Anomaly: The Power of Spinoza's Metaphysics and Politics*. Minneapolis: University of Minnesota Press.

———. 2008. *Reflections on Empire*. Trans. E. Emery. Cambridge: Polity Press.

Noys, B. 2012. *The Persistence of the Negative: A Critique of Contemporary Continental Theory*. Cambridge: Cambridge University Press.

Ryan, M. 1992a. Translators' Introductions, Part II. In *Marx Beyond Marx: Lessons on the Grundrisse*, ed. A. Negri, xxviii–xxvxxx. London: Pluto Press.

———. 1992b. Epilogue. In *Marx Beyond Marx: Lessons on the Grundrisse*, ed. A. Negri, 191–221. London: Pluto Press.

Thoburn, N. 2001. Autonomous Production? On Negri's 'New Synthesis'. *Theory, Culture and Society* 18 (5): 75–96.

Turchetto, M. 2003. The Empire Strikes Back: On Hardt and Negri. *Historical Materialism* 11 (1): 23–26.

CHAPTER 7

The Fragment on Machines

7.1　Introduction

In this chapter, I survey the significance of Marx's 'Fragment on Machines', a short passage in his notebooks for *Capital*, the *Grundrisse*, for the postoperaist prospectus of capitalist collapse. The reception of this discarded and provisional outline of a future development of capitalism beyond a society organised around the expenditure of concrete labour-time and the rule of exchange-value allies, in this prospectus, with the assessment of novel empirical possibilities granted by the New Economy, producing an optimistic portrait of imminent collapse and incipient communism within the present. But, theoretically, this extrapolation from Marx's Fragment of a crisis in the law of value – recoded elsewhere, as we will go on to see, as a 'crisis of measurability' – rests on the absence of any serious attempt to read the Fragment within the full unfolding of Marx's value theory beyond the *Grundrisse*, in its highest stage of development – and that Marx committed to public consumption – in *Capital*. And, empirically, it reads far too much into the favourable unfolding of events in the direction of travel the Fragment specifies, suggesting the conditions Marx describes are of the here and now rather than the far-off future – if, indeed, at all. This chapter suggests that this is analytically and politically disastrous, emphasising perpetual change and novelty in a world where continuities of both form and content carry over.

In the first section of the chapter, I introduce the Fragment and chart its reception in both postoperaist literature and its currently fashionable

© The Author(s) 2018　　　　　　　　　　　　　　　　169
F.H. Pitts, *Critiquing Capitalism Today*, Marx, Engels, and Marxisms,
DOI 10.1007/978-3-319-62633-8_7

'postcapitalist' echo on the contemporary left – a modern manifestation I return to with greater critical focus in the Conclusion of this book. I then discuss how the Fragment's conceptualisation of a breakdown in the law of value is mobilised to suggest the conditions for such a breakdown are present today, associating this with the Spinozist celebration of the constituent capacities of the multitude covered in the previous chapter. In the third section, I continue this thread by assaying the 'affirmationist' tenor of postoperaist pronouncements on the relationship of human activity and the limits placed upon it by capitalist social forms and relations. I also clarify the function of what Hardt and Negri characterise as 'molar' and 'molecular' ways of comprehending history, suggesting that a focus on the immediate intricacies of the latter obstructs any critical perspective on the overarching continuities of the former. Finally, I apply this to the contention, tied to the conceptualisation of a crisis of measurability that flows from the Fragment and is covered in greater detail in the next chapter, that, in the succession of paradigm shifts the molecular vantage point proposes, measurement comes to be replaced first by control, then command and then direct violence. This, I suggest, shows how, by emphasising novelty over impermeable negativity, and the unfolding forward force of history rather than its negative-dialectical inversion in on itself, postoperaismo misses that capitalism is and continues to be all these supposed historically specific forms of domination at once.

7.2   FRAGMENT-THINKING

Like others through time, our political moment may well rest on the inheritance of a few slender pages from the oeuvre of Marx. The 'Fragment on Machines' (1993, pp. 704–6) is a small section of his *Grundrisse*, the notebooks for what would later become *Capital*. In it, Marx presents a future scenario where the use of machines and knowledge in production expands. Production revolves more around knowledge than physical effort. Machines liberate humans from labour, and the role of direct labour time in life shrinks to a minimum. Free time proliferates. The divorce of labour-time from exchange value sparks capitalist crisis. But this technological leap brings about the possibility of a social development on a massive scale. Freed from physical subordination to the means of production, workers grow intellectually and cooperatively. This freely generated 'general intellect' reinserts itself, uncoerced, into production as fixed capital. The worker is incorporated only at a distance, rather than as a constituent part of the capital relation. The potential for an incipient communism arises.

In the 1980s and 1990s, the Fragment inspired postoperaist analyses of the New Economy and 'immaterial labour'. Popularised by Hardt and Negri's bestseller *Empire* (2001), it wielded influence on early 2000s alter-globalisation struggles. Its echoes carried through, post-crisis, to Occupy and its intellectuals. And, as the left moved towards a state-oriented politics of populism and electoralism in the mid-2010s, it reached a peak, specifically in the UK. Postcapitalism (Mason 2015a), accelerationism (Mackay and Avanessian 2015; Srnicek and Williams 2015a; see also Negri's response 2015), Fully Automated Luxury Communism (Bastani 2015): all owe their roots to the Fragment. In their name, the Fragment has gained a foothold in the popular consciousness. Media personalities accrue it broadsheet inches, directly (see for instance Mason 2015b) or by inference (Harris 2016; Jones 2016).

The most unexpected turn has been the uptake of ideas stemming from it in the UK parliamentary political world. Under Corbyn, Labour's shadow treasury team has embraced an economic agenda of 'Socialism with an iPad' (Wintour 2015) and the basic income (Stewart 2016). Shadow Chancellor John McDonnell routinely invites leading postcapitalists and accelerationists to address policy workshops, such as the Labour Party's 'New Economy' Shadow Chancellor's Conference at Imperial College London in May 2016. The intellectuals disseminating Fragment-thought number among Corbyn's leading supporters (see Mason 2016). This cross-fertilisation with the calculation of party policy marks high-water for the Fragment's reception. It has wended a strange and unconventional route to prominence in which Marx is often a silent partner. It is one part of this route, in the work of Negri and the postoperaists, I seek to chart here.

To the Italian operaist milieu, the Fragment's interpretation, Thoburn (2003, p. 80) writes, has been 'akin to biblical exegesis'. This interpretation rests less on 'reification of authorial truth' than its 'iteration' in 'different sociohistorical contexts as part of the composition of varying political forms'. Its early apogee was Negri's 1978 Paris lectures on the *Grundrisse*, published as *Marx Beyond Marx* (1992). A political weapon from the start, it was not until *Empire* (2001) that its lasting sociohistorical iteration was set out. The New Economy drew Negri to conclude that the conditions described in the Fragment were already present.

In this way, postoperaist receptions of the Fragment seize upon contemporary transformations in work (Noys 2012, pp. 113–14). The positing of an already-existing crisis of measurability rests upon the advent of 'immaterial labour' (Lazzarato 1996). This puts to work elements formerly, we are told, extraneous to the production process. Cognitive, affective and cooperative capacities and free time factor in value production. What the Fragment foretells becomes reality.

Hardt and Negri define immaterial labour as transcending 'the expropriation of value measured by individual or collective labor time'. This, of course, rests on an understanding whereby value was measured thus previously – which was never the case to begin with (see Chap. 8). Regardless, they inform us that, today, labour is no longer subject to capitalist control. It is a self-organised function of the 'multitude'. For Hardt and Negri, the multitude is what happens when the proletariat and the labour movement alters radically from its paradigmatic figure of the white, male manual worker to a multifarious, mobile body of so-called singularities (2001, p. 53). The multitude's immeasurable productivity is enacted through communicative and affective networks. In this way, labour holds the potential of 'valorizing itself' through its own activity. '[H]uman faculties, competences and knowledge' are 'directly productive of value', rather than requiring the superintendence of capital (2009, pp. 132–3). This, Virno notes (1996, pp. 22–3), is the current form assumed by what Marx referred to in the *Fragment* as 'general intellect'.

Its autonomous activities, Lazzarato writes, are located in the 'immaterial basin' of 'society at large'. This labour, then, is 'not obviously apparent to the eye', undefined by the four walls of a factory. It thus 'becomes increasingly difficult to distinguish leisure time from work time. In a sense, life becomes inseparable from work' (1996, pp. 137–8). And, postoperaists suggest, this potentiates the crisis of value *qua* labour-time described in the Fragment. This is synonymous with the 'crisis of measurability' contested in this book.

In this chapter, I confront the postoperaist positing of the existing realisation of the Fragment. As we will see further in the next chapter, postoperaists elide the persistence of the real abstraction of value and the social relations of production it expresses and proceeds through. I challenge the assertion that the crisis and redundancy of value associated with the Fragment is realised. This is because we still, in a contradictory way turned against us, subsist through the value-form. Where postoperaists see a 'communism of capital' already existing, I contend that we live, work, starve and suffer still under its rule. An alternative strand of Marxist theorising – that of the NRM – brings its full horror home. But as we saw in Chap. 6, recognition of this negativity is necessary to develop the theoretical and practical tools to overcome it.

Read against the radically revisionist Marx exegetically defined by the NRM, there are two problems with the postoperaist account of the Fragment. The first relates to Marx himself. As Heinrich (2013) asserts, the Fragment's temporary formulation fails against the standards of Marx's own work as set out in Chap. 2. Its fragmentary status owes to this. The Fragment was one part of Marx's working discarded as his theory developed in sophistication and coherence. The most complete statement of this theory is that we find in the still-unfinished iteration given in *Capital*.

Postoperaists have us believe value relates not to abstract social forms, but quantities of inputs and outputs. In this, their work bears out a disavowed productivist temptation towards the factory. In a brief critique, Moishe Postone (2012) assays Hardt's suggestion that 'the question of measurability is a function of the nature of that which is measured – material or immaterial'. Rather, 'the question of measurability is, basically, one of commensurability'. This relates not to specific objects or practices, but 'the social context within which they exist'. The grounds for 'mutual exchangeability' are 'historically specific and social'. For instance, how two distinct items are rendered commensurable will change through time. Today, this is value, what Postone calls 'a historically specific form of social mediation'. This 'crystallisation' occurs in spite of any change in the material or immaterial basis of that which it mediates. We will explore this further in the next chapter.

Recognition of this socially mediated form destabilises the Fragment-interpretations hegemonic within new strands of popular Marxism. It shows that the situation set out in the Fragment is contrary to the development of Marx's own theory. And his interpreters since do not do any better, the law of value they claim redundant rendered resistant to its purported 'crisis'.

Postoperaist claims as to the realisation of the Fragment's conditions in the present are possible not only by virtue of a misunderstanding of the value-form. They also elide the persistence of the social relations it conceals and implies.

As we have seen in Part 1, the NRM radically diverges from the Marx one finds represented in receptions of the Fragment on Machines. In the Fragment, Marx describes how the increase in machinery in the labour-process displaces human labour. This weakens the role of labour-time as the measure of human productive activity. In this it carries echoes of the 'falling rate of profit' account of crisis covered at the end of Chap. 5, with all the political and theoretical baggage this entails. In the scenario presented in the

Fragment, these conditions cause the quantitative connection between labour-time and exchange value to break down. For postoperaists, this 'crisis of measurability' or 'crisis of the law of value' afflicts capitalism today.

The critique of political economy, therefore, is, as Bonefeld (2014) puts it, fully a critical theory of society as a whole. It refuses to accept at face value the objective forms taken by congealed social relations in capitalist society. It does not reflect the world back at itself with the same objectified economic and social forms that dominate us. In what follows, I suggest that postoperaist receptions of the Fragment do precisely that. And this complicity with the present state of things may account for the Fragment's popularity with policymakers and media movers-and-shakers today. In the subsequent discussion, I return to the roots of this popularity to destabilise them. In so doing, I hope to contribute to the unfolding debate over the possibilities of a post-work, postcapitalist utopia in the present day.

7.3   THE COMMUNISM OF CAPITAL

The modern tribunes of postcapitalism derive their wayward theorising from the postoperaist proliferation of Marx's Fragment. But I suggest that readings of Marx that sit the Fragment front-and-centre are misplaced. They extrapolate from it a situation impossible in the present according to the letter of his value theory. Heinrich (2013) recommends we treat it as exactly what it is: a fragment. The scenario it presents remains untouched as Marx develops his theory of value towards *Capital*, which, as we have seen in Chaps. 2 and 3, and will explore further in Chap. 8, rests on much different assumptions about what value is and how it comes about.

Tony Smith (2013) suggests another basis on which to situate the Fragment within Marx's wider body of work. Smith suggests that the Fragment describes a *future* communism, not a current capitalism. This would explain how radically the prospectus breaks with what we know of Marx's theory of value as a theory of social form.

Problematically, modern popularisations of the Fragment run counter to this periodisation. As Caffentzis notes, what Marx sees happening at some point in the future, Negri sees holding in the here and now (2005, p. 89). This was not always the case. In *Marx Beyond Marx*, for instance, Negri suggests that communism is defined in the transition towards it (1992, p. 115), with no implication this transition is complete. It is underway, perhaps, but in no meaningful sense realised. Here, Negri suggests that only communism's realisation fulfils the conditions the Fragment describes. It brings an end to the law of value, through 'the negation of all measure, the affirmation of the most exasperated plurality – creativity' (1992, p. 33). But, at this stage, Negri makes no intimation that this point has been reached.

But, by *Empire*, this 'exasperated plurality' reappears as the basis for a shift in stress from Marx to Spinoza. Drawing on the latter, Negri conceives creative desire immanently driving capitalist development towards Fragment-conditions. Empirical changes in the world of work express what we can call, following Beverungen, Murtola and Schwartz (2013), a 'communism of capital'. Immaterial labour – creative, communicative, cognitive – 'seems to provide the potential for a kind of spontaneous and elementary communism' (Hardt and Negri 2001, p. 294).

Earlier, in his *Grundrisse* lectures, Negri describes the Fragment as 'the highest example of the use of an antagonistic and constituting dialectic' in Marx's work (1992, p. 139). But in the switch to Spinoza, the antagonism and the dialectic disappear. Only constitution remains. The difference relates to how Negri periodises historical transition. In *Marx Beyond Marx*, he characterises the Fragment as prophesising a 'communism' reached through the constituting power of working-class subjectivity. '*Communism has the form of subjectivity*', he writes, '*communism is a constituting praxis*'. This is a movement in opposition to the present: 'There is no part of capital that is not destroyed by the impetuous development of the new subject' (1992, p. 163). But, by *Empire*, the struggle seeps away. The new subjectivity – that of the multitude – is in compliance, not conflict, with the present. This is because, by virtue of its immanent creative power, the present is in its own image. As such, the communism foretold in the Fragment is no longer subject to a struggle through which to attain it. It is, rather, a current with which one conforms. As we considered at the end of the last chapter, this shows how close postoperaismo remains to the productivist, teleological Marxist orthodoxy with which it auspiciously claims to break. Despite appearing as a countervailing intellectual trend to traditional Marxism, it ends up repeating many of its mistakes.

That postoperaismo insufficiently breaks with the conventional Marxism it claims to relates to the position of workers and class struggle in its theoretical worldview. In delineating a 'communism of capital', Negri pays lip service to the worker-led struggle of Tronti's Copernican reversal (Cleaver 1992) that sits at the very inception of the operaist tradition encountered in Chap. 6. But the account of change and crisis in *Empire* ultimately writes history without it. Multitude and Empire move in syncopation – and, vice versa. Whatever happens in the world is a result of the unfolding of the multitude's 'creativity of desire' (Hardt and Negri 2001, pp. 51–2) conceptually derived from Spinoza.

Here the 'affirmationism' that Noys (2012) skewers is plain to see. It illuminates the contemporary resonances of Negri's interpretation of the Fragment's present-day realisation. Take the 'accelerationist' current, with which Negri himself engages (2015, see also Mackay and Avanessian 2015; Srnicek and Williams 2015a). Here Fragment-thinking endows a nihilist optimism whereby whatever happens, however bad, is for the good. What accelerates subsumption and crisis (of measurability and otherwise) represents a liberation. Srnicek and Williams (2015b), for instance, herald a time where newscasters report firm closures and job losses not as tragedies, but victories. When the immanent driving force of multitude stands behind every twist and turn in capitalist misery, it is easy to see a silver lining to the fraying thread that links life ever less with labour. A crisis in social reproduction is misread as post-work possibility. How one sees this situation produces quite different politics. One emphasises human questions of how we access the things we need to live. The other places faith in robots and machines to liberate us from what we need to do to get them instead.

This myopia around work and production unwittingly reproduces the stale communism and social democracy operaismo originally sought to escape. On one hand, there is teleology. The orthodoxy stood sure in the knowledge that history unfolds precisely to plan: an inevitable collapse of capitalism propelled by outdated irrationality and technological change. Workers were expected to move with the current, rather than against it. But, as Benjamin wrote of the social democracy of his time in Thesis XI of his *Theses on the Philosophy of History* (1999), its conformism to what is 'attaches not only to its political tactics but to its economic views as well… Nothing has corrupted the German working class so much as the notion that it was moving with the current. It regarded technological developments as the fall of the stream with which it thought it was moving' (Benjamin, quoted in Noys 2012, p. 115).

As Noys suggests, a 'key symptom' of this conformism was the celebration of labour (2012, p. 115). This reappears again, today, in the affirmationist Fragment-thinking of postoperaists like Negri. It betrays a reverse productivism, whereby all change in capitalist hangs on the workplace. Only here, its end is posited as opposed to its liberation. Today's postoperaist-inspired radicals hold post-work to be synonymous with postcapitalism. A kind of work, with a kind of worker, is taken to portend a new world. In this case, it is the 'immaterial labourer'. This displays a traditionalist productivism inherited, as Caffentzis astutely notes, from Marxist-Leninism. Here, 'the revolutionary subject in any era is synthesised from the most "productive" elements of the class' (2013, p. 79).

But, in postoperaismo, this is augmented by a 'Spinozist metaphysic' that 'affirms the productive force of humankind', as Ryan puts it (1992b, p. 218). Everyone is the most productive element of the class, which is now 'multitude'. Spinozist monism, which suggests everything is as one, grants Negri a convenient alibi. Unremitting positivity greets a world wherein whatever happens results from a multitudinous 'creativity of desire'. And the hypothesis that this is so is by its nature indisputable. Its only proof is what is. 'History' becomes synonymous with 'multitude', and just as elusive. The political message echoes through bided time: sit back, and let teleology do the rest. Whatever you are doing is good enough. But is it? In the next section, I will evaluate the limitations of the kind of popular action Negri champions, and places at the heart of the supposed changes in labour and capital he and his followers posit.

7.4   Too Unlimited

As we touched on in Chap. 6, in eulogising the multitude's capacity to create the world around it, Negri and other postoperaists end up affirming that world. This neutralises their ability to critically get to grips with a world in which human creativity is turned against itself. Noys's concept of 'affirmationism' is important here. In realising the Fragment, for postoperaists like Negri the multitude's actions wield an 'affirmative' dimension (Noys 2012). Capital is subject to its drives, we are told, which are the immanent motor of all change. This is as true when capitalism is working as when it is not. On one hand, globalisation responds to the border-hopping boundlessness of the nomadic multitude. The New Economy arises from the autonomous and cooperative creativity of that multitude. On the other hand, crisis springs from the multitude's challenge to capital's limits. As Noys notes, the crisis of measurability springs from an excess of life made 'directly and immeasurably productive' (2012, pp. 113–14). So the multitude both compels capitalist development, and its crisis. The positivity of this process is made clear in *Empire*. Hardt and Negri celebrate the immanent force of the multitude, writing that

> Immanence is defined as the absence of every external limit from the trajectories of the action of the multitude, and immanence is tied only, in its

affirmations and destructions, to regimes of possibility that constitute its formation and development... If Empire is always an absolute positivity, the realization of a government of the multitude, and an absolutely immanent apparatus, then it is exposed to crisis precisely on the terrain of this definition, and not for any other necessity or transcendence opposed to it. Crisis is the sign of an alternative possibility on the plane of immanence – a crisis that is not necessary but always possible... Since the spatial and temporal dimensions of political action are no longer the limits but the constructive mechanisms of imperial government, the coexistence of the positive and the negative on the terrain of immanence is now configured as an open alternative. Today the same movements and tendencies constitute both the rise and the decline of Empire. (2001, pp. 373–4)

The crisis, then, is in no way forced by the *negation* of the unfolding of capitalist social relations. Rather, it confronts capitalism with an *excess* of things already present within it *positively*. These elements are a positive part of its functioning – free time, productivity, value, creativity, desire, labour and non-labour – and of life, which under capital is nothing other than labour-power and its reproduction. In *exceeding* them, the multitude *affirms* (Noys 2012, pp. 113–14) what exceeds these limits and the limits themselves. And, by extension, it affirms the relations and things that usually proceed with reasonable bounds of those same limits. Which is to say, value, labour, capital and so on.

One reading might have the multitude affirming what meets the limits, but not the limits themselves. But this chicken-and-egg scenario implies the pre-existence of a constituted power. This suspends the Copernican Inversion, springing not from constituent power but something prior. Thus the undialectical core of the idea of constitutive power is exposed.

In a critique of Negri, Bonefeld (1994) restates how the perverted forms taken by the products of human practice dominate and cajole us. In Negri, only the provenance of that which pushes against the limits of valorisation is explained. The origin of those limits themselves is lacking. And it lies in perverted forms of human practice assuming alien power above and beyond us.

A dialectical orientation can grasp this. It comprehends the contradictory unity of, on the one hand, the conceptuality of abstract social form, and, on the other, the non-conceptuality of the struggle to subsist on the other. But Negri's Spinozist immanentism sees only one, uncomplicated monad. It lacks the dialectical sensitivity to contradiction and mediation capable of accessing the nature of the limits it claims the multitude transcends. This relates to an understanding of history and its progression and periodisation centring on Hardt and Negri's distinction between 'molar' and 'molecular' approaches. By advocating the latter over the former, Hardt and Negri are able to posit changes impossible in a capitalism that in many respects remains the same, in spite of alterations in the immediate content of labour.

Negri positively associates the multitude with the breaking of capital's quantitative boundaries. But in embracing what challenges its limits, he loses critical focus on the nature of those limits themselves. This disregards how the perverted forms resulting from human practice continue imposing themselves anew. The activities that ebb at the limits of capital are one and the same as those that constitute those limits to begin with. Human practice takes the form of abstract labour in a society mediated by the exchange relation of value. This relates not only to an analysis of social processes at their most abstract. Rather, those processes express the essence contained, denied, within their appearance – which is to say, concrete social relations, of antagonism, coercion and separation from subsistence outside selling one's labour-power.

Their elision in Negri's account of the Fragment's unfolding is curious. The conceptualisation of the crisis of the law of value is historicist in its presentation. The conditions that make it possible are embedded in a changing set of concrete realities. The crisis of measurability attends changes in the relations of production. And these are, for Negri, synonymous with the forces of production. Workers set the rules under which they labour. The Italian situation in the 1960s and 1970s is central to this prognosis. A constituent power-grab led to the breakdown of the Keynesian accord on wages and productivity. Operaists watched closely as wage demands rocketed and work refusal proliferated. Workers abandoned agreements submitting their productivity to capitalist command (Cleaver 2000, p. 68). This eventually resulted in a new kind of economy, immaterial and factory-free. For the postoperaists, the revolt of these forces was also a revolution in the relations of production. This is not a dialectical relationship, but one shared by two sides of the Copernican Inversion. Negri's embrace of Spinozist immanence makes this clear. It gives a philosophical basis to render two as one. Where multitude leads, Empire not only follows, but moves as one. But the historical analysis remains more or less the same. The change is rooted in concrete circumstances, their *form* unconsidered.

But this historicity leaves postoperaismo no more capable of capturing capitalism's overwhelming continuities. It emphasises only change. This is a deliberate choice. Hardt and Negri set out to distance themselves from a *molar* perspective (Hardt and Negri 2008, p. 50) that explains history along the lines of 'large aggregates or statistical groupings'. This, they claim, results in a world portrayed as one of continuity rather than change, 'a history of purely quantitative differences' (2008, pp. 51–2). On the other hand, a *molecular* perspective is a qualitative approach revealing change rather than continuity. It refers to 'micromultiplicities, or rather singularities, which form unbounded constellations or networks' (2008, p. 51). This is the approach Hardt and Negri choose.

This molecular perspective moors accounts of the Fragment's unfolding in a rejection of continuity. This is so on two counts. On one hand, it elides the persistence of the abstract rule of value. Hence measure itself is done away with. On the other, it elides the continuation of the social relations that undergird it. In other words, it ignores its antagonistic undertow in separation, hunger and dispossession.

The molecular vantage point allies in important ways with Negri's reverse productivism. It permits the extrapolation from compositional changes in labour's content systemic observations about capitalism. But the labour process is merely a carrier of the valorisation process (Arthur 2013). This implies the persistence of certain social forms and relations. The content of a given labour process matters less than the form it assumes at the level of capitalist reproduction as a whole. If a molar perspective is necessary to comprehend this, then so be it.

From the molecular perspective, crisis issues from the constituting movement of the multitude. The historically specific conditions under which this occurs owe to this immanent correlation. The multitude's movements are those of capital, too. This is so 'not for any other necessity or transcendence opposed to it' (Hardt and Negri 2001, pp. 373–4). Value moves beyond measure because the multitude makes it so.

Understanding value as quantity rather than a social relation, this eschews the 'molar' dimension. Measurability is always in the condition of 'crisis' ascribed to it in Fragment-thought. Capital permanently confronts its inability to fully negate life's concrete specificity in the value-form. For Negri, the challenge posed to measurability is historically specific. The multitude's immeasurable productivity is a novel fact. Its 'immeasurable powers of life' express not an existential vitalism but the contemporary rise to prominence of a 'multitude of singularities' (Noys 2012, p. 112).

But the truth is that there was always an excess, with or without the multitude. There is a remainder of human dignity the value relation cannot contain through denial. This is a critical position Hardt and Negri consciously set out to refute in a missing insert from *Empire* (see Noys 2012, p. 110). Critiques of capitalist totality rally to the defence of principles 'totally Other' to it. But this 'otherness' implies antagonism and contradiction alien to an immanentist viewpoint. This renders out of bounds the positing of a humanity that constantly evades capture.

From Negri's molecular and immanentist perspective, any excess is historically temporary. But, contrary to this periodisation, the domination of the particular by totality is permanent. The molecular resonates with pop-intellectual eulogies for a long line of 'new economies'. It celebrates change, at the expense of critiquing capitalist continuities that must be overcome. Politically, this has us hang our hopes on the affirmation and acceleration of historical change, and not its halt-cord. Hence the bad political efficacy of the Fragment and its postoperaist reception on the left today, and its resonance with bourgeois celebrations of contemporary digital and creative labour as the harbingers of a new concord with work.

Reading history molecularly allows Negri to view the present through the prism of the Fragment. The rise of immaterial labour seems to realise the conditions Marx describes. But the ascription of novelty elides how value persists, and the social relations this implies. This extends to the positing of 'paradigm shifts'. As Holloway (2002) asserts, Hardt and Negri alight upon this idea to explain social change. But parsing one from another – Fordism from post-Fordism, for instance – overlooks how common features carry over.

This parsing is easy when one sees all change issuing from the workplace. As Aufheben note (2007), these paradigms are defined along productivist lines. They pass by in accordance with superficial transformations in the content of labour. This overlooks the stability of the social form productive activities assume. It is this aspect that is crucial for Marx's critique of political economy. Postoperaists focus on only the immediate guise taken by productive activity. But, to see the Fragment within the context of Marx's work, focus must fall on the social form mediating this immediacy. What characterises capitalism is not the specific kind of productive activity that takes place. Rather, it is characterised by the forms taken by its results: value, money, capital. This is the specificity of the social formation in which we find ourselves, which is to say, capitalism. And understanding this is key to investigating it.

Bypassing this specificity, postoperaists conceive a capitalism they cannot grasp undergoing a crisis it cannot suffer. The same theoretical imprecision

blights the new politics of 'postcapitalism.' Misunderstanding what capitalism is produces misunderstandings over the possibilities of its replacement.
And this leads to bad politics. But these foreshortened forms of praxis stem
from analytical weaknesses in the first instance, of which I say more in the
next chapter.

7.5   MEASUREMENT AND VIOLENCE

As I showed in the last section, faulty conceptualising follows from the
molecular succession of paradigm shifts. Its immanentist and productivist
analysis of change leads it down many blind alleys. Postoperaist attempts to
explain capitalism's reproduction after the unfolding of the Fragment demonstrate this. How does capitalism carry on once its forms of measure enter
crisis? To answer this, postoperaists reach for a string of concepts – command, control and violence. They propose a transition from measurement
to pure coercion. This suggests that the two are not already implicit within
each other. This owes to a misreading of how value and social domination
function in the first place.

The progression through command, control and violence mirrors the
development of autonomist Marxism. The operaist–postoperaist transition
centred on a changing interpretation of class struggle and capitalist development. The first-generation operaists saw a role for capitalist planning of
production. This implied measurement, rationalisation, quantification and
so on. But this related less to top-down control than capital's reaction to
class struggle. Mario Tronti's so-called 'Copernican Inversion' was ground-
breaking in this regard (Cleaver 2000, pp. 65–6). It placed workers as the
prime mover in capitalist development. But, essentially, capital could still act
in response, channelling production to its ends.

With Negri's lectures on the *Grundrisse* came a bold contention to the
contrary. An 'empty form of capitalist command' replaced the law of value
(Negri 1992, pp. 147–8). The planning and regulation of production gave
way to 'a direct relation of force', as Ryan puts it (1992a, p. xxix). The
exchange relationship between the buyer and seller of labour power – in
production a relationship of exploitation – passes over into a relationship of
pure command over which the struggle is no longer economic but 'purely
political' (1992a, p. xxix).

Later, Negri substitutes command for control. With Hardt, he follows
Deleuze in positing a transition from disciplinary society to one of control.
The former saw power enforced within the four walls of the factory, the

prison and the school. In the latter, their carceral and exploitative logics seep out of their four walls into society as a whole (Deleuze 1990; Hardt and Negri 2001). The conduit for this is the disciplined subjects themselves. Rather than coming from without, at the hands of the capitalist, discipline comes from within. Foucauldian biopolitics meets the Spinozist 'creativity of desire' through which the multitude propels history. The immaterial labourer's self-valorising self-production reappears as a consensual self-exploitation. Under 'command', power is extensified. But in the society of control, it is intensified, through subjectivity itself.

In a recent iteration, Bifo situates violence as measurability's resolution in contemporary capitalism. Capitalist reproduction holds not through planning, command or control, but through brute force alone. Bifo writes, referring to the end of the Gold Standard under Richard Nixon, that

> [a]fter Nixon's decision, measurement ended. Standardization ended. The possibility of determining the average amount of time necessary to produce a good ended. Of course, that means that the United States of America, its president, Richard Nixon, decided that violence would take the place of measurement. In conditions of aleatory, what is the condition of the final decision? What is the action or process of determining value? Strength, force, violence. What is the final way of deciding something – for instance, deciding the exchange rate of the dollar? Violence, of course... There can be no financial economy without violence, because violence has now become the one single method of decision in the absence of the standard. (Berardi 2013, p. 88)

The problem with each of these novel replacements for measure is they imply measurement is not always already based in relationships of command, control and violence. This owes to the absence of a social-form appreciation of value in postoperaismo. Postoperaists see capitalist measure relating to a quantitative process of valorisation. Hence it enters into crisis when things cannot be counted. But value is a social relation, not a property of things. It appears as a relationship between things. But it contains within this appearance its essence in relationships between people. Postoperaists remain stuck with the objective economic forms of appearance.

Scrutinising the relationships between people clarifies the link between measurement and violence. The question central to the CPECTS is 'why does this content take this form?' (Bonefeld 2001, p. 5). But this is never posed, foreclosing a grasp of how measure and labour relate. The appearance of objective economic forms contains, sublated, that which it denies. Which is to say, historically grounded concrete social relations. These are the product of an original and sustained violence of brute phys-icality contained within the outward niceties of contracts and commodity exchange. They express the radical dispossession whereby whether we eat or starve is arbitrated by the coins in our pocket (see Marx 1993, pp. 156–7). The socially synthetic function of money and value considered in Chap. 3 rests in forceful separation. Continuously, people are deprived of indepen-dent individual and collective means to reproduce themselves (see Bonefeld 2014). The sale of labour-power is last resort. Only by means of this bloody fact do we live in a world of objective economic categories. Measure carries within it this background.

The continuous character of this dispossession institutionalises violence or the threat of it. It is present not only in the continually reproduced material and social preconditions of a world ruled by value. It is also present in the policing of the measures by and through which value manifests. Measurement *is* violence. Postoperaists posit its lapse into crisis and the replacement of one by the other only by wilfully eliding this. As Lukacs writes, the value abstraction 'has the same ontological facticity as a car that runs you over' (quoted in Lotz 2014, p. xiv).

We can see this dimension implied in the etymology of the word 'abstract'. '*Abs*' comes from the Latin for 'away', 'tract' '*trahere*', or move. To 'abstract', then, is 'to transport into a formal, calculative space' (Muniesa et al. 2007). Even in the most basic and primitive instances of calculation, this meaning is significant. As David Graeber writes, the 'vio-lence of quantification' (2012, p. 14) present in forms of debt 'turns human relations into mathematics'. Violence might 'appear secondary' to measure, money and the abstraction it implies. But, writes Graeber, they have 'a capacity to turn morality into a matter of impersonal arithmetic'. This permits the exertion of force in their pursuit. Graeber uses the example of tribal 'sister exchange'. The forceful removal of things from their context implicated in abstract measurement is clear:

> to make a human being an object of exchange, one woman equivalent to another, for example, requires first of all ripping her from her context; that is, tearing her away from that web of relations that makes her the unique conflux of relations that she is, and thus, into a generic value capable of being added and subtracted and used as a means to measure debt. This requires a certain violence. To make her equivalent to a bar of camwood

takes even more violence, and it takes an enormous amount of sustained and systematic violence to rip her so completely from her context that she becomes a slave. (Graeber 2012, p. 159)

Problematically, Graeber's method is to extrapolate from non-capitalist society insights about a very different social formation. But the link remains. The divergence rests in the fact that, in capitalist society, this violence is sublated in the value-form. But the exchange abstraction still 'liquidates' the concrete, as Adorno and Horkheimer suggest. It is disappeared, as surely as fate was held to dispatch with human subjects pre-Enlightenment (1972, p. 13). Measurement not only denies the concrete chaos of reality, transforming quality into quantity. It also denies the concrete social relations that undergird value. The capitalist state enshrines the rule of equivalence in law whilst implicitly threatening violence to enforce it. The sublated principle is negated but retained in the mode of denial. As Kunkel writes of the quantitative obligations of debt (2014, p. 116), 'the violence wielded by mafias or the state enforces the abstraction' by which value is ascribed to things, and by which money mediates relationship between individuals. Violence is measurement, and vice versa. It is not, as postoperaists suggest, an alternative to it in the form of command, control or outright force. Once again, change wins out analytically over continuity, to the detriment of critique and praxis. The idea that crisis is around the corner consoles us that change is afoot. If capitalism is seen as in a state of permanent crisis and uncertainty, the easy belief in its coming collapse seems far less tenable.

By seeing measurement as a functioning part of capitalism, postoperaists portend its breakdown. But, I argue in the next chapter, its death cannot be announced so brusquely. Postoperaists see capitalism as functioning perfectly until crisis comes. But this ignores the uncertainty capital must constantly confront, in creating, commensurating and circulating commodities, an aspect central to the analysis of productiveness and unproductiveness within the circuit of capital given in Chap. 9. And, I suggest, its persistence in light of this uncertainty indicates, contrary to Negri and his modern followers, that capitalism is far from done.

For postoperaismo, command, control and violence step in only when measurability breaks down. This elides the continuity of measurability's crisis-ridden fragility. Pure quantity can never capture the chaos of reality, and nor does it claim to. Force is always needed to bend reality to its expectations and ease of measurement. This force often issues from the state, and from the law. And force undergirds that which is measured in the first place. Constant struggle marks the condition by which we cannot eat except by the buying and selling of commodities. Violence is meted out in support of it. What the molecular positing of change implies is that all this is novel. But it is not.

The Fragment's scenario of a crisis in the law of value is thinkable only on the basis of a kind of functionalism. Postoperaists perceive breakdown in the functioning of something that, in normal conditions, 'functions' freely and without contradiction. But, where measurement sublates antagonistic social relations of production, contradiction, not function, reigns. Where capitalism seems to function, it teeters on the brink of a social basis that exists in the mode of being denied. It struggles to negate what is concrete in abstraction. This is a permanent crisis where postoperaists see only a recent one.

Key here is Negri's attack on dialectics in the name of a Spinozist embrace of immanence and monism. With this disappears the ability to grasp contradiction. Things cannot be two things at once, or contain within them the essence of another. Form analysis is impossible. The strange situation whereby the results of human practice should assume transcendent forms of social domination slides entirely from view. Contradiction is mistakenly seen as relating to crisis, rather than capitalism itself. The ascription of crisis portrays a normal functioning broken by contradiction. Whereas in fact capitalism, to the extent it 'functions' in the way suggested, does so via contradiction. The same creativity and spontaneity on which human industry relies must be stifled and reshaped to fit within controllable and commensurable constraints.

Negri's 'molecular' positing of a succession of self-contained paradigms, as Holloway notes (2002), has the effect of rendering his argument functionalist. All things in a given historical juncture must always correspond to the correct paradigm. Even crises come to play their part in their unfolding. The paradigm is a framework to which all parts of reality must fit. There is no room for contradiction, or conflict.

But capital always struggles to measure, and what is measured always struggles back. The value-form sublates the qualitative incommensurability of feelings, dignity, desires – but never totally. There is *always* an excess left over that cannot be captured. This is not a novelty of Empire. It is as true for the industrial factory, where sabotage and subordination was rife, as it is for the social factory. And, confounding paradigms, it is as true for Fordism as for so-called 'post-Fordism'. This is where a 'molecular' micro-focus on the immediate forms taken by concrete labour fails. The forms of social mediation persist. And with them lasting contradictions Fragment-thinkers optimistically see as a sudden and liberatory crisis.

Marx's critique of political economy is all about understanding the *form* productive activity assumes. Crucial here is abstract labour – and not immediate concrete labour. Changes in labour-time and the composition of the labour cannot create in themselves a crisis of measurability. It is comforting to contend an incipient communism is around the corner owing to such changes. But placing the Fragment on Machines in the context of Marx's work as a whole gives little cause for comfort. Capitalism is characterised by categories of social mediation. They persist regardless of whether a worker uses a keyboard or a hammer, ideas or nuts and bolts. And in this is implied the persistence of means of measure and time discipline familiar to the pre-'social' factory. The social form assumed by labour in and through value's practical abstraction wields an effect on the content of labour – so the ways of measuring a given kind of labour do not live and die by changes in that labour, but in fact restructure it to conform to its metrics.

This gives pause for thought to those projecting Fragment-inspired pipedreams. The epochal crisis they posit is no crisis at all. On their terms, capitalism *is* crisis, for all involved. No amount of Spinozist optimism is capable of coming to terms with the theory and practice required to change it. And, I conclude, we must look to elements of Marx's work other than the Fragment to overcome this impasse.

7.6   CONCLUSION

Just as this chapter searched for the philosophical roots of the postoperaist attack on the law of value, this chapter has located its textual and exegetical authority. In dispensing with a Marxist dialectical method for Spinozist immanence, postoperaismo under the watchful eye of Antonio Negri retains only those parts of Marx for which it can find further use – in this case, the Fragment on Machines. But in abstraction from the development of Marx's work as a whole the myopic reading of this small element of his oeuvre alone can only lead prospectors of a postcapitalist future down a blind alley. There is no direct relationship between labour-time and exchange value around which to hitch hopeful analyses of a coming liberation from capitalism. Such a prospectus hinges on a silence over money, abstract labour, socially necessary labour-time and a whole host of other concepts central to the NRM but largely neglected in postoperaist readings of the Marxian inheritance.

At a time where Fragment-thinking has filtered through from the pages of *Empire* to criss-cross the utopian contours of contemporary left thought, this is no minor exegetical or theoretical quibble, but one with real political consequence. The Fragment suggests we can let capitalism's technological advancement unfold so as to break through the limits that stand between us and communism. Its adherents interpret the conditions for this to not only already be present today, but already in motion, fully realised. This induces us to comply with capitalist development and pliantly bide our time for utopia to arrive. For all its revisionist bluster, this is not so different to the hopes traditional Marxism invested in a profit-deprived capitalist collapse and the proletarian revolution to come. The difference consists in the absence of any such antagonism in today's teleological pipedreams. The NRM, despite often refraining from explicit political commitments and the populist temptation to pick a side in the class struggle, suggests that capitalism will not go of its own accord, its abstract social rule historically specific but totalising. Working through abstraction, capitalism refashions what is real and concrete in the image of the value-form. The analysis of this form-determination, I will suggest in the next chapter, forecloses hope in the kind of 'crisis of measurability' set out in the Fragment and on which postoperaist political aspirations rest.

Bibliography

Adorno, T.W., and M. Horkheimer. 1972. *Dialectic of Enlightenment*. London: Verso.

Arthur, C. 2013. The Practical Truth of Abstract Labour. In *Marx's Laboratory: Critical Interpretations of the Grundrisse*, ed. R. Bellofiore, G. Starosta, and P. Thomas, 101–120. Leiden: Brill.

Aufheben. 2007. Keep on Smiling: Questions on Immaterial Labour. *Aufheben* #14: 23–44.

Bastani, A. 2015. We Don't Need More Austerity, We Need Luxury Communism. *Vice Magazine*. June 12. http://www.vice.com/en_uk/read/luxury-communism-933. Accessed 29 Oct 2016.

Benjamin, W. 1999. Theses on the Philosophy of History. In *Illuminations: Essays and Reflections*, ed. H. Arendt, 245–255. London: Pimlico.

Berardi, F. 2013. *The Uprising: On Poetry and Finance*. Los Angeles: Semiotext(e).

Beverungen, A., A.-M. Murtola, and G. Schwartz. 2013. The Communism of Capital? *Ephemera* 13 (3): 483–495.

Bonefeld, W. 1994. Human Practice and Perversion: Between Autonomy and Structure. *Common Sense* 15: 43–52.

———. 2001. *The Politics of Europe: Monetary Union and Class*. London: Palgrave.

———. 2014. *Critical Theory and the Critique of Political Economy: On Subversion and Negative Reason*. London: Bloomsbury.

Caffentzis, G. 2005. Immeasurable Value? An Essay on Marx's Legacy. *The Commoner* 10: 87–114.

———. 2013. *In Letters of Blood and Fire: Work, Machines, and Value*. Oakland: PM Press.

Cleaver, H. 1992. The Inversion of Class Perspective in Marxian Theory: From Valorisation to Self-Valorisation. In *Open Marxism Vol. II: Theory and Practice*, ed. W. Bonefeld, R. Gunn, and K. Psychopedis, 107–144. London: Pluto Press.

———. 2000. *Reading* Capital *Politically*. Edinburgh: AK Press.

Deleuze, G. 1990. Society of Control. *L'autre Journal* 1. https://www.nadir.org/nadir/archiv/netzkritik/societyofcontrol.html. Accessed 29 Oct 2016.

Graeber, D. 2012. *Debt: The First 5,000 Years*. Brooklyn: Melville House.

Hardt, M., and A. Negri. 2001. *Empire*. Cambridge, MA: Harvard University Press.

———. 2008. Sovereignty. In *Reflections on Empire*, ed. A. Negri, 49–59. Cambridge: Polity Press.

———. 2009. *Commonwealth*. Cambridge: Harvard University Press.

Harris, J. 2016. Should We Scrap Benefits and Pay Everyone £100 a Week? *The Guardian*. April 13. http://www.theguardian.com/politics/2016/apr/13/should-we-scrap-benefits-and-pay-everyone-100-a-week-whether-they-work-or-not. Accessed 29 Oct 2016.

Heinrich, M. 2013. The 'Fragment on Machines': A Marxian Misconception in the Grundrisse and Its Overcoming in Capital. In *Marx's Laboratory: Critical Interpretations of the Grundrisse*, ed. R. Bellofiore, G. Starosta, and P. Thomas, 197–212. Leiden: Brill.

Holloway, J. 2002. Going in the Wrong Direction; Or, Mephistopheles – Not Saint Francis of Assisi. *Historical Materialism* 10 (1): 79–91.

Jones, O. 2016. We Should Be Striving to Work Less, Not Toiling Until We Drop. *The Guardian*. March 3. https://www.theguardian.com/commentisfree/2016/mar/03/retirement-retiring-age-77-strive-work-less-progress-challenge-bleak-prospect. Accessed 29 Oct 2016.

Kunkel, B. 2014. *Utopia or Bust: A Guide to the Present Crisis*. London: Verso.

Lazzarato, M. 1996. Immaterial Labor. In *Radical Thought in Italy*, ed. P. Virno and M. Hardt, 133–150. Minneapolis: University of Minnesota Press.

Lotz, C. 2014. *The Capitalist Schema: Time, Money, and the Culture of Abstraction*. Lanham: Lexington Books.

Mackay, R., and A. Avanessian, eds. 2015. *#Accelerate: The Accelerationist Reader*. Falmouth: Urbanomic.

Marx, K. 1992. *Capital*. Vol. II. London: Penguin.

———. 1993. *Grundrisse*. London: Penguin.

Mason, P. 2015a. The End of Capitalism Has Begun. *The Guardian*. July 17. https://www.theguardian.com/books/2015/jul/17/postcapitalism-end-of-capitalism-begun. Accessed 29 Oct 2016.

———. 2015b. *Postcapitalism: A Guide to Our Future*. London: Allen Lane.

———. 2016. Corbyn: The Summer of Hierarchical Things. *Mosquito Ridge*. https://medium.com/mosquito-ridge/corbyn-the-summer-of-hierarchical-things-ab1368959b80#.f8e5z4k82. Accessed 29 Oct 2016.

Muniesa, F., Y. Millo, and M. Callon. 2007. An Introduction to Market Devices. In *Market Devices*, ed. M. Callon, Y. Millo, and F. Muniesa, 1–13. Oxford: Blackwell.

Negri, A. 1992. *Marx Beyond Marx: Lessons on the Grundrisse*. London: Pluto.

———. 2015. Some Reflections on the #Accelerate Manifesto. In *#Accelerate: The Accelerationist Manifesto*, ed. R. Mckay and A. Avanessian, 363–378. Falmouth: Urbanomic.

Noys, B. 2012. *The Persistence of the Negative: A Critique of Contemporary Continental Theory*. Cambridge: Cambridge University Press.

Postone, M. 2012. Thinking the Global Crisis. *The South Atlantic Quarterly* 111 (2): 227–249.

Ryan, M. 1992a. Translators' Introductions, Part II. In *Marx Beyond Marx: Lessons on the Grundrisse*, ed. A. Negri, xxviii–xxvxxx. London: Pluto Press.

———. 1992b. Epilogue. In *Marx Beyond Marx: Lessons on the Grundrisse*, ed. A. Negri, 191–221. London: Pluto Press.

Smith, T. 2013. The 'General Intellect' in the *Grundrisse* and Beyond. *Historical Materialism* 21 (4): 235–255.

Srnicek, N., and A. Williams. 2015a. #Accelerate: Manifesto for an Accelerationist Politics. In *#Accelerate: The Accelerationist Reader*, ed. R. Mackay and A. Avanessian, 347–362. Falmouth: Urbanomic.

———. 2015b. Remembering the Future. *BAMN #1*. Available from http://www.weareplanc.org/bamn/remembering-the-future/. Accessed 29 Oct 2016.

Stewart, H. 2016. John McDonnell: Labour Taking a Close Look at Universal Basic Income. *The Guardian*. June 6. http://www.theguardian.com/politics/2016/jun/05/john-mcdonnell-labour-universal-basic-income-welfare-benefits-compass-report. Accessed 29 Oct 2016.

Thoburn, N. 2003. *Deleuze, Marx and Politics*. London: Routledge.

Virno, P. 1996. The Ambivalence of Disenchantment. In *Radical Thought in Italy: A Potential Politics*, ed. P. Virno and M. Hardt, 13–36. Minneapolis: University of Minnesota Press.

Wintour, P. 2015. John McDonnell to Unveil 'Socialism with an iPad' Economic Plan. *The Guardian*. Nov 20. http://www.theguardian.com/politics/2015/nov/20/john-mcdonnell-to-unveil-socialism-with-an-ipad-economic-plan. Accessed 29 Oct 2016.

CHAPTER 8

A Crisis of Measurability

8.1 Introduction

The ideas around Empire and multitude discussed in Chaps. 6 and 7 have gained increasing resonances as the first decades of the twenty-first century progress, with interest and application in activist circles and elsewhere. Hardt and Negri's popularisation of postoperaist theories of immaterial labour, however, had a subtler impact, largely confined to academia and the art world (Graeber 2008). Ideas akin to 'immaterial labour' are, after all, common currency in public discourse. The mainstream is well abreast of the same empirical shifts as described by Hardt and Negri. The move towards a service economy. The development of the creative industries. The prominence of cognition and emotional connection in contemporary workplaces. The fragmentation and dispersal of work time. The blurred line between work and leisure. The rise of information technology. The immense power of communicative networks. The proliferation of non-standard forms of employment and contractual arrangements. The trends to which theorists of immaterial labour react in delineating the concept are stark enough to have been covered extensively elsewhere. As such, the significance of the theory is mainly limited to the development of academic research agendas, and to debates about the changing face of labour. The latter in particular are driving a renewal of left thought around the prospect of a coming postwork society. The concept's relevance to debates in Marxian value theory receives less attention. In this chapter, I seek to rectify this by foregrounding this aspect.

© The Author(s) 2018   191
F.H. Pitts, *Critiquing Capitalism Today*, Marx, Engels, and Marxisms,
DOI 10.1007/978-3-319-62633-8_8

As noted in the Introduction to this book, the postoperaist tradition of autonomist Marxism and the world of Marxian value theory seldom meet. Noting the absence of any engagement with recent interpretations of Marx's theory of value, I bring such a meeting together in my analysis. Through a conventional application of the categories of Marx's theory of value, postoperaist theorists like Negri overlook both the abstract quality of value-producing labour and the social relations of domination and coercion undergirding it. Measure, in other words – in its dimension as value and means of control – is still very much in force. This book contests the claim made in postoperaist literature that immaterial labour precipitates a crisis in measurability that renders the theory of value redundant.

In this chapter, I will use the theoretical approach developed in Part 1, particularly in the first two chapters, to contest this claim. This opens up critique on two fronts. First, by emphasising value as subject to an abstraction owing to the move from concrete to abstract labour rather than the expenditure of concrete labour, the NRM interpretation of Marx's theory of value overcomes any objections based on the supposed immeasurability of labour-time in contemporary capitalism. Second, by emphasising the persistence of the social relations of production – of subsistence, social reproduction, labour-power, time discipline and so forth – Bonefeld's Open Marxist critique of the NRM suggests that the violence concealed in the value-form continues, despite the claims of postoperaists on its empirical and theoretical crisis. My critique has four prongs.

First, postoperaist theorists emphasise the novelty of the way in which immaterial labour surpasses and exceeds the law of value. Yet the thesis of immaterial labour, rather than surpassing the theory of value, does not go far enough. It is hamstrung by its insistence upon the novelty of that which it describes. A theory of value based upon the process by which value appears through the social validation of abstract labour negates the novelty of immaterial labour. It suggests instead that labour has always been in some way immaterial.

Second, Hardt and Negri suggest that immaterial labour renders all labour immediately abstract. But this attempt is hamstrung by their reliance upon an explanation of the abstract sociality of labour as consisting in the realm of production (or even prior to it). A more radical viewpoint suggests that it is instead constituted retrospectively in exchange, with only the tentative and pre-emptory existence described in Chap. 4 becoming apparent in the workplace itself, preceding the point of its culmination with the commodity moment.

Third, what postoperaists such as Hardt and Negri describe as 'immaterial labour' is not immediately abstract in its concrete performance. Concrete labour is productive of value only by means of its immaterial abstraction. This is a process of becoming which culminates away from the workplace in the sphere of exchange. This account disputes the association of immaterial labour with the production of immeasurable value. It thereby also negates the threat immaterial labour poses to the basis of capitalist valorisation.

Fourth, measure is validated in the same act of exchange which grants it its existence. Value and abstract labour exist only through their measure, by means of the social validation of labour as productive of value via the exchange of products of labour as commodities in the marketplace. Yet this measure is always struggled for in production itself. The capitalist need for commensuration always faces the qualitative complexity of reality. But this is a crisis so permanent so as not to be one at all. It proceeds initially in production, where the drive to measure manifests in early pre-emptory abstractions and ways of disciplining workers. And these are ungirded by the 'social relations of production' – in class, exploitation, struggle, violence, coercion and so forth – that we considered in Chap. 5.

8.2   IMMATERIAL LABOUR AND THE CRISIS OF MEASURABILITY

The immaterial labour thesis was originally formulated by Maurizio Lazzarato (1996). It depicts a transformation of work in late capitalist economies. For Hardt and Negri, these changes are not so much numerically significant as cultural and social. The transition to immaterial, post-industrial labour is not a quantitative shift, but a change in the hegemony of certain kinds of activity within the world of work (2004, pp. 107–9). According to Hardt and Negri, 'industrial production is no longer expanding its dominance', economically and socially (2001, pp. 285–6). Take, for instance, the move from secondary to tertiary occupations characterised by 'the central role played by knowledge, information, affect and communication'. For Hardt and Negri, this shift does not mean that industrial production has ceased or will cease. Older forms of labour, such as manufacturing, become infused with an informational aspect, akin to how industrial production came to infuse agriculture in the past.

The first aspect of the transformation in the quality and the nature of labour that Hardt and Negri cite is the change from a Fordist to a post-Fordist model (2001, p. 289). Under this new paradigm, labour is flexible, mobile and precarious (2004, p. 112). In the rapid feedback loop of the Toyotist model, communication and information play for a pivotal role. The service sectors reveal an even 'richer model of productive communication'. This is immaterial labour, of which Hardt and Negri distinguish three types (2001, p. 293). The first is where industrial production has been informationalised, incorporating communication technologies. This turns manufacturing into more of a service, mixing durable goods with the immaterial. For instance, the most advanced automobile manufacturers incorporate the creative labour of designers and advertising professionals at an early stage. The second is the immaterial labour of analytical and symbolic tasks, broken down into a division between manipulation and routine. This division could be applied to, on the one hand, games designers, and, on the other, games programmers. The third is the production and manipulation of affect, whether through virtual or actual human contact, of which care workers are one example.

Thus, postoperaist theorists suggest that labour becomes synonymous with the creation and manipulation of ideas, symbols, selves, emotions and relationships. Work comes to inhabit the full range of human capacities and activities. As such, the boundary blurs between work time engaged in immaterial labour and spare time away from paid employment. The activities of work take on the characteristics of those of leisure and of everyday life, and those of leisure and everyday life assume the characteristics of work. Immaterial labour thus transcends the formal confines of the working day to invest the whole of life with its value-producing processes. In response to this, theorists of immaterial labour posit a 'crisis of measurability' (Marazzi 2008, p. 43). The crisis arises from the impossibility of the quantification of work-time and value. This afflicts any application of the LTOV (Vercellone 2010). As Andrea Fumagalli and Sandro Mezzadra assert, '[w]ith the advent of cognitive capitalism, the process of valorization loses all quantitative measuring units connected with material production' (2010, pp. 238–9).

The theorisation of immaterial labour and immeasurability gained historical impetus not only from the changes in contemporary work post-operaists seek to describe with the theory, but with the conditions of economic crisis that accompanied these changes. The analysis of immeasurability at the heart of the post-operaist treatment of immaterial labour was clarified with the rise of 'financialisation' and the two twenty-first-century financial crises with which post-operaist theorists engaged most seriously: the Dot.Com boom and bust and the 2008 credit crunch.

According to Marazzi, financialisation is an extension of the widespread attempts on the part of capital to capture the immeasurable value produced by the free labour of the digital, decentred workplace. The contemporary capitalist organisation of production is structured so as to fulfil the primary purpose of capturing the value produced in society at large. For Marazzi, such 'crowdsourcing' Web 2.0 phenomena as Facebook and Google represent the 'the totality of linguistic machines' that act in society at large to capture 'the totality of sociality, emotions, desires, relational capacity [and] free labor'. These 'linguistic machines' extend the working day with their acquisitive search (2010, p. 56).

Marazzi claims that the new forms of immaterial production secure an 'economy of increasing returns', working against an underlying fall in the rate of profit (see section 5.6). The tendencies described above, the 'putting to work of the language of social relations, the activation of productive cooperation beyond the factory gate' and the extension of the working day are presented therefore as countertendencies to falling profitability, 'respond [ing] to declining profit rates by intensifying the exploitation of the communicative-relational cooperation of the workforce' (2008, p. 60).

A good example is the provision of stock options as a form of compensation exercised by many Dot.Com enterprises. At the firm that Andrew Ross observed in his research, tickers were installed on computer desktops updating workers on the movements of the NASDAQ Index with which their interest had been suddenly entwined. This was a source of 'motivation' and 'anxiety' for the workers, with important implications for labour-time: 'Where once the working day had been dictated by the regimen of the factory clock, now it was regulated by the flux of the stock index' (2003, pp. 199–200). The financial infrastructure is the only such institution adaptable and fluid enough to operate within the similarly flexible and elusive logic of the new means of creating value through decentred and extended labour-time. Financialisation coheres with, and brings under a degree of mathematical control, an economically immeasurable return to absolute surplus-value cultivated with the new immaterial production.

The combination of these factors suggests that financialisation issues from the conditions of production. This insight is an important one, running counter to left-Keynesian conceptualisations of a 'real' economy infringed by the 'false', but also indicative of postoperaismo's productivist inclination to read off from changes in labour changes in society and the economy as a whole. From this perspective, financialisation is the only method adequate to the new quality of labour and value because it can institute a framework through which the 'crisis of measurability' of contemporary capitalism can be temporarily resolved (Marazzi 2008, p. 43). The impact of the immeasurability of labour and value has significant implications upon the estimation of productivity, in which, as Berardi contends, 'the relation between time and quantity of produced value is difficult to determine' (2009, p. 75). Furthermore, as Hardt and Negri suggest, the familiar characteristics of the commodity are thrown into flux. The products of immaterial labour, '[i]ntangible values and…assets…pose a problem because the methods of economic analysis generally rely on quantitative measures and calculate the value of objects that can be counted, such as cars, computers and tons of wheat.' In light of this, autonomist thought questions the validity of the approach to labour-time exhibited in orthodox Marxism, throwing a simple quantitative appreciation of the working day into relief against the infinitude of immaterial labour conducted in cyber-time. Immaterial products 'tend to exceed all quantitative measurement and take common forms', Hardt and Negri contend (2009, pp. 135–6).

With respect to this, Vercellone comments that the production of 'social relations' is much harder to quantify than the production of material goods, juxtaposing the latter 'traditional goods' with what he labels 'fictitious commodities'. What renders the financial markets so well-suited to this new mode of production is its willing and exuberant embrace of this fictitiousness. As with so many other crises, the crisis of measurability presents itself as an opportunity to the markets. The markets help bring order to the swelling and fluid mass of immaterial production conducted in the social sphere, rationalising fictitious commodities in a formal set of figures that are themselves similarly fictitious. Vercellone contends that the 'collective intelligence' at the heart of the new production 'escapes any objective measurement', the attempts at which in the arena of finance existing only as extravagant illusions. The value of this collective intelligence is 'the subjective expression of the expectation for future profits effectuated by financial markets who procure themselves rent in this way. This helps to explain why the "market" value is essentially fictitious' (2010, pp. 110–11).

The self-referential and subjective attributing of market values to anticipated future profit exposes the disjuncture that exists in the timeframe of a production process founded upon immeasurable quantities of unpaid labour-time. For Fumagalli, 'the exploitation and expropriation of "general intellect"' finds 'immediate valorization on the markets'. This is because markets hastily institute their fictionalised fix to render interpretable a 'process of valorization…not immediately computable at the time of production' (2010, p. 66). However, the determination of labour and value by financial markets is achievable only up to that stage at which the grand fiction of measurability conjured through the self-referential and subjective activity of financial players runs up against the essential underlying impossibility of exerting economic discipline upon intangible, immaterial and infinite forms of production. The possibility of crisis is therefore ever-present; and, as Fumagalli and Mezzadra assert, the 'subsumption of the common' that fuels this financial processes promises a permanent crisis marked by an all-pervasive infinitude reflective of its roots in the deepest fabric of human cognition and sociality (2010, p. 241).

So, a general 'readability crisis' on the part of capital affects its 'capacity to read the composition of labor on whose exploitation it depends', as Mezzadra suggests (2010, p. 14). Financialisation, expressed morbidly in stock-market crises, is an attempt upon the part of capital to read this composition. For Marazzi, it is the expression of an intangible and immaterial form of production whose content and, most important, time, is effectively beyond measure, but which finds a degree of reconciliation in the symbolic and communicative content of the share price. In this regard, stock prices are not 'the reflection of the irrational exuberance of speculation', but instead represent 'the real growth in social production' and the time that it occupies (2008, p. 134). The valuation of an enterprise based upon a balance sheet only reflecting the results of the recordable hours of labour expended in the workplace is unable to estimate the immense value created by the combined efforts of users, consumers and producers in time outside work. Thus, for Marazzi, only the financial markets possess the elusive capacity to quantify what is immeasurable, expressing the growth in social production. Hence the hegemony of immaterial labour and the resultant crisis of measurability is taken to express and explain the financialised character of contemporary capitalism.

This theorisation has had the welcome effect of counterbalancing contemporary left critiques of crisis capitalism on the basis of a dichotomy between real and false economies. But the concept of the crisis of measurability, on which the entire edifice rests, requires a foreshortened and impoverished application of Marx's theory of value to succeed. In a recent iteration (2013, pp. 75, 87), Franco 'Bifo' Berardi indicates the theorisation of value and labour that such an account rests on. 'When you want to establish the average time that is needed to produce a material object', he writes, 'you just have to do a simple calculation: how much physical labor time is needed to turn matter into that good'. It is impossible to 'decide how much time it takes to produce an idea', or 'a project, a style, an innovation'. In their production, 'the relationship between labor-time and value suddenly evaporates, dissolves into thin air'. This is because 'the productivity of the general intellect' is 'virtually unlimited' (2013, p. 75). It 'cannot be quantified [or] standardized' and, ultimately, value cannot be measured in terms of time. But, posing a simple resemblance between labour-time and value, Bifo elides the abstract mediation of concrete labour in the value-form. These claims rest on a fundamental misreading of Marx's theorisation of the law of value, aided by the wider attack on mediation in the name of immediacy that we find in Negri and his cognate thinkers.

In this chapter I argue that the immaterial labour thesis brings into dispute only a traditional, orthodox LTOV. The conditions it describes leave intact the abstract law of value by which capitalism operates. Theorists of immaterial labour are correct to say that the LTOV is redundant. Indeed, it was ever thus. Capital has always struggled in its attempts to render human labour productive against a 'crisis' of measurability. But it is *abstract* labour that enters into and sustains the social relationship of value, more so than that expended in the realm of production. Thus, capital has always faced the immateriality of the process of abstraction as a potential crisis of measurability. In this way, the existence of immaterial labour poses no threat to critical reinterpretations of value theory such as the NRM. Postoperaists see immaterial labour as stealing away the empirical and theoretical foundations of the law of value. But an approach to value oriented around the 'social validation' of abstract labour (Heinrich 2012, pp. 50–1) places little importance on the possibility or impossibility of the quantification of working hours. This approach transcends the crisis of measurability posited in the postoperaist literature. It conceives of such a crisis as a permanent and in no way novel feature of valorisation.

8.3   CRITIQUES OF IMMATERIAL LABOUR

Previous attacks on the conceptual apparatus of 'immaterial labour' adopt a much different critique than I do here, highlighting enduring materiality (Banks et al. 2013, Pt 2) or attempting the 'rematerialisation' of discourse around the topic (Doogan 2009, p. 6). My approach does neither, emphasising instead an even greater immateriality that both rests on the sublation of definite material relations and is expressed in them. In so doing, it contends that the concept of immaterial labour does not go far enough. The postoperaist theorisation of the relationship between labour, value and

their measure inhabits an orthodoxy that is too 'materialist' by far, preoccupied only with the concrete and not the social forms it assumes. In this, I
build on critical fragments concerning Hardt and Negri in Heinrich's work.
The distinctiveness of this critique can best be examined by comparing it
with another notable critique of Hardt and Negri from the perspective of
unorthodox Marxism, in the work of the autonomist George Caffentzis.

George Caffentzis, from the autonomist perspective, has produced some
of the most sustained value-theoretical engagements with Hardt and
Negri's claims about immaterial labour and immeasurability. His criticisms
arrive from a broadly similar scepticism as those voiced here, but with
significant differences that help clarify the specificities of my approach.

Caffentzis dismisses both the concept of immaterial labour and that of
the crisis of measurability, but differently to how I dismiss them here. In the
first case, Caffentzis takes a 'materialist' perspective with reference to immaterial labour, assuming what he calls an 'extreme position' on its alleged
non-existence. The immaterial labour thesis is wrong, he contends, because
'services, cultural products, knowledge and communication are "material
goods" and the labour that produces them is material aswell', although, he
admits, 'it might not always be tangible' (2013, p. 177). However, here he
refers not to the material undergirding of abstract labour in the sublated
'actual conditions of life' presupposing value production and commodity
exchange, but more simplistically to the physical activities that produce the
commodities and the concrete processes and forms through which they are
consumed.

> The products of services, from stylish haircuts to massages, are embodied
> material goods; cultural products like paintings, films, and books are quite
> material; communication requires perfectly material channels (even though
> the material might be 'invisible' electrons); and finally, knowledge as presently
> understood is, like goals in soccer games, a specific material transformation of
> social reality. (Caffentzis 2013, p. 177)

But, as I will go on to show, such a critique of immaterial labour misses the
mark. The problem with immaterial labour is not that it elides the material
substrate of labour, but that that it focuses too much on transitions in the
material substrate of labour – of changes in the character and composition of
the physical activities of concrete labour, and not enough on the significance
of this activity under capitalism – which is to say, that its results appear in the
value-bearing form of commodities, and the implications this presents for

how we think about labours relating to one another as 'labour'. The crucial thing here, then, is not concrete labour but abstract labour. The immateriality ascribed to contemporary labour and its products by postoperaists is insufficiently accommodating of the true immateriality that consists at the heart of abstract labour. And Caffentzis's critique of postoperaismo on this point makes what is essentially the same mistake – an inability to conceptualise labour in its specificity under the law of value, which is to say, as abstract labour.

This mistake extends to Caffentzis's defence of the law of value, and Marx's theory of it, against the claim of redundancy that issue from postoperaists like Negri. His critique of the purported 'crisis of measurability' focuses on the persistence of the law of value as a quantitative process and, more problematically, Marx's theory of value as a quantitative theory. This disregards the qualitative nature of both in their association with value as an abstract social relation of all things with all other things that assumes, via money, an objective economic form. It defends against the postoperaists something that is not really there to defend in the first place, and overlooks the social form dimension of value and the objective economic categories through which it moves and rules. Yet, despite this, Caffentzis's critique is, second to Heinrich, among the most sophisticated of immaterial labour and the crisis of measurability, against which the critique I pose here can be fruitfully compared in order to clarify my own approach.

Caffentzis makes three claims with which my own critique of immaterial labour and the immeasurability thesis broadly concurs. First, he argues that postoperaists like Vercellone are not concerned with the study of the real abstractions of capitalist rationality, as were forerunners of the NRM like Sohn-Rethel (2013, p. 97). As Caffentzis notes, in the assertions postoperaists make about the obsolescence of the law of value, they miss how Marx was 'the original "immaterialist"'. '[A]s far as capitalism is concerned', Caffentzis argues (2013), Marx saw capitalists as 'not interested in things, but…their quantitative value' which is 'hardly a material stuff!' Postoperaists render obsolete the law of value only by holding to its most productivist interpretation, rather than the properly 'immaterialist' Marx. It is this 'immaterialist' Marx my own approach, in line with that of the NRM, stresses. As we saw in Chap. 7, contrary to this Marx, postoperaist claims of the Fragment's realisation rest on a disavowed orthodoxy build around a wholly materialist Marx. Despite their professed anti-productivism, they present a conventional LTOV. This incorrectly emphasises labour's concrete expenditure over its abstraction in exchange. By conceiving it contrary to its reality, postoperaists can then challenge the continuing role of the rule of value.

Caffentzis points to the everyday persistence of measurement in all kinds of work. Far from crisis, it continues to function, just as necessary for capital as ever before. At the most basic level, 'the process of creating propositions, objects, ideas and forms and other so-called "immaterial products"...is a process in time that can be (and is) measured' (2013, p. 111). This may differ from, say, the 'material' factory labour of Marx's own time. But it occupies time and is subject to measurement on this basis all the same. Caffentzis captures this well when he writes that the crisis of measurability 'does not seem to refer to what billions of people across the planet do every day under the surveillance of bosses vitally concerned about how much time the workers are at their job and how well they do it again and again' (2005, p. 97).

Third, Caffentzis contends, measurability has always endured the uncertainty ascribed in the Fragment scenario. No commodity has ever had its value seamlessly read off from the amount of direct labour-time that went into its production. As Caffentzis contends (2013, p. 112), this is as true for material commodities as it is for the immaterial goods and services emphasised by the postoperaists. This is because, as we saw in Part 1, the labour represented in the value of a commodity is abstract labour. This is measured on the basis of SNLT. This is determined by, as Marx writes (1976, p. 129), 'the conditions of production normal for a given society and with the average degree of skill and intensity of labour prevalent in that society'. In other words, it is arbitrated not by direct, concrete labour time, but through social validation in monetary exchange. Value, on this count, always contends with crisis.

The *problems* with Caffentzis's critique of Hardt and Negri come when he engages with the value-theoretical foundations of the claims they make about immaterial labour and the crisis of measurability. Caffentzis (2005, p. 96) periodises Negri's work as having rejected 'value discourse' in *Marx Beyond Marx*, graduating to an acceptance of value – although not its measurability – in his later work with Hardt. Whereas in the former, Caffentzis contends, Negri 'espoused excising the whole value discourse from the "usable" part of the Marxist canon' (2005, p. 100), by *Empire*, value is back again, although not, Caffentzis asserts, in a conventional form recognisable from the Marxist tradition of value theory. In *Empire*, what Caffentzis labels the 'LTOV' is replaced by a theory of value as 'both immeasurable and beyond measure' (2005, p. 96).

I differ on this interpretation of Negri. In spite of wider shifts, I see a common value theory uniting Negri's work pre- and post-Hardt, a conventional account of the relationship between value and labour that serves as handmaiden to the historical claims about immaterial labour and immeasurability that he eventually makes. This value theory is by no means unrecognisable from what has gone before in the Marxist tradition, but actually represents, once one strips away the lip-service paid to work refusal and anti-productivism, only the latest – and, admittedly, most interesting – appearance of a vulgar materialist, essentially substantialist understanding of the relationship between labour and value.

Caffentzis is correct to differentiate Hardt and Negri's account of the relationship between labour and value from Marx's, but incorrect as concerns (a) the novelty of their position within the Marxist tradition as a whole, where substantialist readings of the LTOV are dominant, and (b) precisely *why* Hardt and Negri's account of value deviates from Marx's theory as set out in *Capital*. The latter issue rests in Caffentzis's own reading of what Marx is talking about when he talks about value. Caffentzis critiques Hardt and Negri for discarding anything quantitative from the theory of value and retaining only that which is qualitative, so that labour and value are always 'unmeasurable "things-in-themselves"' (2005, p. 100). This is contrary, Caffentzis says, to Marx's 'commit[ment] to creating a theory that could explain capital's quantitative character'. In this book, I advocate a Marx along these lines, interested in exploding the objective quantitative appearance of social forms. But Caffentzis seems to mean something quite different: a Marx that works with quantity rather than explodes it. For Caffentzis, although Marx was 'not a professional mathematician', his work lends itself profitably to 'an enormous amount of mathematical analyses of capitalism' (2005, pp. 100–1). And, in Hardt and Negri, the 'assumption of measurability', which Caffentzis sees as crucial to the mathematical possibilities afforded by Marx's quantitative theory of value, is done away with.

There are two issues here. The first is that Caffentzis characterises Marx's theory of value as *quantitative* theory of economics, an alternative political economy to the political economy he immanently critiques in *Capital*. But, as Bonefeld contends, the critique of political economy is not an alternative to its object but a *critical theory of society*, geared towards a theoretical confrontation not only with political economy but the objective economic categories it describes, as they present themselves under the abstract social rule of value. It is not an attempt to work, in a positive way, with these categories in the name of quantitative measure, but a means to explode, negatively, the equivalence and commensurability posited in quantity itself.

This is clear when one reads between the lines of Marx's immanent critique of political economy in *Capital*. As Jameson highlights, Marx persistently draws a 'chiasmic' kind of equivalence between the two terms of an equation. According to Jameson, Marx 'undermine[s]' the 'static or synchronic function of the equals sign'. This he does by relativising each term based upon its position in the equation. By comparing two seemingly incomparable things, Marx generates a 'surrealist image'. The image achieves its surreal effect by 'juxtapos[ing] two objects as far from each other as possible' (2013, p. 24). A fine example of this quoted by Jameson is Marx's equation consisting of 'one volume of Propertius and eight ounces of snuff' (Marx 1976, p. 28) Through such flourishes, Marx undermines the abstraction upon which equation depends. Marx abstracts from concrete properties so as to render absurd the practice by which this abstraction proceeds in society itself. These quantitative forays do not represent earnest appeals to mathematics or science. Rather the often humorous equations presented by Marx are fragments of an immanent critique of the equation itself.

Thus, Marx, as the critical theorist of capitalist society par excellence, can be seen not as an advocate of quantity but as its fiercest critic. Caffentzis pre-empts this objection by addressing directly the critical strands of Marxism, from Lukacs to, in the latter day, Holloway (to which we can add Bonefeld, Arthur et al.) that seek to undermine the economic objectivity of capitalist social forms. For Caffentzis (2005, p. 103), 'this skepticism towards the "false" objectivity of value, however, is often confused with a skepticism towards the value of objectivity itself. Whatever one might think about the value of objectivity, one should not confuse skepticism with regard to it and skepticism with regard to the value of commodity values.' Here Caffentzis equates economic objectivity with a kind of neutral, instrumental rationality.

This is best exhibited where he writes that 'bread baking does require knowing how many cups of flour must be mixed with how many cups of water to make dough, i.e., there is a value to objectivity' (2005, p. 104). But what this spurious, simplistic example elides is that the objectivity involved in the measurement of ingredients for baking bread is not the same as the monetary and temporal measurement of value and abstract labour that, via the coins in our pockets and the clocks on the workplace wall, governs life and work under capitalism. The 'objectivity' of a bread recipe implies no necessarily coercive social relations, no impoverished actual conditions of life, and, most importantly, no totalising abstract social rule of value that brings all things into relation with all other things in a false equivalence.

Caffentzis seeks to save an idea of objectivity that, he suggests, is seemingly absent in claims that this or that thing is 'immeasurable'. For, he asks, how can we 'prove' what is or is not immeasurable without an objective benchmark for doing so (2005, p. 101)? He places Hardt and Negri within the tradition of Lukacs, Holloway et al. by virtue of what Caffentzis sees as their 'questioning and even putting a curse on measurement, scientificity, and any other objectifying process' (2005, p. 103). In this, Caffentzis contends, Hardt and Negri discard any objective yardstick by which claims about what is and is not within or beyond measure can be verified. But this conflation of the claims of, on one hand, the critical Marxist tradition of Open Marxism and the NRM, with, on the other, postoperaist accounts of immeasurability and the irrelevance of the law of value, obscures more than it reveals.

Where Caffentzis defends economic objectivity explicitly, it remains present in Hardt and Negri implicitly. Caffentzis acclaims the quantitative aspect of Marx's theory of value, where Hardt and Negri silently advocate a reading of the LTOV as a theory of quantity, as a necessary foundation for their refutation of it – a refutation, let us note, that is based less upon a theoretical rejection than a historically specific crisis in the supposedly quantitative functioning of the law of value Hardt and Negri hold Marx's theory to describe.

Thus, Caffentzis's critique has much in common with its object. On one hand, Caffentzis posits a simple, unmediated relationship between measure and quantity, free of a social form determination, and fit to work with at the level of mathematics, uncompromised by fetishism. On the other, Hardt and Negri can only refute the law of value and the theory with which Marx analyses it on the basis of a most reductive understanding of its normal functioning where conditions of crisis are not present. This reductive understanding describes a process of objective measurement that can be analysed quantitatively under normal conditions, contrary to what the heretical, critical strand of Marx-interpretation I follow here would contend is the case: namely, that value is an abstract social relation understood qualitatively in order to explode the apparent objectivity of economic categories, rather than assuming their existence as neutral tools with which to work and understand the world better.

Caffentzis and Negri draw radically different conclusions from a similar reading of a very specific iteration of Marx's theory of value. Where the former announces its rude health, the latter announces its demise. As we shall see, the theoretical resources afforded by the NRM constitute a much stronger basis to critique claims about immaterial labour and the crisis of measurement at the level of the value-form.

Heinrich's 'social validation' reading of Marx's value theory refutes postoperaist critiques of the relevancy of the law of value. Against Hardt and Negri's extrapolation from changes in the immediate form of labour a theory of the obsolescence of the law of value, Heinrich focuses instead on the analysis of value's social form. The central movement of the law of value is the translation of multiple different and heterogeneous concrete labours into an abstract average. This is necessitated by the exchange relation. Hardt and Negri suggest this translation is redundant in the immaterial production of contemporary capitalism. The 'informatization of production and the emergence of immaterial labor' have led to a 'real homogenization of laboring processes'. This renders labour immediately abstract. It does not, as in Heinrich, become abstract via a process of social validation internal to the law of value.

What this shows is that one can concede the redundancy of the LTOV only when one takes it to refer to the attempted quantitative measurement of inputs and outputs. As Heinrich suggests, against their protestations to have surpassed the proletarian condition, they 'equat[e] value-constituting "abstract labor" with temporal, measurable factory labor'. But, as Heinrich states (2007), 'Marx's concept of "abstract labor" is not at all identical with a particular type of labor expenditure', but is rather 'a category of social mediation'. This applies 'regardless of whether th[e] commodity is a steel tube or care giving labor in a nursing home'. If Marx's theory of value relates not to quantification but to the analysis of form, there is little difference between material and immaterial labours. The value-form relates not to labour but to its commensuration in commodity exchange.

It is through recognition of this socially mediated form that the continuing relevancy of value theory is resistant to Hardt and Negri's claim of redundancy. Heinrich argues that the status of being a commodity relates not to anything material with regards to make-up or the character of the labour involved in a product's creation. Rather it relates to their '*social form*', namely, 'whether objects and services are exchanged' (2012, p. 44). Thus, to a value theory geared towards the understanding of social validation, Hardt and Negri's empirical claims look different. The move from a society based upon the production and consumption of goods to one based upon the production and consumption of services poses no threat to the law of value.

The different kinds of labour that these two phases imply matters little to their interpretation using the tools provided by Marx's theory.

To survive such attempts upon its validity, value theory must come down to an analysis of the value form, such as that introduced in Chap. 2. What Heinrich shows is that value theory in the 'traditional Marxist' vein has not always granted the form of value the attention necessary to ensure this validity. But the NRM secures the application of Marxian value theory to contemporary capitalism, including to apparently novel areas of capitalist activity like the creative industries, as we shall see in Chap. 9. It does so in spite of the changes highlighted in postoperaist analyses.

8.4   Within and Against the Labour Theory of Value

The specificity of my critique of Hardt and Negri is clarified by its distance from that of Caffentzis. Where he critiques Hardt and Negri on the basis of materiality and objectivity, the critique I offer, inspired by Heinrich, unpicks both.

Let us assume that value stems from measurable, concrete, performed chunks of labour time. On the basis of such an assumption, 'immaterial production' calls into question the LTOV. But the trouble posed to the LTOV owes not to the new status of immaterial labour, but the inadequacies of just such a 'labour' theory of value. Theorists of immaterial labour tend to affirm this orthodox 'labour' theory of value only to refute it. They repeat its uncritical ascription of value production to human labour and the time in which it takes place. This disavowed repetition then allows them to criticise other implications of that orthodoxy. Vercellone, for instance, sees the crisis of measurability rendering the theory of value redundant. But he can only do this by retaining an orthodox understanding of the basic fact of that theory of value. This is that labour is the 'substance and the source of the creation of value and surplus value'. In this account, value results from human labour, rather than as a residue of human labour in exchange (2010, p. 92). It is this positive claim about value that facilitates the negative claim vis-à-vis the obsolescence of Marx's theory of it.

In a more upfront way, Negri accepts that his 'critique actively embraces the Marxian point of view' by foregrounding the concrete form of labour in the creation of value. The fact that he endows this concrete labour with an 'immaterial' aspect renders it no less concrete (2008, pp. 67–8). Negri is emphatic that *labour still remains the fundamental and sole element of value creation*' (2008, p. 183). The only difference with past renditions is the nature of the new labour. It renders the theory of value irrelevant. It is boundless and immaterial, its value 'determined deep in the viscera of life' (Hardt and Negri 2001, p. 365). In the 'productive excess' that results (2001, p. 357), the law of value 'reveals itself in its greatest expansion' (Negri 2008, p. 183). This assertion is interesting. It suggests that only one part of the law of value and the theory that describes it suffers in this expansion: the criterion of measurability, of the ability of capital to measure and abstract value from labour. What expands, Hardt and Negri imply, is the status of labour as the source and substance of all value. Their insistence upon the latter makes possible their insistence on the former. But it also invites a critique of the conceptual framework that they use to make this argument. Claiming that the law of value expands when applied to labour beyond measure grants misplaced importance to labour and too little to measure. The reason that the law of value can stay intact at all is because measurement is still possible, in spite of the immaterial labour thesis.

Hardt and Negri, Vercellone and others remain wedded to an orthodox interpretation of the concept of the LTOV. At the same time, they seek to overcome it with 'new' facts. As Weeks (2011, p. 93) suggests, 'there is a fidelity to Marx in Negri's work that might be construed to be as orthodox as any other'. Interpreted differently, the Marxian theory of value is harder to refute. My interpretation stresses not the material measurement of specifically *concrete* labour-time, but *abstract* labour. Such a 'value-form' perspective accommodates a much greater degree of immateriality. This enables us to perform the same manoeuvre as that I attribute to Hardt and Negri, only in reverse. I accept their understanding of the 'fact' of immaterial labour. But in the same movement I overcome it with a new conceptualisation of the relationship between labour-time and value. I dispute the special, unique and novel status afforded to immaterial labour, delineating how a theory of the value-form broadens the ascription of immateriality to *all* capitalist labour, and not, as I go on to suggest in the next chapter, some productive subsection of it.

I will now use this wider theoretical context as a springboard for the critique of three claims: the novelty of immaterial labour, the concrete existence of immaterial labour as immediately abstract and the status of immaterial labour as productive of immeasurable value. The critique of these claims challenges the terms of the mooted 'crisis of measurability'.

8.5   THE NOVELTY OF IMMATERIAL LABOUR

Postoperaists emphasise the novelty of immaterial labour and how it exceeds the law of value. New communicative, cognitive, and affective forms of immaterial production generate an immeasurable plenitude of value that capitalist frameworks cannot capture. In this rendition, immaterial labour is something completely new to capitalism. The practices and results of work appear as having been primarily material in the past. But today, such accounts suggest, a new immaterial aspect suffuses every step from labour to exchange.

Yet the thesis of immaterial labour, rather than surpassing the theory of value, does not go far enough. It is hamstrung by its insistence upon the novelty of that which it describes. This is because labour, value and exchange – and the interrelationship between them – have always had an immaterial existence.

A theory of value based upon the process by which value appears through the social validation of abstract labour negates the novelty of immaterial labour. It suggests instead that labour has always been in some way immaterial. This is especially so when we consider labour in the form in which it comes to the fore in capitalist production. This is as abstract labour, socially validated as value-producing in exchange. This hinges upon acceptance of the view that abstract labour has no concrete existence. Abstract labour does not 'happen', it is not 'performed', it is not observable. It exists only in process, in its becoming, and manifests only in exchange.

Thus, immaterial labour is nothing new, when thought of as a kind of labour with no material existence rather than a set of working practices incorporating emotion, cognition and affect instead of handiwork and physicality. On the understanding advanced here, value is incredulous to the specific activities of commodity creation. What is significant is the way in which these labours result in value. And the way in which these labours result in value is through their abstraction and validation as part of total social labour. This totality is ultimately immaterial, expressed in commodities and the proportions in which they exchange with one another. It is brought into existence only by means of the successful sale of a given product – which we will interrogate more fully in the next chapter.

8.6   CONCRETE EXISTENCE AND IMMEDIATE ABSTRACTNESS

In postoperaist accounts of immaterial labour, there is a recurring claim that changes in the composition and character of labouring tasks renders concrete labour immediately abstract. Take Bifo, for instance, who suggests that the 'immaterialization of the labour process' witnesses a passage from 'the industrial abstraction of work to the digital abstraction of work' (2013, p. 135), where the former constitutes an unfolding of abstraction, and the latter an immediate abstraction. What this implies is a literalist understanding of abstract labour whereby it has a concrete existence in production itself. This is exemplified where, for instance, Bifo suggests that 'Marx's theory of value is based on the concept of *abstract work*' (2013, p. 137, my italics). The linguistic lapse from 'labour' to 'work' is deliberate and all-too-telling, locating the abstraction of labour at the level of physical, concrete 'work', rather than the congealed factor of production 'labour'. Bifo elaborates further on this point, contending that, to be the 'source and measure' of value, this 'work' must 'sever its relation to the concrete usefulness of its activity and product'.

But whilst, as we have seen in Chap. 4, the *abstraction of* labour has a practical existence within the sphere of production by means of the practices of measurement and valuation inaugurated by the placing of a value on labour via the wage, it is by no means the case that *abstract labour itself* is 'done' in the form of 'work'. It is cohered through 'practically abstract' processes of measurement.

This category mistake makes possible a number of historical claims about the digitalisation or informationalisation of 'immaterial labour' potentiating an increased abstraction of labour *in its very doing*. We will deal with this due course. First, it is important to see these claims about immediate abstractness within the progression of Negri's path-breaking contributions to the development of postoperaismo, and specifically the philosophical revolt against mediation, abstraction and transcendence that we covered in Chap. 6.

We can trace the understanding of labour as immediately abstract in its concrete existence to Negri's 1978 lectures on the *Grundrisse*. Negri writes of the 'definition of work' that 'work appears as immediately abstract labour' (1992, p. 10). Negri extracts from the *Grundrisse* a theory of the law of value whereby, rather than the law containing in a mediated, sublated way the exploitation of the workplace, it is immediately synonymous with it. The law of value is thus one and the same as the law of exploitation, as the worker experiences it, in the workplace, entirely free of any layers of mediation (1992, p. 24). Between commodities and surplus value, Negri writes, there is no 'middle term' of value – rather the law of value relates directly and immediately to social antagonisms themselves, without any mediating or sublating 'other'.

In expressing, without mediation, social antagonism, abstract labour, Negri writes, 'traces a constituting process' whereby the abstraction and socialisation of labour – which, for Negri, takes place *within* production rather than exchange – expresses the class struggle over the needs of the working class, which they expand and demand capital through their immanent urges for less work and greater and more cooperative productivity and consumption. This 'progressive expansion' of needs gives a 'concretization' to the 'progression of abstract and social labour' – in other words, giving it a real, lived form (1992, p. 133).

Such insights weld Negri's nascent Spinozist elaboration of Tronti's Copernican Inversion into the threads of a future theory present in Marx's *Grundrisse*. As Arthur (2013, pp. 4–5) rues, '[u]nfortunately, at one point [in the *Grundrisse*], Marx plays with the notion that the actuality of abstract labour requires the empirical emptiness of all labours', with this emptiness achieved in their concrete existence, via automation or deskilling, for instance. Somehow, this says, concrete labour can be emptied of content at the material level in order to make it more 'abstract', and not owing to its practical abstraction. However, as Arthur contends – and this is really a crucial point in all discussions of postoperaist claims about immaterial labour and so on – 'it is the social abstraction itself that is real, regardless of any change in material production' (2013, pp. 4–5). By focusing so intensely on changes in the way we work, rather than the significance that work takes in the form of its results, and by relying so myopically on the *Grundrisse*, a series of sketches and fragments for what would later become *Capital*, postoperaists attain only a partial perspective on the development of Marx's theory in full, and conceive value and labour in a way that deviates from Marx's theory only so as to dismiss it.

Having said this, at certain points in his earlier work, Negri does provide some sops to the conceptualisation of social mediation that makes the most developed iteration of Marx's theory of value possible. At one point in *Marx Beyond Marx*, Negri writes that '[w]ork is abstract in so far as it is only perceptible at the level of social relations of production' (1992, p. 10). This suggests, at first glance, that work (read: labour) becomes abstract at a level removed from its immediate, concrete existence. But on closer inspection, the 'production' part is crucial. Negri appears to be saying that work is abstract at the level of its existence in production. But despite this, some sense of mediation remains. Negri gets close to a delineation of social form, but steps back again. And then, later in his lectures on the *Grundrisse*, Negri suggests that abstract labour 'concerns the mediation between the time of work and social production', which we can take to mean production for the purposes of commodity exchange (1992, p. 162).

But these are outliers to the general thrust of Negri's gradual shaking off of Marx's value theory. As we saw in Chap. 6, by the time of *Empire*, these few vestiges of mediation are gone. With mediation goes the possibility of analysing the law of value in anything but the most rudimentary way. But 'immediacy', as we will go on to consider, offers an incomplete understanding of the strange and abstract world of value. The refutation of mediation serves as the handmaiden to a series of historical claims about the advent of immaterial labour and its immediate abstractness *qua* concrete existence.

Hardt and Negri suggest that immaterial labour renders all labour immediately abstract. Immateriality and informationality result in the 'real homogenization of laboring processes'. Diverse productive activities once attained parity through capitalist practices of measurement and valuation, with the ultimate arbiter the exchange of distinct commodities for money. But today, according to Hardt and Negri, concrete heterogeneity is abstracted from immediately, different labours commensurated in their very doing. Hardt and Negri posit that tools have 'always abstracted labour power'. The computer, as the 'universal tool', creates the possibility of this immediate abstraction (2001, p. 292). Hardt and Negri are correct to say that 'abstraction is essential to both the functioning of capital and the critique of it', and to recognise the centrality of abstract labour in Marx's explanation of how value operates (2009, p. 159). But they situate the abstract sociality of labour as consisting only in the realm of production (or even prior to it), whereas it is really constituted in a process of practical abstraction culminating in exchange, as conceptualised in Part 1. The historical emphasis upon the value-creating capacities of concrete labour expresses a political belief in the power of the working class. Hardt and Negri's insistence upon the antecedent nature of both abstraction and sociality vis-à-vis exchange is no different. It expresses a belief in the power of their own revolutionary subject: the multitude, the collective force of immanently cooperative immaterial labourers.

For Hardt and Negri, things *begin* from social labour (2004, p. 144). They note that social labour is an abstraction. But they posit it in two problematic ways. It is first an abstraction forged *before* production in the cooperation immanent to immaterial labour. Second, it is an abstraction forged *within* production as the result of this labouring in common. Yet what I suggest here is that labour becomes social only when its various individual, private manifestations enter into abstract relation. This takes place by means of the exchange of commodities in the marketplace. This is the means by which the sociality of labour is attained, even though it is 'posited' in production itself.

Labour is *ideally* social before becoming fully so. Capitalist production processes begin with money. And, as we saw in Chap. 2, money grants an early, anticipatory universality to the labour-power it acquires (Bellofiore 2009). But things cannot *begin* with social labour in anything other than this ideal sense. Practices of measurement, quantification and classification are set in place within production to help this cohere. But, ultimately, social labour arises through a process of gradual becoming. It cannot be realised until after exchange has taken place. And through this the sphere of exchange structures, rather than passively reflects, the direct and immediate character of concrete labour in production.

Hardt and Negri's conceptualisation of social labour builds upon the claim of novelty. They ascribe to present-day capitalism completely new characteristics that render obsolete the terms of its previous functioning. But these changes simply better exemplify that which was always true. There *are* existing assumptions to be invalidated. But it is not the perceived newness of contemporary capitalism that makes this invalidation necessary. Rather, capitalism past and present demands a more profound rethinking than that attempted by Hardt and Negri. To some they travel too far in their immaterialising portrayal of present-day conditions of labour and valorisation (Doogan 2009). But, perhaps, this portrayal is nowhere near immaterial enough.

According to Hardt and Negri, the law of value Marx describes is irrelevant. An 'important difference between Marx's time and ours' is the changed relationship between labour and value. A certain quantity of time no longer translates into a corresponding quantity of value. The measurability this assumes is no longer attainable in immaterial production. This is because the latter transcends all temporal boundaries (2004, p. 145). But I would argue that abstract labour-time has no necessary relation to expended concrete labour. It does not matter where or for how long labour takes place. As we will see in the next chapter with reference to how creative industries like advertising intervene in the buying and selling of commodities, the forces of capital abstract from labour a measure regardless of its reality, constructing a fresh one anew. This accepts the difficulty of translating labour-time accurately into an abstract quantitative measure. But I depart from the novelty and crisis Hardt and Negri ascribe to this. The process actually *works*, in spite of the seeming impossibility and immeasurability that confront it. Hardt and Negri have no theoretical resources to ask how.

Hardt and Negri associate abstract labour with an amount of expended labour-time. But abstract labour does not take place. Although the process of practical abstraction can be experienced, which gives us ground to investigate it empirically in the first place, we deal here with an essentially 'non-empirical reality' as described in Chap. 3. As set out in Chap. 2, abstract labour has no concrete existence from which to establish a measure of its temporal duration. Although, as discussed in Chap. 5, it contains a definite non-conceptuality within this conceptuality, rooting it in real, concrete social relations, abstract labour is a conceptual residue of the act of exchanging two distinct commodities. Owing to this act – which is carried out preliminarily in production too – the labours that contributed to the production of these commodities enter a social relationship with each other, via an abstraction that irons out their specificities. The way Hardt and Negri phrase matters leads us to believe instead that, somehow, abstract labour is actually *performed*. Take the purported evolution of a body of workers for whom all work is a possibility, and for whom work can take place anywhere and everywhere in the entire fabric of life. This may be in advance of the abstraction of labour. It offers new potential for the commensuration of heterogeneous concrete labours in *exchange*. But Hardt and Negri seem to suggest that the abstraction is complete in the very *doing* of that labour. Hardt and Negri give a reductive reading of the abstraction central to Marx's analysis of the relationship between labour and value. Because of this, they are able to claim to have done away with that analysis. Immaterial labour is taken to be a new fact that defies the underlying laws of capitalist society. But Hardt and Negri do not go far enough in the immateriality they ascribe. This failure blinds them to the continuing relevancy of what they contend is obsolete.

The underlying laws of capitalist society have been enduringly more immaterial than Hardt and Negri acknowledge. Negri may indeed be right in saying 'immaterial labour is abstract labour in its higher expression' (2008, p. 75), but only insofar as abstract labour has *always been* immaterial. Abstract labour has no material, concrete form, only an immaterial, conceptual quality. It posits expended labour as somehow similar and commensurable, when in fact it is anything but. Practical abstraction in production helps serve to make this so, and value is 'posited' ideally at the commencement of production. Indeed, the changes in production Hardt and Negri describe may make this conceptual abstraction easier, establishing an informational infrastructure upon which all labours rely and through which they may be more easily compared. But this does nothing to contest the abstract functioning of capitalism Marx describes. Rather, it exemplifies its most developed manifestation.

In summary, Hardt and Negri go too far and not far enough. The main constraint is their conceptualisation of the compromised relationship between labour and value. They argue that in Marx's time, heterogeneous labour required equalisation in order for exchange to take place, but today diverse labours do not need homogenisation through the exchange abstraction. They become homogeneous by the computerisation of production. By investing all labour with an informational aspect, this reduces labouring activity to abstract labour in its performance. There is thus no need for the process Marx describes.

But immaterial labour is not abstract labour in its performance. This is because abstract labour, as noted above, has no concrete existence in which it can be performed, observed or measured. Hardt and Negri get close to this with their claim of immeasurability, but with a misplaced focus. Rather than something that can occur in the guise of immaterial labour, abstract labour is a category of social mediation (Heinrich 2007). Concrete labour-time is abstracted from and validated through the process of exchange. What is described as 'immaterial labour' is not abstract labour, because abstract labour has no concrete existence.

8.7   IMMEASURABLE PRODUCTIVENESS

What postoperaists such as Hardt and Negri describe as 'immaterial labour' is not immediately abstract in its concrete performance. Concrete labour is productive of value only by means of its abstraction. This is a process of becoming which culminates away from the workplace in the sphere of exchange. This account disputes the association of immaterial labour with the production of immeasurable value. It thereby also negates the threat immaterial labour poses to the basis of capitalist valorisation.

Ironically, the ascription of powers of value production to immaterial labour coincides with past physicalist readings of Marx's theory of value.

Both imagine value to be created with every hour that the worker spends expending energy. In the new version, immeasurable value is sent spiralling into the ether for capital to attempt to capture. There are further similarities. For Hardt and Negri, the cooperative self-valorisation of immaterial labour is part of the revolutionary promise of a new class subject. This is akin to how physicalist accounts endowed workers with immense power by means of a supposedly scientific LTOV. The ascription of value production to one class was politically advantageous. Hardt and Negri and their theoretical companions are as productivist as the vulgar Marxism they wish to escape. Doogan (2009, pp. 7–8) notes the prolific use of manufacturing as an example in accounts of post-industrial society. Points are extracted from this sector and extrapolated to the labour market as a whole. Similarly, *Empire* drips with fascination over the ins and outs of restructuring, downsizing and outsourcing. It expresses a materialist flipside of the unabashed productivist belief in the cooperative creativity of human activity, in spite of postoperaismo's apparent anti-work ethos.

Vercellone (2010, p. 105) contends that 'the source of the "wealth of nations" rests on...productive cooperation', or 'living labour'. I deny this value-productivity not only to immaterial labour, but to all labour in and of itself. I would suggest instead that the types of cooperative sociality heralded by the multitude blossom only in the market, in exchange. Up to the point at which it is validated as such by successful exchange of the good or service it renders, labour is not social, cooperative or productive. To repeat: labour produces value only in its appearance as abstract labour, and this is a factor of exchange rather than of production. Abstract labour may assume an early, anticipatory existence during the time in which work takes place (Harvie 2005). But the point remains the same: productiveness is a feature of exchange rather than of production, as we will see in the next chapter. Imperatives from outside production in the market structure what goes on in the workplace, and it is via the practical abstraction enforced by management that the cooperative sociality coheres, and not, as dismissed in Chaps. 6 and 7, any autonomous or multitudinous constituent power.

The postoperaists place great importance upon a productivist belief in human labour as the source and substance of all value. But like any series of concrete actions, expended immaterial labour does not produce value in and of itself. This has significant implications for other aspects of the postoperaist treatment of immaterial labour. Not least among these is the claim that contemporary capitalism finds itself faced with a crisis of measurability. Hardt and Negri's eulogising of immaterial labour rests on the assumption that immaterial labour is productive of value. But it is productive on an unquantifiable and unrepresentable scale, resulting in a 'crisis of measurability'.

There is an air of celebration in the postoperaist treatment of the immeasurable self-valorisation of immaterial labourers. The outcome is that they champion value as a positive category rather than a relation to be negated and destroyed. This is serviced by the situating of immaterial production within the realm of concrete labour. However, as we have seen, a theory of value emphasising the social validation of abstract labour tells a different story. It holds that it is abstract labour that determines value, rather than concrete. I conceive abstract labour to be something fully established only by the exchange relation to which the practical abstractions that populate production are subservient. It comes about as heterogeneous individual labours enter into abstract equivalence with one another. In this movement they become properly 'social'. Abstract labour both produces value and is produced by it. It acquires existence as value in the successful sale or exchange which ascribes value or worth to something. That something then becomes a commodity, where once it was only a mere product of labour.

Immaterial labour is not immeasurable, because value relates to labour's abstract residue in exchange and not its concrete practice. In this sense, it has always been impossible to effectively measure value in relation to concrete labour, only mere guesswork and estimation pending exchange. Value's measurement occurs in the same act of exchange which brings it into existence, by means of the social validation of labour as productive of value via the exchange of products of labour as commodities in the marketplace. Yet, as noted already, this measure is always struggled for. The uphill struggle to commensurate in conditions of qualitative heterogeneity continues.

8.8   CONCLUSION

The conceptualisation I have presented in this chapter escapes the threat posed to orthodox versions of Marx's value theory by the thesis of immaterial labour. Against postoperaist perspectives, this recalibrated theory of value reinstates the ability to speak of measure. One can do so regardless of any mooted 'crisis' afflicting its application. Indeed, I have identified this crisis as a largely constant factor against which capital must struggle. Value itself comes into being at one and the same time as its measure. What 'crisis' there is in this process of becoming is that crisis faced by the circuit of capital when bringing this measure into existence.

In this chapter I have extended an understanding of the immateriality of production to the nature of capitalist valorisation in its pure form through time. This surpasses the thesis of immaterial labour. It reveals the crisis of measurability to be conditional on a certain understanding of how labour and value interrelate. Immaterial labour's purported challenge to the theory of value feeds upon a traditionalist interpretation of what the law of value is and can be. Any orthodox representation of the possibilities of Marxian value theory stands wide open to the challenge mounted by immaterial labour. An interpretation informed by the NRM is better equipped to deal with it.

From an analysis of the value abstraction, one can craft a theorisation of value that accommodates and extends the conceptualisation of immaterial labour. By means of this extension, we *exceed* existing conceptualisations of immaterial production as concrete practice. It is instead possible to situate immateriality in the capitalist process of valorisation as a whole. The redundancy of the theory of value is conceded on this terrain only when taken to refer to the attempted quantitative measurement of inputs and outputs. When it becomes a question of what Heinrich (2007) calls a 'category of social mediation' things take a different complexion. What matters is that concrete labour is abstracted from and validated through the process of exchange which confirms a good or service as a saleable commodity. As we will see in the next chapter, this could be the provision of a car, a viral ad, or a brand strategy. It is in recognition of this that I state the continuing relevancy of value theory, and resist any claim of redundancy founded upon a crisis of measurability.

It is important to note that Lazzarato, Negri and others have played a significant part in highlighting profound changes in the sphere of production in capitalist societies. But they have made the error of extrapolating from these changes the notion of a crisis of measurability. They confuse the changes that *have* taken place in production with a crisis of measurability that has not. This is because they misunderstand the nature of labour, of value and of measure. Value's measurability lies elsewhere than in production. It arises in and through social validation. Therefore, the changes in concrete labour matter little to the form that measure takes, or the degree of its possibility or impossibility. What counts and is counted is abstract labour, regardless of evolutions in the world of work.

BIBLIOGRAPHY

Arthur, C. 2013. The Practical Truth of Abstract Labour. In *Marx's Laboratory: Critical Interpretations of the Grundrisse*, ed. R. Bellofiore, G. Starosta, and P. Thomas, 101–120. Leiden: Brill.

Banks, M., R. Gill, and S. Taylor, eds. 2013. *Theorizing Cultural Work: Labour, Continuity & Change in the Cultural & Creative Industries*. London: Routledge.

Bellofiore, R. 2009. A Ghost Turning into a Vampire: The Concept of Capital and Living Labour. In *Re-reading Marx: New Perspectives After the Critical Edition*, ed. R. Bellofiore and R. Fineschi, 178–194. London: Palgrave Macmillan.

Berardi, F. 2009. *The Soul at Work*. Trans. F. Cadel and G. Mecchia. Los Angeles: Semiotext(e).

———. 2013. *The Uprising: On Poetry and Finance*. Los Angeles: Semiotext(e).

Caffentzis, G. 2005. Immeasurable Value? An Essay on Marx's Legacy. *The Commoner* 10: 87–114.

———. 2013. *In Letters of Blood and Fire: Work, Machines, and Value*. Oakland: PM Press.

Doogan, K. 2009. *New Capitalism? The Transformation of Work*. Cambridge: Polity.

Fumagalli, A. 2010. The Global Economic Crisis and Socioeconomic Governance. In *Crisis in the Global Economy*, ed. A. Fumagalli and S. Mezzadra, 61–84. Trans. Jason Francis McGimsey. Los Angeles: Semiotext(e).

Fumagalli, A., and S. Mezzadra. 2010. Nothing Will Ever Be the Same: Ten Theses on the Financial Crisis. In *Crisis in the Global Economy*, 237–272. Los Angeles: Semiotext(e).

Graeber, D. 2008. The Sadness of Post-Workerism, or "Art and Immaterial Labour" Conference: A Sort of Review. *The Commoner*. http://www.commoner.org.uk/?p=33. Accessed 29 Oct 2016.

Hardt, M., and A. Negri. 2001. *Empire*. Cambridge, MA: Harvard University Press.

———. 2004. *Multitude*. London: Penguin.

———. 2009. *Commonwealth*. Cambridge: Harvard University Press.

Harvie, D. 2005. All Labour Produces Value for Capital and We All Struggle Against Value. *The Commoner* 10: 132–171.

Heinrich, M. 2007. Invaders from Marx: On the Uses of Marxian Theory, and the Difficulties of a Contemporary Reading. *Left Curve* 31. http://www.oekonomiekritik.de/205Invaders.htm. Accessed 29 Oct 2016.

———. 2012. *An Introduction to the Three Volumes of Karl Marx's Capital*. New York: Monthly Review Press.

Lazzarato, M. 1996. Immaterial Labor. In *Radical Thought in Italy*, ed. P. Virno and M. Hardt, 133–150. Minneapolis: University of Minnesota Press.

Marazzi, C. 2008. *Capital and Language*. Los Angeles: Semiotext(e).

———. 2010. *The Violence of Financial Capitalism*. Trans. K. Lebedeva. Los Angeles: Semiotext(e).

Marx, K. 1976. *Capital*. Vol. I. London: Penguin.

———. 2013. Workers' Inquiry. In *A Workers' Inquiry Reader*. Assembled to Accompany. The Politics of Workers' Inquiry Conference, ed. S. Shukaitis, J. Figiel and A. Walker, 8–15. Wivenhoe: Ephemera.

Mezzadra, S. 2010. Introduction. In *Crisis in the Global Economy*, ed. A. Fumagalli and S. Mezzadra, 7–16. Trans. J.F. McGimsey. Los Angeles: Semiotext(e).

Negri, A. 1992. *Marx Beyond Marx: Lessons on the Grundrisse*. London: Pluto.

———. 2008. *Reflections on Empire*. Trans. E. Emery. Cambridge: Polity Press.

———. 2009. *The Savage Anomaly: The Power of Spinoza's Metaphysics and Politics*. Minneapolis: University of Minnesota Press.

Ross, A. 2003. *No-Collar: The Humane Workplace and Its Hidden Costs*. New York: Basic Books.

Vercellone, C. 2010. The Crisis of the Law of Value and the Becoming-Rent of Profit. In *Crisis in the Global Economy*, ed. A. Fumagalli and S. Mezzadra, 85–118. Los Angeles: Semiotext(e).

Weeks, K. 2011. *The Problem with Work*. Durham/London: Duke University Press.

CHAPTER 9

Creative Industries and Commodity Exchange

9.1 Introduction

In this chapter, we will consider the practical ways in which the culture industry – in this instance, the so-called 'creative industries' of advertising and cognate fields – help bring the exchange relation together, as a means by which postoperaist claims about immaterial labour and the kind of work that takes place in creative industries can be challenged. Their claims, it will be seen, both go too far and not far enough.

I first demonstrate how the creative industries have functioned as an archetypal example of immaterial production in postoperaist literature, with reference specifically to the work of Andrea Fumagalli. Fumagalli suggests, in line with the analyses we have critically traversed in the last three chapters, that the specific kind of immaterial labour found in 'knowledge work' like that in the creative industries produces an immeasurable surplus of added value by means of the 'general intellect' of which Marx writes in the Fragment. However, I suggest that, in attributing an immeasurable productiveness to such work as graphic design, advertising and branding, this remains stuck within the logic of some well-worn debates about productive and unproductive labour. Whilst correctly opening out this classification beyond the sphere of production to circulation, in ascribing more or less productiveness to certain kinds of worker it is squarely contained within the continuities of traditional Marxist parlour games of who or what is productive. The main mistake of such thinking is the assumption that

© The Author(s) 2018
F.H. Pitts, *Critiquing Capitalism Today*, Marx, Engels, and Marxisms,
DOI 10.1007/978-3-319-62633-8_9

productiveness logically pre-exists the law of value, rather than any criteria for what is classed under the former being subject to the determination of the latter.

In the second section, I turn to Marx's treatment of circulation and productive and unproductive labour in *Capital* Vol. 2, focusing on a passage about the 'work of combustion' which furnishes us with textual support to contest the relegation of the activities that take place in circulation – selling, marketing and so on – to a purely secondary, unproductive role. Rather, what the passages in Marx on the work of combustion suggest is that sectors like the creative industries actually defy the rubric of productiveness and unproductiveness by making the exchange relation in which value is arbitrated possible in the first place by encouraging the buying and selling of commodities. Fields like advertising, branding and graphic design do so by giving commodity 'form' to the pure content of what, upon leaving production, are mere products of labour. For this I draw critical resources from the work of Jonathan Nitzan and Shimshon Bichler, Asger Jorn's use of Marx's concept of labour's 'form-giving fire' in his conceptualisation of the 'creative elite', David Harvie's probing recapitulation of debates around productive and unproductive labour, and further fragmentary writings by Marx on the topic, including in *Theories of Surplus Value* and the treatment of transportation in the second volume of *Capital*. In the third section of the chapter I use this discussion of transportation as an example through which to draw an analogy between the spatial moving of goods to people and the emotional moving of people to buy goods engaged in by advertising and branding. By doing so I reconceptualise the specific productive role of circulatory activity in the terms of Marx's own characterisation of a sector also in circulation but also playing an indispensable role in allowing value to be realised as a category of social mediation.

The central role thus ascribed to the creative industries in the exchange of commodities resonates with the dynamics of capitalist crisis discussed at the end of Chap. 5. In the fourth and final section of the chapter we return to this topic. In conditions of constrained consumption owing to the classed social basis of capitalist society, creative industries assist in resolving the two-sided contradiction of underconsumption and overproduction by generating and securing the attachment of new needs and wants to unsold stock inventories, in what, as we will see, Baran and Sweezy called the 'sales effort'.

I conclude that placing the creative industries within the circuit of capital in this way confounds traditional Marxist and postoperaist claims as to the relative productiveness of different kinds of industrial sector and labouring activity owing to their location within either the sphere of production or that of circulation. Rather, by situating the arbitration of what is and is not productive within the logic of the law of value, we can see that, far from alternately adding immeasurably productive value or exerting an unproductive drain on profit or revenue, creative industries bound to circulation like advertising, branding and marketing actually make possible value's appearance in the exchange of commodities in the first place, especially where conditions for buying and selling are unfavourable. This role – highlighted, as we will see, in Raymond Williams's conceptualisation of advertising's 'organising' effect in the circuit of capital – corresponds to Adorno's association of the culture industry with the capitalist schema covered in Chap. 3, whereby, by means of exchange, all things are brought into relation with all others things and the chaos of reality is organised along commensurable lines.

9.2   IMMATERIAL LABOUR AND THE CREATIVE INDUSTRIES

As Ursula Huws notes, the shift to a marketplace of immaterial goods and services has led some to re-evaluate the relevancy of Marx's LTOV (2014, p. 81). 'If value is observably being generated from some activity', she writes, 'the tendency is to search for the commodity at its source' (2014, p. 87). The creative industries – among them fields such as advertising, branding and graphic design – exemplify much of what is at stake in the ongoing re-evaluations of Marx's theory of value examined in the last three chapters. As we have seen, some interpret these changes using postoperaist theories of immaterial labour. For such approaches, creative industries represent the novel immateriality of post-Fordist production. According to Lazzarato, immaterial labour is 'the labor that produces the informational and cultural content of the commodity'. It incorporates 'activities involved in defining and fixing cultural and artistic standards, fashions, tastes, consumer norms, and, more strategically, public opinion' (1996, p. 133). The cooperativity of this labour is immediate and immanent, rather than coerced. Thus, it creates value beyond measure. Theorists of immaterial labour endow the kind of practices found in the creative industries with novelty and inventiveness. They suggest that their powers of value production are novel and inventive in three ways. First, they are greater than other industrial contributions. Second, they are immeasurably so. Third, in this regard, they are something new and unseen.

The creative industries suggest themselves as a perfect arena for a study of the theoretical preoccupations I have derived from the work of Marx, namely the reconstruction and reinterpretation of his theory of value away from labour and towards abstraction. In the first instance, and on a superficial level at least, their conditions are sufficiently different from the primarily factory-oriented production that Marx had in mind when he constructed what was later interpreted in its orthodox form as the LTOV. The creative industries constitute a very different environment and set of problems than the predominantly industrial context in which Marx's theorisations were initially hatched.

There has been a tentative return to Marx in studies of communication, media and cultural industries. Fuchs and Mosco (2012) defend Marxist analyses against Jean Baudrillard's assertion that Marx's theory of value cannot extend to culture and media. Against Baudrillard, the theory of value is not 'strictly homogeneous with its object'. For Baudrillard, this object is 'material production' (2012, p. 129). Rather, it extends to many fields. One such field is the creative industries. Nicole Cohen (2012, p. 141) notes the way in which the dawning of the 'creative economy' has led to the unfair dismissal of the relevancy of Marx's work. Scholars do use Marx to understand the creative industries, Cohen notes. But they often draw upon the 'new' concepts so important to recent revisionist approaches. One such concept is the 'general intellect'. Discussed in Chaps. 6 and 7, this gained popular usage with the English translation of the *Grundrisse* in the mid-twentieth century (1993). Cohen (2012, p. 142, n. 3) is astute in highlighting that the 'old' conceptual apparatus, centring upon the theory of value, enjoys less favour. As we have seen in previous chapters, the uptake of the *Grundrisse* over *Capital*, and specifically the theoretical baggage that follows a narrow focus on the Fragment on Machines, has unfortunate analytical and political implications. But the 'old' Marx should not be so easily discounted. What this book shows is that a changing world of work by no means obstructs our application of Marx's categories to understand it. But theoretical work needs to be done to get to this position.

Marx considered capital through a series of abstract categories. This has secured his theory's longevity outside the immediate context and specificities of his time. Thus Marx employs a frame of understanding which pertains above and beyond its particularities. But to understand the particularities of our own time, we have to perform some work ourselves. This may sometimes involve leaving behind parts of Marx's theories, or illuminating new or misunderstood aspects. The study of the creative industries helps in this process of selection. It sheds more light upon some of the things that Marx was trying to get at than did the industrial work processes preoccupying his mature output. Indeed, the concrete capitalism that we witness in our day may be much closer to Marx's abstract model of capitalism than the concrete capitalism of his own (Mandel, quoted in Jameson 2011, p. 9).

In this sense, the creative industries, far from bringing into question Marx's theory of value, may allow us to do much more with that theory of value. The creative industries expose elements of the production and circulation of commodities opaque in the industrial work of Marx's time.

Further, creative industries, it may be argued, occupy a similar position in developed Western capitalist economies as did manufacturing in Marx's time. The writing of *Capital* was conducted in response not to the overwhelming quantitative prevalence of factories, but to their increasingly hegemonic qualitative status. Factories were not the most numerous type of production, but seemed as if they would exert a hegemonic influence on how production in the rest of the economy would develop.

The creative industries and their working practices constitute a worthwhile object of analysis in the contemporary era precisely due to the possibility of their occupying a similarly hegemonic status vis-à-vis the economy as a whole, carrying a series of traits which display characteristics that, however tentatively, have a tendency to be adopted in other industrial contexts and circumstances. In this, areas like graphic design, advertising and branding are among the most exemplary manifestations of the kinds of activities grouped under the banner of 'immaterial labour' by the postoperaists. Therefore, they are a perfect territory upon which to critically examine claims about immateriality and immeasurability.

In assessing the theory of immaterial labour as it applies to the creative industries, I will focus on the work of one postoperaist thinker in particular, Andrea Fumagalli. Within that tradition, Fumagalli's work stands out as an attempt to apply postoperaist categories to fields such as the creative industries. Fumagalli engages, in a series of papers published over the last decade (Fumagalli 2011; Fumagalli and Lucarelli 2008; Fumagalli and Morini 2010, 2013), with the shift towards 'cognitive capitalism'. His work explores what this entails for value theory.

Fumagalli focuses on the hegemonic position of 'knowledge work' in contemporary capitalism. He associates this with increases in productivity. For Fumagalli, productivity gains arise from the 'increasing return effects and absence of scarcity' in knowledge work. This is because knowledge 'is not a rival but a cumulative commodity' (2011, p. 86). Industrial activities based on knowledge include advertising, design, marketing and branding. Fumagalli holds them to be unassimilable to the notions of productivity found in previous industrial paradigms. This owes to the 'general intellect' of immediate cooperative creation that the thesis of immaterial labour describes. This, Fumagalli suggests, increases 'the achievable level of social productivity'. In so doing, it surpasses existing understandings of what productivity is and can be (Fumagalli and Lucarelli 2008, p. 8). There are 'new factors that generate the gain of productivity' in so-called 'cognitive capitalism'. These entail the 'non-measurability of the productivity of knowledge through the traditional quantitative methods' (2008, p. 10). This crisis of measurability puts at risk the applicability of a Marxian theory of value. Value transcends the sphere of production. It is now generated by a novel dispersion of cooperative creative capacities through informational networks. This is very relevant to creative industries such as branding, design and advertising. In these sectors, Fumagalli (2011, p. 90, 97) suggests, the symbolic imaginary integrates consumption more closely within the productive moment. Valorisation occurs not only in production, but in realisation, by means of consumption. Fumagalli writes that

> the value of a commodity is no longer merely definable by 'the necessary working time'; to the value...should be added the value deriving from the degree of social symbolic nature that it contains. When its immateriality increases, the symbolic value of commodity becomes even more apparent. It is on this edge that the relationship between production and realization...is played. The valorization of the commodity no longer occurs within the productive process alone but, as the immaterial production has become production of imaginaries, it occurs when the imaginary realized itself, at the very point of consum[ption]: it is the result of what we can define the *brandization* process [...]. It does not relate to the mere act of consumption. When the commodity becomes a symbol, there is no difference between production and consumption, namely: there is no clear cut between production and realization. (2011, p. 90)

Fumagalli asserts that this process leads to a situation whereby 'brandization' does not only realise value, but *adds* it to the commodity. This occurs through 'the increase of its symbolic significance and to the capacity to generate a shared imaginary on the part of consumers'. To this 'corresponds an increase of the value of commodity'. This proceeds through 'common relational activities'. These occur through immaterial production's dispersed cooperative and communicative networks (2011, p. 97).

I will return to Fumagalli at the end of the chapter. But first, I will draw on some of Marx's writing around the issue of production and unproductive labour, read through a NRM prism, in order to situate what exactly it is creative industries do in the production and circulation of value. I find that Fumagalli's fixation on the novelty of the 'added value' they create is wide of the mark, and does not quite capture the fundamental role they assume in the selling of goods and services as commodities, the *sine qua non* of value. Through this we can conceptualise the specificity of the market-mediated exchange relationships into which capitalist enterprises enter, which in turn are the context for the concrete social relations and practical abstractions to which, following Part 1, workers on the ground are subject.

9.3   THE WORK OF COMBUSTION AND THE FORM-GIVING FIRE

It is in Marx's considerations of productive and unproductive labour that we find his most direct engagement with the labour of circulation, such as that found in graphic design, advertising and branding, and its role in value production. Inflecting the interpretation of these passages with a NRM-inspired understanding of social validation, my account moves away from an intrinsic picture of where productiveness lies. Instead, it gravitates towards one that describes a process of abstraction whereby labour is rendered productive.

Although it has a gradually cohering identity at earlier stages, the category of productiveness is an assessment achieved only at the culmination of this process. Where many orthodox treatments of the topic see the distinction between productive and unproductive labour *prior to* the law of value (Mohun 1996), I support David Harvie's contention (2005, p. 61) that the opposite is the case: whether something is productive or not is arbitrated internally to the value relation, and cannot pre-exist it. Productiveness is an outcome of the movement of the law of value, the abstraction of concrete, private labour as a part of the social whole in exchange. The exchange of commodities by means of money is the movement by which labours enter into the social totality of abstract labour. And, by helping this happen, I argue, creative industries like graphic design, branding and advertising play a central part in the value abstraction.

I therefore situate the creative industries at a pivotal position crucial for the understanding of the particular economic context in which they sit. Their pivotal role relates to their endowment of goods and services with a sellability that, when successful, renders in retrospect the labour expended in their production socially valid as productive of value. This it does by effecting successful exchange, which, as we have seen in Chap. 2, is the criterion for social validity. It determines whether a given good or service can be said to be value-bearing or not, and the labour expended in its production productive of value. But for this to happen, there is a considerable effort to endow a commodity with a social dimension whereby it can stand in relationship with other commodities through the mediation of monetary exchange. I attribute this contribution to the labour that takes place in the realm of circulation. In this case, this includes graphic design, advertising and branding.

This labour of circulation is traditionally conceptualised as 'unproductive' in the Marxist canon. As Nitzan and Bichler contend (2009, pp. 112–14), this has problematic implications. The 'standard Marxist view', they suggest, has typically taken production to 'mediate the relationship between society and nature' and circulation to merely operate on society itself, reordering relations therein. This, they point out, excludes employees of advertising conglomerates like InterRepublic Group (as well as many others) from the category 'productive', relegating them to the ranks of the unproductive.

However, they assert that things are not that simple. Advertising does not only 'promote sales', but also, today, participates in the 'incessant remodelling of automobiles, clothing, detergents, cosmetics, architecture, news media and what not' (2009, p. 112). Indeed, this work now represents, according to some accounts, some 25 per cent of the costs of production. This is circulation-facing activity based around concepts and the consumer bond, classed as unproductive but hardwired increasingly into the sphere of production itself. The Toyotist feedback loop between production and consumption that Lazzarato (1996) identifies, for instance, now sees advertising professionals intervene in the development of automobile designs and customers enter workshops to specify their preferences before production.

Reflecting on this, Nitzan and Bichler question how cleanly traditional Marxists can parse the circulation of 'existing values' and the creation of 'new values'. As they point out, one manoeuvre by which Marxists have circumnavigated the issue is by 'conceding that circulation activities [like] advertising. . .do have an impact on the. . .reproduction of the social order as a whole, and therefore the *overall* magnitude of value and surplus value'. But this generality is not in any way synonymous with the 'relative magnitudes of *specific* values and surplus values', and is hence unproductive. This captures what John Kenneth Galbraith called marketing's 'propaganda on behalf of goods in general' – an aspect we will return to in due course (Galbraith 1967; quoted in Nitzan and Bichler 2009, p. 114). But how then to explain the '*differential*' aspect whereby advertising is engaged by firms in a competitive struggle with one another, benefitting certain capitalist enterprises and sectoral arms more than others? The 'consequences' of Galbraith's propaganda 'vary along production chains', Nitzan and Bichler suggest (2009, pp. 113–14). Clearly there is more going on than meets the traditional Marxist eye. The amount spent and accrued through advertising complicates its casual dismissal as an unproductive drain on revenue bound to the sphere of circulation:

> Capitalists worldwide are estimated to spend up to $600 billion annually just to remind us of [our] options. If we assume a 15 per cent markup on these advertising expenditures, we get $90 billion of net profit. This sum represents roughly 5 per cent of global net corporate income and a comparable portion of global market capitalization. The computations of course are tentative ('half my advertising is wasted, but I don't know which half', goes the famous Madison Avenue saying). They also exclude sales promoting expenditures buried in the 'cost of production'… But the very fact that so much is spent on persuasion suggests that a significant chunk of outstanding corporate assets discounts the very ability of capitalists to shape human hopes and fears. (Nitzan and Bichler 2009, p. 161)

For Nitzan and Bichler, such issues are enough to precipitate a break with Marx completely. But their work takes no account of the innovations of the NRM, and the flexibility with which a 'social validation' approach to value theory can approach the activities of circulation. By a close reading of Marx's writings on what he called the 'work of combustion' in the second volume of *Capital* (1992), we can craft a radically different interpretation, from squarely within the Marxian value theory unfolded in this book, of the determination of production and unproductive labour that places this combustive work front and centre. And for us, this work is synonymous with that of graphic designers, brand strategists and other creatives.

In *Capital* Vol. 2, Marx at one point refers to the labour that takes place in the sphere of circulation as that of the 'work of combustion'. This work of combustion, Marx asserts, produces no value. But the work of combustion is essential for value to come about. He uses a scientific analogy to illustrate this. 'This work of combustion does not generate any heat', Marx writes, 'although it is a necessary element in the process' by which combustion takes place. It uses up energy but is necessary for heat's generation (1992, pp. 132–3).

So, although combustion uses up energy in a supposedly 'unproductive' way, it would be hard to deny that it is a prerequisite for the production of heat. Departing from Marx, I suggest that it does this by realising the potential heat-productiveness of the different elements involved. We might situate the creative agencies covered in the next chapter in an analogous relationship to the production of value. They bring about value through their facilitation of opportunities for the exchange of products of labour as commodities. In so doing, they help make possible the production of value. This gives them a pivotal position vis-à-vis capitalist valorisation.

I will go on to delineate the theoretical basis of this assertion further. But for now it is worth considering the practical dimensions of this 'work of combustion' as it exists in the creative industries. One might draw a parallel between Marx's utterances on the 'work of combustion' and those he makes on the subject of labour's 'form-giving fire'. He writes in the *Grundrisse* that '[l]abour is the living, form-giving fire; it is the transitoriness of things'. In turn, 'the transitoriness of the forms of things is used to posit their usefulness' (1993, pp. 360–1).

The work of combustion may be seen as precisely this 'form-giving fire'. It posits transitory usefulness in the way described above. It gives exchangeable 'forms' to the various heterogeneous 'contents' passed on from the realm of production proper. It makes these forms desirable on the basis of their difference or specific quality. In so doing, the combustive work of advertising, branding and graphic design helps organise the monetary exchange of products of labour as commodities. This exchange grants them value and attaches to them a price. Without this, no value would come about.

In his critical treatment of Marxist political economy, Asger Jorn develops this notion of 'form-giving fire' (2002). He suggests that creative workers perform an essential function in capitalism. They create the specific forms which commodities take on the market. The basis for Jorn's contention is that creative workers do not make value in and of themselves, but rather value persists in the difference that they create. This difference manifests in the plenitude of styles, fashions and trends one finds for consumption on the capitalist commodity market. It is brought into being by Jorn's creative elite (Wark 2011, p. 89). It is this creative elite that 'give[s] form to value', by 'renew[ing] the form of things' and creating the difference in which value consists (2011, pp. 84–5). The creative elite are the producers of the form rather than the content of commodities (2011, p. 89, n. 33). Indeed, the commodity as it sells in its fetishised existence is pure form, pure symbol, incredulous to content. It need only be desired to be successfully exchanged in the marketplace, regardless of underlying characteristics. It is owing to this that value can attach itself to something in the first place.

Jorn touches upon something important and significant in the role that creative workers and creative industries play in capitalism. He reasserts that which Marx only implied in his discussions of 'form-giving fire' and the 'work of combustion'. Valorisation proceeds not through the manufacture of specific goods or services. Rather, it proceeds through the manufacture of desirable forms, irrespective of content.

Jorn's thesis of the creative elite and their production of forms harkens back to a distinction which Marx himself makes. This is that between form and content in productive and unproductive labour. Marx suggests that productive labour is pure form without content. He writes in his *Theories of Surplus Value* (1861–63) that 'the designation of labour as productive labour has absolutely nothing to do with the determinate content of that labour, its special utility, or the particular use-value in which it manifests itself. The same kind of labour may be productive or unproductive.' Thus, it does not matter whether labour is productive or not. Labour itself may in fact be entirely peripheral. Its content must be given form to be said to be productive of value. Advertising and other such industries oriented towards exchange in the sphere of circulation create this sellable form. This pure symbolic form is indifferent to its particular content. This is an aspect which becomes apparent in the periodic scandals about consumer goods purporting to be something that they are not. This may be horsemeat masquerading as beefsteak or quack medicine masquerading as miracle cures. As Baran and Sweezy (2013) note,

> advertising campaigns if sufficiently large, persistent, and unscrupulous (availing themselves of such methods as subliminal suggestion and the like) can sell to the consumer 'almost anything.' This contention is supported by some of the most authoritative experts in marketing techniques, one of whom observes that 'a superior product means superior in the eyes of the consumers. It does not necessarily mean superior in terms of objective value or according to laboratory standards'... The most striking examples of the capacity of advertising to generate demand for worthless or even harmful products have recently been provided in the area of pharmaceuticals, cosmetic products, and the like.

The particular content of the commodity that is sold is not at stake. The specific labour to which it owes its material existence, as good or service, matters little. What counts is the form in which it sells. As we have seen, Marx implies the irrelevance of labour's content. We might infer that the latter depends on the particular form the labour takes, in its guise as abstract labour. It is by being abstracted from, after the fact, that labour attains full 'productiveness'. This abstraction is possible only through the exchange of products of labour as commodities. But this requires a considerable effort to create a commodity in its full social dimension, as pure form without content. It is to the labour that takes place in the realm of circulation, such as advertising, that we can attribute this contribution, and it is to this that we can attribute their pivotal position along the circuit of capital.

This fundamental role is similar, in some way, to how Adorno conceived of the part the culture industry plays in allowing the capitalist schema to cohere. In Chap. 3, we saw how monetary exchange plays a synthesising role in capitalist society as a whole in a way akin to the Kantian transcendental synthesis. Proposing that we seek in society itself 'that fundamental reality which in traditional philosophy had been constituted by eternal essences of Mind' (1976 [1962], p. 237), Adorno builds on the association Sohn-Rethel and Horkheimer draw between exchange and ways of thinking with reference to the culture industry. Lotz surveys upon a 'side note' from the *Dialectic of Enlightenment* (1972), whereby Adorno and Horkheimer suggest that Hollywood and the culture industry are 'foreshadowed' by the Kantian schematism (Lotz 2014, p. 2). Adorno suggests that, in capitalist society, the culture industry comes to take an active role in organising social reality along the lines of the schema. It establishes the basis upon which experience is schematised, patterned and pre-formed in the minds of consuming subjects under capitalism (Bernstein 2001, p. 11). Lotz identifies two central issues with Adorno's perspective here. The first is that the culture industry is seen as a purely psychological 'filtering' and 'prefiguring' of 'what can be conceived meaningfully' in capitalist culture, rather than as an element of a '*social-material schema*' that is itself specifically capitalist. Second, Lotz suggests that Adorno's analysis remains stuck at surface level, insofar as it treats *exchange* as the 'central concept of capitalism', whereas in fact exchange is itself 'derive[d] from other social categories' – namely, for the purposes of Lotz's approach, money (2014, p. xiv). Put simply, concrete and contingent human action must take place in order for the exchange relation to come together – and it is this work to which the circulation activities of the creative industries like graphic design, advertising and branding are committed, placing all things on a plane of formal equivalence with all other things.

9.4   CREATING COMMODITIES FROM PRODUCTS OF LABOUR

The implicit tendency of orthodox approaches is to relegate the labour of circulation to a secondary position vis-à-vis the realm of production. Thinking about practices as advertising and graphic design, I challenge this relegation. In an important contribution to existing debates, Harvie (2005) makes the claim that all labour is productive of value. He suggests that the labour involved in circulation such as advertising and other professional services is as productive as any other labour.

The labour that exists in the realm of production produces the goods that are later sold as commodities – the future bearers of value, posited as such by the monetary beginnings of the production process. But it is non-productive in the sense that it does not really matter whether or how much of it takes place. All that matters is that something attracts a price at the end of it all. It is helpful, of course, that labour is expended to create a specific use-value that can hold a distinct appeal to consumers. Yet it is not necessary to generate a specific use-value for it to retail as one on the market. A clever and well-targeted advertising campaign can achieve this, for instance. Furthermore, it is helpful that labour is expended in order to subject it to measurement. We examined why labour taking place in time and space is considered important for capitalist measurement in our assessment of the eight 'c's in Chap. 2. Measurement is part of the process of abstraction which brings all things into social relation with all other things. But even here, the abstraction and commensuration of labours as parts of the total social whole can be effected in retrospect. This can occur with or without a corresponding expenditure of labour at its basis. Thus, it may be a precondition of the production of value that the thing sold should have had some kind of labour input into its production. Certainly, labour creates many things that *carry* and *bear* value, if not value itself. But it is neither necessary nor sufficient that such labour should take place. As long as something sells, value appears, regardless of the specific practical activity by which the thing consumed is distinguished.

One might just as easily say, then, that due to the quintessence of its role, the labour of circulation is the only labour productive of value. But this would be to adopt an understanding of productiveness entangled in the conceptual framework of orthodox approaches. Value is 'produced', if we wish to use the traditional understanding, on a continuum that includes the labour that takes place in the realm of production. But this continuum has its culmination only in exchange. This culmination comes via those who service the ends of exchange, i.e. those involved in the labour that takes place in circulation, Marx's 'work of combustion'.

Without this culmination, value would not be present to have the understanding of its having been produced applied to it. The labour that goes into the production of a value-generating commodity does not produce this value, but, as we saw in Chap. 4, produces the *bearer* of value. Value itself is a social relation between these bearers. And, in order for this social relation to be fully established, commodities must exchange by being sold for money. Graphic design, advertising and branding, by intervening in the images and meanings applied to goods and services in order to sell them, are central to capital's attempts to bring this social relation into existence. Therefore, I do not claim that Marx's 'work of combustion' is the *only* productive labour, or represents a way of 'adding value' in the manner Fumagalli contends. Rather it intervenes on a deeper level, on the possibility of pinpointing 'production' itself, owing to its pivotal role in cohering the social relationship between commodities that makes value apparent, and thus the labour that produced its bearer.

Thus, rather than anything intrinsic to concrete labour itself, the productiveness of labour is a factor of its end result. Its ultimate arbiter is whether the good or service it produces sells as a commodity. It is this that brings the labour performed into relation with all the other labours of society as part of an abstract whole. This validates the labour as part of the 'socially necessary' labour of society. It confers upon it the standard of productiveness. This is as a result of the good or service it produces gaining its own confirmation of its status as a full commodity, an object of exchange or sale. This is a principally retrospective activity. The 'validation' of past labour as productive conjures a new purely symbolic and abstract quantity of labour. This is nothing but a conceptual, imaginary device by which the social totality of productive activity is pictured. It helps bring its goods and services into a relationship of commensuration and equivalence with one another.

I therefore agree with Harvie, who contends that '[l]abour which is 'unproductive' is…categorised as such because commensuration through market exchange does not take place' (2005, p. 150). That labour is productive by commensuration through commodity exchange is not restricted to the moment that a product hits the market. The commensuration is that by which different concrete labours enter into a relationship of equivalence with one another. They thus attain abstractness, sociality and productiveness. This is a process that unfolds gradually within production and without, culminating fully only in exchange. As Harvie writes, 'a thing – commodity – is produced, and then it just is, until it is sold – its value realized'. Helping this come together are those recruited by the capitalist, such as 'marketers and advertisers, credit-providers and retailers' (2005, p. 152). Without these functionaries, the commodity moment would not come, and nothing would be 'productive' in any real sense at all.

Harvie uses advertising as an example of this. The particular use-value that the service commodity of advertising offers to the capitalist is that it facilitates exchange, validating abstract labour as productive, and thus bringing value into full reality. This it does by means of the sale of a product of labour as a commodity on the market. Thus advertising and marketing insulates the capitalist against the uncertainties of circulation. Not least among these is that of whether a commodity will sell. Advertising also produces use-values for consumers. It conjures 'imagined, non-corporeal qualities of products', such as the brands with which one identifies when buying a material good. The two, Harvie suggests, cannot be 'disentangled'. The brand is completely tied up with, part of and implicated in the specific product purchased. We 'buy not only the tangible good, but the identity too' (2005, p. 153). Traditionalist accounts of circulation labour overlook this kind of production. This provokes Harvie (2005, p. 144) to pose an important question:

> How do we understand the fact, for example, that a pair of Nike trainers costs four or more times as much as a physically similar 'no logo' pair? If all the creative human activity involved in designing (beyond the physical design of the shoes) and marketing the Nike product is unproductive, adding nothing to the shoes' value, then the values of the Nike and 'no logo' trainers will be similar. A significant divergence of price from value is the only result. How is this to be explained?

Something is missing in accounts that cast the circulation labour that creates the Nike brand as somehow irrelevant to value and its production. It is not simply that advertising and its counterparts add a 'cultural content' (Lazzarato 1996) to the commodity, on top of an objective sphere of use-value. Rather, they actively intervene in the latter. The production of a use-value may be the original impetus out of which a good or service arises. It furthermore grants the basis for a good or service exchanging as a commodity with a specific purpose or desirability attached to it. But more must be done to create this desirability than simply to produce something useful. Use is the basis of this desirability. But it may not be quite enough to foster the conditions by which a product of labour can be sold and thus attain the fully fledged status of a commodity. Something more must happen to grant the good full commodity status and render the labour expended abstract and, thus, productive.

The facilitation of use is a precondition of something being desirable and specific enough in its attributes to constitute a worthwhile purchase. Creative industries help create the correct environment in which use-value means something. This establishes the basis around which exchange-value can cohere, and defines the creative industries' specificity within commodity circulation and the circuit of capital, and, with this corporate context, the labour that takes place within them.

Value depends upon the creation of an exchange relation between commodities (and thus the labours attached to them) through the mediation of money. This is, as we have stated, based upon someone wanting something. Use-value is one part of this, but the category of use is a potentiality unlocked only with the conditions in place for use to actually happen. Things will not be used unless they sell. Things will not sell unless they are desirable in some way. Indeed, Marx suggests as much. He writes that the production of a commodity succeeds by 'creating in consumers a want for its products as objects of consumption' (Marx, quoted in Gough 1972). Desire, and the want that Marx contends it 'implies', are not extraneous to the production and consumption of use-values, but rather essential to it.

In *Capital* Volume 2 (1992), Marx spends some time discussing the role of the transport sector in capitalist valorisation. Marx's treatment of transportation parallels what I have offered so far on the role the creative industries assume in the production of value. Marx situates transportation in production rather than circulation. This is because it does not present itself as a loss or deduction to the capitalist, unlike other ancillary functions. Noting that 'the transport industry sells. . .the actual change of place', Marx focuses on the movement of people to commodities and commodities to people. This constitutes both a production process and an act of consumption. Movement is a very specific and particular commodity in itself (1992, p. 135).

Marx writes that 'the use-value of things is only realized in their consumption, and their consumption may make a change of location necessary, and thus, in addition, the additional production process of the transport industry. The productive capital invested in this industry thus adds value to the products transported' (1992, pp. 226–7). Transportation, then, helps in the production and realisation of value by bringing goods to people and people to goods. It both produces a commodity – the movement of goods and people – and helps in the production and realisation of value – by bringing goods to people and people to goods. It does not present itself to capital as a loss in the same way as the activities of circulation.

The service performed by transportation would not appear to be something limited exclusively to trains, planes and automobiles. We can associate Marx's remarks with the development of a much different infrastructure of activities and industries. Advertising, and branding are similarly committed to bringing products to people and people to products.

According to Raymond Williams, advertising organises the market. It helps standardise, rationalise and render predictable the patterns of consumer behaviour and choice. Williams highlights the role taken by the advertising industry in the regulation and reportage of the distribution and consumption of goods. This is a crucial response to the organisational difficulties of disconnected, large-scale industrial production. Advertising is a device for smoothing and steadying distributive channels. It is a lightning rod for demand, establishing clear indications for capital to act upon (2005 [1980], p. 186).

Fields such as marketing, advertising, graphic design and sales bring products to people and people to products. In so doing they turn simple products of labour into commodities. They create the bond and the conditions by which it is possible that something exchanges or sells as a commodity in the first place.

Marx isolates transportation as inhabiting a separate realm of value-productiveness that somehow eludes all the other activities of 'circulation'. But can the same not be said of those circulation functions such as marketing, advertising and sales? Do they not perform such a similar movement of goods and people to increase the possibility of products of labour exchanging as commodities? Marx's reading of transportation extends to the roles he relegates to the realm of circulation. Consumption, after all, is necessary for value to come about. Whatever contributes towards, induces or facilitates consumption is thus a component of the *production* of value. It *realises* the potential productiveness of the labour that has gone into fashioning or performing the good or service sold as a commodity.

My understanding of Marx on transportation resonates with that of Huws. Huws (2014, n. 31, p. 106) notes that the 'special exception' Marx makes for transport workers may owe to the revolutionary potential they possessed at the time. They were at the forefront of class struggle, with strong organisation and frequent participation in industrial action. But, for Huws, this 'special exception' can extend to 'other forms of labour involved in getting products to market'. She cites Marx's statement in the *Grundrisse* (1993, pp. 533–4) that 'the bringing of the product to the market...belongs to the production process itself. The product is really finished only when it is on the market'. As Huws notes, on this basis, 'a wide range of functions to be found in a modern corporation can be assigned to this directly productive category'. This includes 'marketing, logistics management, distribution, transport, customer service, retail and wholesale sales' (Huws 2014, p. 93).

From this reconstruction of Marx's thought one can see that the category of what produces value in capitalist society is potentially much wider. It exceeds activities such as transportation that Marx singles out for special treatment. To drive this home, we might play upon the dual meaning of the verb to move. One can move goods in a spatial sense, as in transportation, but one can move people in an emotional one. I speak of a specific sense of movement – to move people, to stimulate emotion, identification, loyalty, desire and want towards some product or brand. This marks the truly valorising force not just in the sphere of circulation but within the entire stretch of the circuit of capital as a whole. This applies just as much to the acquisition of means of production and raw materials by businesses as it does to the acquisition of consumer goods by individuals.

It is not enough for a product to be made and used. It is then only a use-value, a product of labour. It must sell and to sell must warrant desire. It is the latter that gives it value, that validates it as something worth exchanging. Orthodox presentations see intrinsic value given osmosis-like to the object. But what is important here is the generation of meaning, desirability, significance around it. It is this that 'creates' the commodity, if we consider the commodity to be that which is sold, and the mere product of labour only a potential commodity. The labour of circulation, in creative industries and elsewhere, stimulates meaning, desire and attachment. This provokes the validation of something as worthy of exchange and grants the attendant status of a commodity. As pointed out in Part 1, this differs from a marginalist account of value by situating these processes under coercive and antagonistic conditions, of human creation beyond our control and not of our choosing.

9.5   CREATIVITY IN CRISIS

In sum, productiveness is situated in what we characterised in Chap. 4 as the 'life trajectory of the commodity' rather than in the activity of labour. In *Theories of Surplus Value* (1861–63) Marx states that 'it is not th[e] concrete character of labour' that 'stamps it as productive labour in the system of capitalist production'. Rather 'only labour which manifests itself in commodities' is properly productive capitalist labour. The emphasis here is upon the production of a commodity as the arbiter of productiveness. Concrete labour, therefore, has little to do with productiveness. In fact, it is the stamping of this labour as productive that counts. And the necessary condition of this is the production of a commodity that someone has some use for. This in turn is the necessary condition of whatever this product of labour is – a good or service – becoming an object of exchange – a formal commodity – in the first place. The condition is that it sells, garners value, bringing its labour into a social relationship of abstraction with other such labours. It thus 'stamps' that labour as part of the productive labour of society.

Thus far, I have applied a value-form perspective to the question of productiveness. This approach stresses an explanation of the origins of value in the social validation of abstract labour in exchange. It entails a crucial shift of emphasis which conceives of the criterion of productiveness as one determined by the law of value rather than determining of it. Through this, I have suggested that the productiveness of a given labour process is an unknown quantity until capital attains the vantage point of the sale of a commodity. We can strip away the practices and procedures that mark the gradual unfolding of the exchange abstraction both within the realm of production and without. Aside from these, value boils down to an encounter forged within the moment of exchange. Thus, the productiveness that gives rise to this value is grasped in retrospect. Indeed, the possibility of the labour that went into the production of this value even being 'productive' comes with the arrival of this value in its fullest form. This form is the outcome of a transaction of two commodities by buyer and seller by means of the mediation of money.

Value is a social relation rather than something intrinsic to labour and its product. The latter is not by some miracle endowed with a valuable quality by the former. No labour is productive or unproductive in its very doing. The ultimate judgement of this comes with the success or failure to sell or exchange the particular commodity that it renders. Previously an ideal category, the production of value is conjured. It has no practical or concrete basis other than in the abstraction of exchange. In this respect, it functions as a conceptual framework through which to assess past concrete activity. Within production itself, tools of abstraction attain early glimpses of this eventuality. But, in the final instance, production is a category not of the realm of production but of the sphere of circulation.

In creating the conditions whereby value can be 'realised', creative industries create the conditions upon which it can be said to be 'produced' at all. They intervene directly in the possibility of the category of productiveness itself. They assist in its attachment to the labour that has generated a given good or service. They do this by intervening in the meanings and images under which goods and services are packaged in order to craft saleable commodities out of the simple products of labour. They attach to pre-existing use-values another layer of significance which styles them in such a way to attract the desire and wants of consumers. They create new use-values by creating new needs where neither were present before. Without this, there is a lessened likelihood of exchange, and without exchange, the impossibility of value. In this respect, circulation activities like creative industries are crucial rather than peripheral to capitalist valorisation, not just in the contemporary age, but in any time.

The interpretation of value and crisis given here implicates fields like the creative industries directly in the maintenance of capitalist reproduction, and not the mere ancillaries of circulation traditional Marxism would characterise them as. As we saw in Chap. 5, crises centre upon the massive accumulation of wealth and commodities without an underlying basis for their valorisation owing to the narrow social basis of the class antagonism. As Clarke suggests (1992, p. 135), crises of overproduction result from the 'develop[ment of] the productive forces without regard to the limit of the market'. Crises of overproduction relate to the inability to socially validate products as exchangeable commodities in the market. Thus, the explanation does not point to contradictions in production. This is the basis of theories concerned with the organic composition of capital and the falling rate of profit. Rather, the contradiction relates to the disjuncture between production and exchange. The former and the latter have a contradictory unity whereby each relies upon whilst denying the other. The moment of exploitation – production – and the moment of its realisation – exchange – are separate in time, space and theory (Marx 1991, pp. 352–3). There is a distance (and contradictory unity) between the foundation of value in production, and its unfolding in exchange. This creates problems of calculation, prediction, projection and uncertainty. Capitalists attempt to bridge these issues in various ways.

The problem of unsold stock is partly resolved by 'aggressive marketing' and the 'develop[ment] of new needs' to expand the market for capitalists' goods (Clarke 1988, pp. 102–3). The principal agents of this are advertising, design and marketing firms. Their continued role owes to the contradictory nature of the situation into which they intervene. The creation of new needs expands production in some sectors, 'opening up new markets' (Clarke 1989). The 'regular destruction of productive capacity' becomes necessary on a sporadic basis, with an attendant 'redundancy of labour'. This is 'expressed in an increased burden of work for those with jobs, alongside a growing "reserve army of labour" who have been made redundant and are condemned to idleness' (Clarke 1991, p. 92). Thus, the crisis theory of overproduction explains the shedding of necessary labour latched onto by celebrants of a coming 'post-work society' sparked by automation. But, rather than seeing liberation, it sees only living labour-power locked in contradiction.

Against the belief of some Marxists and post-Marxists that capitalism will face a final collapse, this conceptualisation of crisis sees a potentially perpetual circularity. All resolutions, according to Clarke, create the conditions for further crises. Production and accumulation increase, defying capitalism's antagonistic distributive basis. A new bout of overproduction ensues. Creative industries and creative destruction once again service the requirements of capital to market aggressively and develop new needs. There is no termination of the necessity of capitalism to break out in sporadic crises. Each time it creates anew the conditions for further occurrences.

On the one hand, for Clarke, as for Heinrich, the inevitability of crisis relates to the antagonistic relations of distribution. As seen in Chap. 5, it relates to the inhibited ability of the vast majority of the population to consume that produced. In this, they surpass the underconsumptionist explanation. The creative industries intervene against these antagonistic conditions. They make consumption happen and cohere the exchange abstraction. On the other hand, the inevitability of crisis relates to competition between capitals. For Clarke (1988, 1989), the 'uneven development' of individual capitals and their sectors is a key factor in the recurrence of overproduction. Marx notes this 'uneven development' when he writes that 'there would be no overproduction, if demand and supply corresponded to each other, if the capital were distributed in such proportions in all spheres of production' (quoted in Grossman 1992, p. 118). Owing to this uneven development, individual capitals seek to gain competitive advantage over one another. They do so initially through productivity gains. But, in revolutionising the forces of production, they invite the future overproduction of commodities (Clarke 1988, p. 105). The greater the success of an advertising campaign, the more the capitalist brushes against the barrier of capitalism's antagonistic social basis. These unequal relations of distribution express themselves as a limit on spending power.

Credit can temporarily overcome this constraint. But, as Clarke (1989) writes, 'sooner or later that barrier will reappear in the form of a limit'. Stock accumulates in warehouses, and, crucially, 'marketing expenses escalate' alongside a fall in prices. This is because capitalists attempt to offload stock. But prices are already low from productivity gains. They finally hit rock bottom as capitalists attempt to conduct a fire-sale of outstanding inventories (Clarke 1988, pp. 102–4). There is no possibility of further competition on the basis of price. This necessitates a greater marketing and sales effort to compete with other capitals in the marketplace. The aim becomes to shift more units.

Among Marxist thinkers, it is Baran and Sweezy who are most attuned to this important function. Of course, they write in the context of 'monopoly capitalism' rather than uneven development. But they identify the link between foreclosure of price competition and advertising's role in valorisation. As John Bellamy Foster and Robert McChesney (2013) note in their introduction to a *Monthly Review* special issue on the cultural industries, 'Baran and Sweezy's take on the "sales effort" and the role of advertising in monopoly capitalism was and is the necessary starting point for any treatment of the subject.' In their political economy, they give a 'central part' to advertising.

For Baran and Sweezy, 'selling what [is] produced' is the key problem of capitalism. Madison Avenue is the response (Foster and McChesney 2013). They see 'insufficiency of demand' as the central issue, rather than the overproduction of commodities. But their analysis of the possible options available to capitalists to overcome this problem resonates with the analysis given here. Competition on the basis of price is impossible, on account of the 'oligopolistic' nature of contemporary capitalism (Baran and Sweezy 2013). Only the sales effort can step in to sell overproduced commodities in the context of the limited capacity to consume. They see this limited capacity to consume as a temporary feature of capitalist crises. Keynesian state measures that bolster effective demand provide a remedy. The analysis presented here, however, sees the limit on consumption as permanent and immanent to capitalism itself. This is in line with Heinrich's critique of underconsumptionist theories of crisis, as covered in Chap. 5.

This boils down to the blunt fact that, as Clarke writes, for capital 'to be realized in the form of money,...commodities have to prove themselves as use-values by finding a consumer' (1988, p. 102). If this does not happen, no value applies. This is an ever-present state of affairs exacerbated in crises. At all times, the production of a product of labour is not enough to bring about value. The product must be validated as a value-bearing commodity. It must enter into a social relationship with other commodities in the market, by means of its exchange and consumption. Rather than new innovations to which Marxist theories of value must adapt or die a death, the creative industries that contain these contradictions exemplify the continuing relevance of Marx's theory of value in the contemporary age.

9.6   CONCLUSION

This chapter has situated the creative industries within the framework of the circuit of capital and the production of value. In this undertaking, I agree with postoperaist accounts that the categories of production and realisation need rethinking in the context of new spheres of economic activity like the creative industries. But this is not so because of new conditions that have only recently come into focus. Rather, creative industries bring to light something that has always been present within the fibre of the value-form. On this basis, my objection to Fumagalli's approach is threefold.

First I object to the idea that branding and so on *adds* value. Fumagalli is right to move the emphasis of valorisation to realisation. But the role of creative industries is far more fundamental. It makes value possible. Fumagalli can only hold to such a view by retaining a traditionalist LTOV that he otherwise paints as redundant. For Fumagalli, one of the 'main novelties of the new accumulation and valorization paradigm' is that 'knowledge and culture diffusion...become productive'. They are *directly* productive of value. In this, Fumagalli holds to a traditional understanding of Marx's 'labour' theory of value. He conceptualises 'productive labour' in a materialist way. Hence: 'productive labour is that which lends its labour to the production of commodities and tangible merchandise which have an exchange value'. In contrast, non-productive labour is that which physically contributes to no value-bearing commodity. Thus, emphasis falls not upon the fulfilment of this value in and through exchange, but takes the conventional path of seeing value as something *added* via labour. Unproductive labour is that which 'adds no value to anything' (Fumagalli and Morini 2013, p. 5). As we have seen, my analysis surpasses this understanding of so-called 'knowledge work' such as that which takes place in the creative industries. I move away from a productivist appreciation of value to one oriented in circulation, with the caveat that this is still rooted in a class antagonism that both precedes and governs the production process itself.

Second, I object to the idea that any aspect of the symbolic imaginary and the importance of consumption to the possibility of value is new or novel. I see these aspects, and their expression in the working of the creative industries, as completely indispensable to the possibility of value itself. They are significant not only in specific or contemporary instances. Unlike Fumagalli, I do not assume the increasing relevance of advertising and graphic design. Rather, I point to the centrality of these activities for commodity exchange itself, at any time and in any place. Their role, even when under other industrial categories, is indispensable for capitalist valorisation. I make no claim of novelty. Statistics testify to the difficulties of approach oriented around the contemporariness of advertising's pre-eminence. Figures from Douglas Galbi's Coen Structured Advertising Expenditure Dataset (see Galbi 2008) show that, between 1919 and 2008, advertising expenditure remained constant at around 2 per cent of total GDP, with the peak years between 1920 and 1932. The statistical insignificance of any changes in the trajectory of advertising spend in the last 100 years does not tell the whole story. As Baran and Sweezy note (2013), it is difficult to accurately capture the industrial activity and resources pumped into each advertisement. The figures represent only the amount spent on advertisements themselves – for instance, the effort getting adverts placed in media and television outlets. But they may not quite convey 'the costs of market research, designing for advertising purposes, and the like carried on *within* the producing or selling concerns themselves'. As Baran and Sweezy assert, for these, 'reliable estimates. . .are not available'. The buying and selling of advertising space constitutes only the most final and obvious expression of a much longer and more complex process of creative work. These concerns aside, the statistics do provide food for thought to those who would suggest that the relationship between advertising and capitalism is anything new. What the statistics show is that it has been there from early on, and remains much the same. As such, and as with so much else, there can be no novelty attached to the current state of things.

Third, and as covered extensively in the previous chapter, I object to the conceptualisation of 'immaterial labour' as an immeasurable cooperative pursuit. I refute the impossibility of capture by both traditional capitalist valorisation processes and Marx's theory of value. Measure manifests fully only with valorisation itself, which is to say in the moment of commodity exchange, the moment of realisation. Of course, measure arises in an anticipatory form within the realm of production. But value brings into existence its own measure by appearing in monetary form upon the successful exchange of commodities. As such, value's measure does not and has never referred to any expenditure of concrete labour. It refers to labour in the abstract. As Heinrich writes, critiquing the postoperaist attachment to Marx's Fragment that we surveyed in Chap. 7, '"labour in the immediate form" is...not the source of wealth. The social substance of wealth or value in capitalism is abstract labor, whereby it does not matter whether this abstract labor can be traced back to labor-power expended in the process of production' (Heinrich 2013a, p. 17). As such, there is no reason why capitalist measurement cannot function as it did before. The supposedly immeasurable cooperative productiveness of immaterial labour would be measured in the same way as all other labour. This is through its abstract expression as monetary value. This measure need not reflect any specific concrete activity in the first instance. As Heinrich writes elsewhere, '[i]mmediate labour-time was at any rate never the measure of value' (2013b, p. 208). The concept of the crisis of measurability falls when confronted with this fact.

Indeed, we have already seen in Chap. 8 that no crisis of measurability afflicts contemporary capitalism. With reference to concrete examples archetypal of the conditions of immaterial labour on which postoperaists centre their analyses, this chapter has explored to what extent this contention holds in the creative industries in contemporary capitalism. Against the postoperaist understanding of the creative industries given in the work of Andrea Fumagalli, this chapter has shown that the conditions described amount to a 'crisis' so permanent as to be no crisis at all. We can still use the categories provided by Marx. Indeed, creative industries illuminate those categories more clearly than industries traditionally scrutinised by Marxists. This chapter is a contribution towards escaping the immaterial labour thesis. It undoes its dominance over discussions of creative industries and other contemporary forms of economic activity. Postoperaismo carries a burden of precisely the same productivist baggage from which it purports to unshackle itself. An account of value informed by the NRM suggests that postoperaist claims to have overthrown value theory go nowhere near far enough, and shed little light on what really goes on in work and life under capitalism today.

BIBLIOGRAPHY

Adorno, T.W. 1976 [1962]. Sociology and Empirical Research. In *Critical Sociology*, ed. P. Connerton, 237–57. London: Penguin.

Adorno, T.W., and M. Horkheimer. 1972. *Dialectic of Enlightenment*. London: Verso.

Baran, P.A., and P.M. Sweezy. 2013. Theses on Advertising. *Monthly Review* 65 (3): 34–42.

Bernstein, J.M. 2001. Introduction to Adorno, T.W. In *The Culture Industry*, 1–28. London: Routledge.

Clarke, S. 1988. *Keynesianism, Monetarism and the Crisis of the State*. Aldershot: Edward Elgar.

———. 1989. The Marxist Theory of Overaccumulation and Crisis. Presentation Given at Conference of Socialist Economists 1989: Value Crisis and the State Stream. https://homepages.warwick.ac.uk/~syrbe/pubs/CSECONF1989.pdf. Accessed 10 Nov 2014.

———. 1991. *Marx, Marginalism and Modern Sociology*. London: Palgrave.

———. 1992. The Global Accumulation of Capital and the Periodisation of the Capitalist State Form. In *Open Marxism Volume I: Dialectics and History*, ed. W. Bonefeld, R. Gunn, and K. Psychopedis, 133–150. London: Pluto Press.

Cohen, N.S. 2012. Cultural Work as a Site of Struggle: Freelancers and Exploitation. *tripleC: Communication, Capitalism & Critique* 10 (2): 141–155.

Foster, J.B., and R.W. McChesney. 2013. The Cultural Apparatus of Monopoly Capital. *Monthly Review* 65: 3. http://monthlyreview.org/2013/07/01/the-cultural-apparatus-of-monopoly-capital/. Accessed 10 Sept 2014.

Fuchs, C., and V. Mosco. 2012. Introduction: Marx Is Back – The Importance of Marxist Theory and Research for Critical Communication Studies Today. *tripleC: Communication, Capitalism & Critique* 10 (2): 127–140.

Fumagalli, A. 2011. Valorization and Financialization in Cognitive Biocapitalism. *Investment Management and Financial Innovation* 8 (1): 88–103.

Fumagalli, A., and S. Lucarelli. 2008. Basic Income and Productivity in Cognitive Capitalism. *Review of Social Economics* LXVI (1): 14–37.

Fumagalli, A., and C. Morini. 2010. Life Put to Work: Towards a Life Theory of Value. *Ephemera* 10 (3/4): 234–252.

———. 2013. Cognitive Bio-capitalism, Social Reproduction and the Precarity Trap: Why Not Basic Income? *Knowledge Cultures* 1 (4): 106–126.

Galbi, D. 2008. U.S. Annual Advertising Spending Since 1919. http://www.galbithink.org/ad-spending.htm. Accessed 31 Mar 2015.

Gough, I. 1972. Marx's Theory of Productive and Unproductive Labour. *New Left Review* I/76: 47–72.

Grossman, H. 1992. *The Law of Accumulation and Breakdown of the Capitalist System*. London: Pluto.

Harvie, D. 2005. All Labour Produces Value for Capital and We All Struggle Against Value. *The Commoner* 10: 132–171.

Heinrich, M. 2013a. Crisis Theory, the Law of the Tendency of the Profit Rate to Fall, and Marx's Studies in the 1870s. *Monthly Review* 2013: 15–32.

———. 2013b. The 'Fragment on Machines': A Marxian Misconception in the Grundrisse and Its Overcoming in Capital. In *Marx's Laboratory: Critical Interpretations of the Grundrisse*, ed. R. Bellofiore, G. Starosta, and P. Thomas, 197–212. Leiden: Brill.

Huws, U. 2014. The Underpinnings of Class in the Digital Age: Living, Labour and Value. *Socialist Register* 50: 80–107.

Jameson, F. 2011. *Representing Capital: A Reading of Volume One*. London: Verso.

Jorn, A. 2002. *The Natural Order and Other Texts: Reconstructing Philosophy from the Artist's Viewpoint*. Trans. P. Shield. Farnham: Ashgate.

Lazzarato, M. 1996. Immaterial Labor. In *Radical Thought in Italy*, ed. P. Virno and M. Hardt, 133–150. Minneapolis: University of Minnesota Press.

Lotz, C. 2014. *The Capitalist Schema: Time, Money, and the Culture of Abstraction*. Lanham: Lexington Books.

Marx, K. 1861–63. *Economic and Philosophical Manuscripts*. http://www.marxists.org/archive/marx/works/1861/economic/ch38.htm. Accessed 29 Oct 2016.

———. 1991. *Capital*. Vol. III. London: Penguin.

———. 1992. *Capital*. Vol. II. London: Penguin.

———. 1993. *Grundrisse*. London: Penguin.

Mohun, S. 1996. Productive and Unproductive Labor in the Labor Theory of Value. *Review of Radical Political Economics* 24 (4): 30–54.

Nitzan, J., and S. Bichler. 2009. *Capital as Power: A Study of Order and Creorder*. New York: Routledge.

Wark, M. 2011. *The Beach Beneath the Street: The Everyday Life and Glorious Times of the Situationist International*. London: Verso.

Williams, R. 2005 [1980]. Advertising: The Magic System. In *Culture and Materialism*, 170–95. London: Verso.

CHAPTER 10

Conclusion: From Postoperaismo to Postcapitalism

The theory of value given in this book has drawn upon work by Marxian theoreticians such as Riccardo Bellofiore, Werner Bonefeld and Michael Heinrich, who broadly coalesce under the banner of the New Reading of Marx, and can be described as holding a broadly 'monetary' theory of value (Fuchs 2014, pp. 40–1) explored at length in Part 1. The NRM, as we have seen, works from a careful reinterpretation of Marx's written output. It inflects its reading of Marx with Frankfurt School social theory derived from the work of Adorno, under which many of its earliest exponents studied. The critique of political economy is thus read as a critical theory of society rather than an alternative economics per se. It presents 'a Marxism stripped of dogmatic certainties and naturalistic conceptions of society' (Bonefeld 2014, pp. 41–2).

In this way, the NRM and its close cousin, Open Marxism, give us 'the critique of political economy as a critical theory of society' opposed to the critique of political economy as an alternative economic theory that one can compare to that of, say, Smith or Ricardo. It rather takes the capitalist social totality as a whole as its object, including the economic categories the relations within this totality assume. This recasts Marx's critique of political economy not as an alternative economic theory, but a demystifying explosion of the objective economic forms specific to capitalism. It focuses, methodologically, on 'the negative dialectics of economic objectivity' (Bonefeld 2016a, b). This demystifies a reality in which the results of human practice pose themselves above and against its performers. It explodes the economic abstractions through which humans subsist in

© The Author(s) 2018
F.H. Pitts, *Critiquing Capitalism Today*, Marx, Engels, and Marxisms,
DOI 10.1007/978-3-319-62633-8_10

capitalist society. Bonefeld's critique of the NRM is particularly important in this regard, advancing an interpretation whereby the abstract unfolding of value theorised by the NRM is rooted in the relations of violence, property, struggle and subsistence.

Using the NRM, I have suggested in this book that postoperaist literature, and its account of immaterial labour and the crisis of measurability, elides two things. These elisions are linked. On the one hand, postoperaismo asserts the redundancy of the law of value and the attempts of Marxian value theory to understand it. Where the immeasurable, immediately abstract productiveness of contemporary labour holds, the possibility of the capitalist capture or measure of value cannot. Second, despite arising from a broad tradition of autonomist thought that places struggle – specifically class struggle – front and centre of its analyses of capitalism and value, with Negri's post-prison work (specifically that with Michael Hardt) postoperaismo falls under the spell of Spinoza, positing monism, immanence and singularity over Hegelian contradiction and dialectics. Everything is cast as one, rather than being at odds with itself. Things are one thing, rather than dialectically potentially two things at once, or one thing appearing in sublated or denied form in some other thing. This diverges from the dialectical perspective that, I would suggest, it is necessary to hold in order to grasp the specificity of value and labour in capitalist society.

Thus, the Spinozist turn in Negri's work has two outcomes. First, it precludes philosophically the capacity to grasp the nature of value in capitalist society. It is no wonder that Negri suggests that value is redundant when the philosophical underpinnings of his thought are rooted in an ontology that does not permit of the theoretical tools necessary to understand, form-analytically, the movement of value through the various social forms it assumes. Second, Negri's monism elides the antagonistic social relations that undergird the value-form. We live in and through a world actively turned against us. The things we do appear one way, but are subverted to serve purposes other than our own. Beyond this, the buying and selling of labour power is presupposed on unequal social relations of ownership, property and distribution that militate against the successful valorisation of products of labour as commodities by squeezing the capacity of workers to absorb the goods capitalist production generates, a contradiction central to the understanding of class and crisis unfolded in Chap. 5, and picked up again in Chap. 9. Moreover, the value-form both expresses and denies – by abstracting from – the antagonistic social basis of the objective economic forms through which life proceeds in capitalist society – commodities, money, the wage, labour and so forth – in the continued and coerced separation of workers from the independent individual and collective ability to reproduce the means of life. Contradiction abounds, and the dialectics that Negri negates are precisely the key capable of decoding it. When all things are one thing, as in postoperaist Spinozism, the conflict-ridden and conflicted relations that undergird value and capitalist society cannot be fully grasped. Antagonism slips from view, despite any appeal to a 'multitude' capable of overthrowing the system.

As charted briefly in Chap. 8, before the 'radical break' between Negri's early Marxism and later Spinozism (Ryan 1992), there is still some concept of social mediation with which to understand the rule of value (1992, p. 162). But the turn to Spinoza is a radical attack on the dialectical understanding of mediation, in the name of pure immediacy. With this comes an unravelling of any idea that capitalism consists in a set of abstract social forms. In Spinoza Negri finds the basis for an interlocking critique of transcendence, dialectics and mediation that becomes central to the claim that Negri and other postoperaists who carry in his wake, make about value and labour under contemporary capitalism.

Looking at value as a category of social mediation changes how we think about the way this relates to what goes on in the world of the workplace. On the one hand, we have theorists like Negri talk about immaterial labour creating a crisis of measurability. Their conceptualisations survey changes in the composition of labour's content and extrapolate from that changes in capitalism, and crises in capitalism. But what the analysis of value as a category of social mediation does is suggest that the immediate form of that labour matters less than the way that the concrete expenditure of labour-time is abstracted from, in the exchange of the commodity it produces with all other commodities by means of money.

In this way, the NRM not only bears analytical import, but has implications for how we act, practically and politically, in, against and beyond capital. In this spirit, I will close with some reflections on what my book offers by the re-evaluation of critical praxis in the wake of the 'postoperaist turn' and the proliferation of policy agendas informed, if only tangentially, by the faulty prognoses of the Fragment.

In the Introduction, I contended that wrong ways of seeing the world can play into wrong ways of thinking politically about how to change it. Postoperaismo, specifically in the work of Negri, manages to strike a perfect synthesis of the two. Analytically, it sees history pass by only at the level of microscopic transitions in the productive base of society. Sweeping revolutions in capital are taken to hinge on immaterial labour of cognition, communication and creativity. They will eventually deliver us liberation. But in this Negri fails to see the persistence of the perverted social forms its results assume in value, money and commodities. This is because they lack the social form analysis of the NRM. They focus as myopically on labour as old-fashioned productivists, despite auspiciously disavowing its politics. In this, they miss the inextricable imbrication of labour and its fortunes within the socially mediated schema of the market.

The political consequences of this consist in a complicity with capitalist vagaries. Whatever form taken by human production becomes not only an explanatory factor. It is eulogised as an example of the free and unburdened 'creativity of desire' that Negri, in pursuit of Spinoza, celebrates. Seeing capitalist production as an expression of the multitude's immanent force, every bump in the road is for the best. This is exemplified today in the many inheritors of Negri's flame, for whom the postoperaist rendering of the Fragment resonates increasingly with what their analysis perceives to be the leading edge of capitalist development. Among the epithets for the various manifestations of current left thinking in which this influence is wielded are 'postcapitalism' (Mason 2015), 'accelerationism' (Mackay and Avanessian 2015) and 'Fully Automated Luxury Communism' (Bastani 2015).

Representing only those dreams the current historical juncture will permit, such accounts concede too much to the ideological self-impression of capital at a time of economic change. They construct an antagonism-free space where, teleologically, communism is made possible within the shell of capital, workers can self-actualise through liberation *at* work rather than only against it, and capitalism meets its final, inevitable crisis, as foretold in Marx's Fragment (see Chap. 6) whereby valorisation and the measurement upon which it depends breaks down. This is true of Hardt and Negri's noughties work, which, as Doogan notes (2009), provided a radical cover for the same celebrations of capitalist dynamism found in the pages of *Wired* magazine and a hundred pop-economic bestsellers. Today the inheritors of Negri's reading of Marx's Fragment perform the same function, crafting radical justifications of Silicon Valley schemes for full automation and the basic income.

This rests, at first glance, on a profound faith in the capacity of the working class – or else the 'people' or 'networked individuals' – to effect change and remodel the world in line with its wishes. But it does so at the expense of any antagonistic moment, seeing capitalist work as the progressive fulfilment of these desires. As we saw in Chap. 6, Negri classifies the working-class capacity to valorise in a 'self-defining, self-determining' way, 'autonomously from capitalist valorization' (Cleaver 1992, p. 129). Negri suggests that it surpasses 'mere resistance to capitalist valorization', amounting to a 'positive project of self-constitution' instead. The activity of the multitude, immanent and not transcendental or contradictory to global order, arises from within the fabric of capitalism as spontaneously organised and autonomous creativity (Hardt and Negri 2001, p. 83). This happens not only through the refusal of work – as was the case in the imbrication of self-valorisation in the anti-labour struggles of the Italian 1970s, but actually 'by working' itself (2001, p. 395). The multitude, in conditions of extant communism within the capitalist shell of the present, can 'produce itself' as a Spinozist 'singularity', through cooperation in the process of *working* (2001, p. 395). This production is spontaneous and cooperative beyond the capacity of capitalists to control, capture or measure it.

This celebration of the multitude's spontaneous productiveness and the unencumbered 'creativity of desire' dovetails with some of the same ideas through which capital understands itself in popular discourse around the creative economy. The notion that the changes in work reflect the immanent drive of workers themselves to self-actualise through more communicative, cognitive and creative work chimes with bourgeois characterisations of contemporary capitalism popular in the same period as this revision in Negri's thinking occurs. We see a fresh uptake of the same ideas in the present day as a series of bestselling books sell radical ideas in rational forms to centre-left policymakers around the 'sharing economy' and the move to a post-work, postcapitalist society (see Mason 2015; Srnicek and Williams 2015b).

By linking the capacity for self-valorisation and the 'creativity of desire' to the rise of immaterial labour current at the time Hardt and Negri were writing *Empire*, they steal work from the antagonistic context in which it sits in the theorisation of the social factory and instead eulogise the capacity to realise oneself *in* the newly socialised workplace in such a manner as to exceed – in a non-negative, non-antagonistic, non-contradictory and entirely immanent way – the ability of capital to measure.

As Caffentzis notes, in common with other treatments of the purported 'end of work', postoperaismo generates a stultifying politics that suggests 'capitalism has already ended at the high-tech end of the system' and all there is to do is 'wake up to it' (2013, p. 81). Today, the so-called 'social movement' (see Bolton 2016) around British Labour leader Jeremy Corbyn exhibits a similar conviction, creating an environment for Negri's ideas to implicitly wend their way into the consciousness of the UK left through inheritors of his legacy like Paul Mason who, foremost among those commentators championing Corbyn, casts the movement as a 'counterpower' within and against capital, driving change (2016). This communicates all the comfort that if you keep on doing what you're doing, everything will be okay. All change will issue from the immanent drive of the vague and ill-defined 'multitude' of which you are a member.

Indeed, we live in an age of upswells rebranded as an authentic 'counterpower' within capital, specifically periodic surges like Occupy, Syriza and Podemos. These tonics reassure the left of immanent, imminent victory. But folk renditions of Negrian political philosophy terminate in a politics of paralysis. All people need to do is keep on doing what they do already. Meanwhile, a crisis of measurability will surely deliver us from capitalism. Incipient communism coexists within the shell of the latter, in the so-called 'sharing economy'. New technologies help regulate a series of demands into fruition. Full automation, working hours reduction, basic income: these demands mimic the suggested reforms hurried in at the end of *Empire* (2001, pp. 393–411).

There is a longer story to this, of which we now see some kind of resolution. In the UK it can be observed that at least part of the intellectual project around Labour leader Jeremy Corbyn springs from the reception of Negri through successive iterations over previous years. His work wielded an influence on the alterglobalisation struggles of the early noughties (White 2009) and later the Occupy milieu (Mason 2011). Today it resounds in the revitalisation of a populist politics of hegemony-building around a techno-utopia of automation and basic income (Srnicek and Williams 2015a, b; see Negri's exchange with the latter in Negri 2015). In each iteration, we see Negri's 'multitude' recoded as, variously, the '99%', 'the people' and 'networked individuals' (Mason 2015).

This ideological environment, I suggest, harkens back in no small way to Negri's turn from Marx to Spinoza covered in Chap. 6. But this does not stand up to scrutiny. Corbynism posits a 'singularity' similar in hue to the multitude. It goes by the name of the 'people'. But this singularity cannot exist in world criss-crossed by antagonistic class relations. There is, translating ideas across times and milieus, a postoperaist hangover operating here. It clings desperately onto the positive and underplays the negative. In the process it obstructs a proper assessment of what is necessary, what is possible, and what is neither in the present. Today, popular analyses celebrate empirical trends in work and economic life in expectation of change. But no substantial critical effort is made to understand capitalism's negativity. The 'actual conditions of life' that characterise capitalism carry over. A crisis, attended by incipient communism, can be conceived only in spite of this.

Wishing all this away theoretically leads to a strategic impasse for left politics. Postoperaismo's inheritors weld the Fragment to a politics too enchanted with the world that is. They assume too much is right, and not enough wrong. Spellbound modes of praxis result, that rub with the grain rather than against it. Positivity is praised, negativity goes un-negated. Policymakers seize upon the false promise of change the radical left heralds. Continuing forms of social domination rest unquestioned. To combat this thinking, we must cap it at its source. In so doing, the second half of the book has reached back into Negri's theoretical development to explore how the mistakes he makes sit also behind the present intellectual succour sustaining Corbynism in the UK and other left movements elsewhere. Its exposure creates critical resources to remedy the latter's errors and build better praxis, to which this book is a contribution.

The theoretical legacy of Marx's Fragment in postoperaismo and its contemporary popularisers matters politically. As such it is necessary to get to grips with where the prognoses derails in theory before it does so in practice. On one hand, postoperaist interpretations of the Fragment's realisation in immaterial labour are seldom immaterial enough. Like the most conventional value theory, they emphasise labour's concrete expenditure over its abstraction. They extrapolate systemic change from the immediate form labour takes, ignoring its mediation. This supports the claim of a crisis mimicking that described in the Fragment. But the novelty it posits is not actually so novel after all. The Fragment provides a faulty map with which to read a mistaken prognosis. Marx would be as much to blame for this as Negri, had he intended it for public consumption.

On the other hand, postoperaist interpretations of the Fragment's realisation are not materialist enough. Negri's Spinoza-derived monism induces him to overlook the persistence of social relations of production. The shiny exterior of workplace change conceals continuing hunger, domination, separation and violence. Both sides – appearance in the value-form and essence sublated within – are missed. And with them the continuing and coercive role played by measurement within and without the sphere of production. This facilitates the claim of a capitalist collapse attended by an incipient communism. A few pages of Marx helped get us here. But more pages still can help us get out. The New Reading of Marx outlined in Part 1 is a theoretical torch shedding light on the path through which to do so, and the application of Marx to new fields of study like the creative industries covered in Chap. 9 is one means to wring new and greater meaning from his work for new times without reinventing the wheel.

The crucial question for the critical strand of Marxism advanced here is 'why does this thing or this process take the form it does?' What we should be talking about when we talk about labour is not necessarily the labour itself but the specificities of that labour insofar as it results in a commodity carrying value, expressed in its price. This, after all, is the specificity of capitalism. In order to understand labour in capitalist society, in its specificity within the social formation in which we find ourselves, we have to understand this, and not whether a worker works with his or her head or his or her hands. This enters into conflict with the claims made by the postoperaists, about immaterial labour, the crisis of measurability and so on, hinging as they do on such microscopic changes. Value is a category of social mediation. It rides upon the successful exchange of the commodity it produces with all the other commodities in the market by means of the mediating force of money. Labour can be comprehended only in its context of that whole valorisation process, with the labour process as a 'carrier' of the valorisation process, as described in Chap. 4.

The relevance of value theory to the study of contemporary work consists in its ability to throw light on how what goes on in the workplace links into a wider nexus of money, wealth, wage and value. The labour process is merely a bearer of this nexus. Utopian visions restricted to its overhaul alone therefore leave the world as it is untouched. Situated within the social mediation of value, the idea that some changes in the way we work – so working with a keyboard instead of with a machine – or working with ideas instead of nuts and bolts – need not necessarily force us to completely throw away everything that we understand previously about the way value works in capitalist society. The ideas of Negri and the postoperaists, on the other hand, emphasise change over continuity, both in the social form of value and also in the concrete social relations that this form implies.

As we have seen, the Fragment on Machines casts a long shadow over postoperaist treatments of value. But, I would suggest, little thought has been given to the coherence of the Fragment within the whole body of Marx's work. Fragment-thinking tends toward a conventional understanding of the relationship between labour and value. Ironically, this productivist perspective belies the avowed post-workerism of its proponents. Their conceptualisation of a crisis of measurability depends upon it. Value must relate directly to expended concrete labour for the latter's reduction to pose a threat. But it instead relates to abstract labour, which, as we saw in Chaps. 2 and 4, has no concrete existence (Bonefeld 2010, p. 260). As such, the Fragment sits uneasily in the development of Marx's value theory (Heinrich 2013). This accounts for its fragmentary, unpublished nature. Its crisis scenario implies a simplistic LTOV that Marx later outgrew. The Fragment can be considered only a partial view-point on value from a Marxian perspective. For this reason, it should not be extrapolated to a theory of the crisis of measurability and the law of value made to fit the conditions before us today. There is more to Marx than his present-day appropriations appear to permit.

Read along the lines set out here, measurement continues the same as always. The optimistic picture the Fragment foretells cannot be the case. The coercive social relations are still there, synonymous with measure, and sublated within it, contradictory and denied. Contra the postoperaists, value, on this account, always faces the conditions of crisis described by those foretelling its downfall. But here what is important is that this crisis cannot be fatal in the way that the Fragment implies. The Fragment runs counter to the whole endeavour of Marx's critique of political economy. We must, therefore, beware the siren calls of those who seek to tear the Fragment from its context within the unfolding of a fuller theory of capi-talism and exploit this for political ends. Its misguided application to the present wields real political efficacy. Its popularity may relate to the reassur-ance it offers to two diverse audiences. To those interested both in capital-ism's continuation, a soothing requiem to its immeasurable productivity and peaceful passage of progress. To those seeking otherwise, the promise of its imminent transformation. From a critical Marxist perspective, both thrive off false hope. We can endow ourselves with real hope only through an initial moment of negativity. This is lacking in the techno-optimism of the Fragment-thinkers.

Today, utopian alternatives consist in the dream of an automated postcapitalist future achieved from the favourable unfolding of the forces of production, and with them the relations around which they are organised (Mason 2015). However, for the critique of political economy as a critical society theory, traditional 'worldview' Marxism, which today takes on the form of a post-work technological determinism, is as much taken in by the appearance of society as an 'objectively unfolding force' as classical political economy or mainstream economics. Take, for instance, the rela-tionship traditional Marxism posits between the forces and the relations of production of which the contemporary postcapitalist followers of the postoperaismo surveyed in the second part of the book are the modern inheritors. The social relations of production are determined by changes in an objective economic law relating to the productive base. Class relations shift as technological or productive changes make it so. Here human action is subordinated analytically to the outcomes of 'an objective framework' (Bonefeld 2014, p. 61). This reads Marx without the subject–object dialectic critical theory reinstates to its rightful place in the analysis of the commodity fetish and social constitution. What is objective can only be objective as a 'socially determinate object' (Bonefeld 2014, p. 63), which is to say as an expression of antagonistic human relations. This object-without-the-subject is as false as the 'Rousseauian' Marxism that G.M. Tamas deplores in his restatement of the foundations of the Marxist theory of class (2009), which, seeing the working class as a subjective force synonymous with the people and sure to assume power, unburdens class struggle of its fateful objectifications in capitalist social forms – a mistake, we have seen, that marks the postoperaist conceptualisation of the 'multitude' and its popularised forms today. This populism coexists in the imaginary of the contemporary left with a postcapitalism fixated on the forces of production. Neither offer a contribution to the critical theory of society and its constitution – only purported remedies for its contradictions in temporary and repressive resolutions that liquidate struggle in an automated post-work future or the rise to power of a classless 'people'.

However, what the critical theory of class and social constitution suggests is that '[t]he critique of class society finds its positive resolution only in the classless society' (Bonefeld 2014, p. 102). It does not do so in a 'fairer' class society in which the relations are reorganised so as to ensure a more equitable distribution of the gains generated by the unfolding forces of production, or when one class rises to prominence to control the wealth it is said to have created. Like authoritarian schemes of national renewal based on the happenstance of blood and soil, post-work utopias and the pursuit of unmediated people power seek only to cleanse the world of its contradictions whilst retaining them in the more abstract form of free money and free subjectivity. In so doing, they temporarily defer the class antagonism's destructive power, where critical theory seeks to abolish it definitively. Marx (1975, p. 159) wrote of class relations, referring to their constitutive function within capitalism as a whole, that is you 'wipe [them] out. . .you annihilate all society'. Yet in this last respect, critical theory confronts the contradiction whereby those dispossessed of all but their capacity to labour count for their subsistence on the successful validation of their exploitation as productive of value and profitable to capital, and hence on class society itself. In and against the class relation, we are really in and against life itself – a stance, as we have seen, postoperaismo lacks the requisite pessimism to live up to.

Uniformly among these torch carriers for postoperaismo, the assumption is shared with Hardt and Negri that work is moving in a generally favourable direction, terminating in a postcapitalist, postwork utopia (Mason 2015; Srnicek and Williams 2015b). This literature is gaining mainstream relevance and informing policy debates. Indeed, as problematic as this analysis is, it would not be nearly so problematic were it not for the forms of political praxis it now invites. Today policymakers obsess over automation, technological unemployment and the basic income. Via its media popularisers, Fragment-thinking wields real influence. It falls most on those forces in favour of those on receiving end of capitalist domination. Social democratic and popular left parties sit under its spell. Protest groups too, as evidenced in the demands at a recent march in London: 'Demand full automation, demand basic income, demand the future' (Harris 2016), read the placards.

But the popularity of these ideas is in inverse proportion to their usefulness. Like Hardt and Negri's original message, they uncomplicatedly place all powers of creation in the hands of people. But this elides how the results of human practice take on forms turned against us in capitalist society. They cast history as unfolding entirely according to our design. But what a critical Marxist analysis tells us is that it might not. We cannot rest on our laurels politically. Contra Pangloss, all is not for the best, and we do not find ourselves in the best of all possible worlds. Proponents of constituent power absent themselves from the necessary negativity to grasp this.

The dissemination of the postoperaist worldview, I suggest, reduces critical resources for a sophisticated, revisionist Marxism. Too positive about prospects for change, it obstructs confrontation with contemporary capitalism's concrete realities. This book suggests that the postoperaismo-inspired paragons of postcapitalism impoverish left politics. We may be better off with the negative dialecticians of the NRM tradition. Through this, we can get closer to capitalism analytically, and further from it historically. The critique of political economy as a critical theory of society allows us to ask: what theoretical imperatives support platforms, such as Negri's and that of the new postcapitalist left, that like to say 'yes'? And, in turn, it poses the question of praxis that Bonefeld identifies (2014): what does it mean to say 'no'? This book has given answers to the first of these questions. Further work must be done, in struggle and scholarship, to find an answer to the second.

BIBLIOGRAPHY

Bastani, A. 2015. We Don't Need More Austerity, We Need Luxury Communism. *Vice Magazine*. June 12. http://www.vice.com/en_uk/read/luxury-communism-933. Accessed 29 Oct 2016.

Bolton, M. 2016. The Terrifying Hubris of Corbynism. *Medium*, July 14. https://medium.com/@matatatatat/the-terrifying-hubris-of-corbynism-6590054a9b57#.ftpsvjg87. Accessed 29 Oct 2016.

Bonefeld, W. 2010. Abstract Labour: Against Its Nature and on Its Time. *Capital and Class* 34 (2): 257–276.

———. 2014. *Critical Theory and the Critique of Political Economy: On Subversion and Negative Reason*. London: Bloomsbury.

———. 2016a. Negative Dialectics and Critique of Economic Objectivity. *History of the Human Sciences* 29 (2): 60–76.

———. 2016b. Bringing Critical Theory Back in at a Time of Misery: Three Beginnings Without Conclusion. *Capital & Class* 40 (2): 233–244.

Caffentzis, G. 2013. *In Letters of Blood and Fire: Work, Machines, and Value*. Oakland: PM Press.

Cleaver, H. 1992. The Inversion of Class Perspective in Marxian Theory: From Valorisation to Self-Valorisation. In *Open Marxism Vol. II: Theory and Practice*, ed. W. Bonefeld, R. Gunn, and K. Psychopedis, 107–144. London: Pluto Press.

Doogan, K. 2009. *New Capitalism? The Transformation of Work*. Cambridge: Polity.

Fuchs, C. 2014. *Digital Labour and Karl Marx*. New York: Routledge.

Hardt, M., and A. Negri. 2001. *Empire*. Cambridge, MA: Harvard University Press.

Harris, J. 2016. Should We Scrap Benefits and Pay Everyone £100 a Week? *The Guardian*. April 13. http://www.theguardian.com/politics/2016/apr/13/should-we-scrap-benefits-and-pay-everyone-100-a-week-whether-they-work-or-not. Accessed 29 Oct 2016.

Heinrich, M. 2013. The 'Fragment on Machines': A Marxian Misconception in the Grundrisse and Its Overcoming in Capital. In *Marx's Laboratory: Critical Interpretations of the Grundrisse*, ed. R. Bellofiore, G. Starosta, and P. Thomas, 197–212. Leiden: Brill.

Mackay, R., and A. Avanessian, eds. 2015. *#Accelerate: The Accelerationist Reader*. Falmouth: Urbanomic.

Marx, K. 1975. The Poverty of Philosophy. In *Collected Works*, ed. K. Marx and F. Engels, vol. 6, 105–234. London: Lawrence and Wishart.

Mason, P. 2011. Twenty Reasons Why It's Kicking Off Everywhere. *Idle Scrawl*, February 5. http://www.bbc.co.uk/blogs/newsnight/paulmason/2011/02/twenty_reasons_why_its_kicking.html. Accessed 29 Oct 2016.

———. 2015. *Postcapitalism: A Guide to Our Future*. London: Allen Lane.

————. 2016. Corbyn: The Summer of Hierarchical Things. *Mosquito Ridge.* https://medium.com/mosquito-ridge/corbyn-the-summer-of-hierarchical -things-ab1368959b80#.f8e5z4k82. Accessed 29 Oct 2016.

Negri, A. 2015. Some Reflections on the #Accelerate Manifesto. In *#Accelerate: The Accelerationist Manifesto*, ed. R. Mckay and A. Avanessian, 363–378. Falmouth: Urbanomic.

Ryan, M. 1992. Translators' Introductions, Part II. In *Marx Beyond Marx: Lessons on the Grundrisse*, ed. A. Negri, xxviii–xxvxxx. London: Pluto Press.

Srnicek, N., and A. Williams. 2015a. #Accelerate: Manifesto for an Accelerationist Politics. In *#Accelerate: The Accelerationist Reader*, ed. R. Mackay and A. Avanessian, 347–362. Falmouth: Urbanomic.

————. 2015b. *Inventing the Future.* London: Verso.

Tamas, G.M. 2009. Telling the Truth About Class. *Socialist Register* 42: 228–268.

White, M.M. 2009. The Politics of Youth. *Adbusters* 82. https://www.adbusters.org /magazine/82/michael_hardt.html. Accessed 29 Oct 2016.

BIBLIOGRAPHY

Abse, T. 2016. Struggle and Postmodern. *Weekly Worker* 1106, May 12, p. 11.

Adorno, T.W. 1941. Spengler Today. *Zeitschrift fur Sozialforschung* 9: 305–324.

———. 1973. *Negative Dialectics.* London: A&C Black.

———. 1974. Commitment. *New Left Review* I/87-88: 75–89.

———. 1976 [1962]. Sociology and Empirical Research. In *Critical Sociology*, ed. P. Connerton, 237–57. London: Penguin.

———. 1990. *Negative Dialectics.* Trans. E.B. Ashton. London: Routledge.

———. 1997. Seminar Mitschrift of 1962. Appendix to Backhaus. In *Dialektik der Wertform*, 501–512. Freiburg: Ca Ira.

———. 2000. *Introduction to Sociology.* Cambridge: Polity Press.

———. 2003a. Late Capitalism or Industrial Society? The Fundamental Question of the Present Structure of Society. In *Can One Live After Auschwitz? A Philosophical Reader*, ed. R. Tiedemann, 111–25. Trans. R. Livingstone. Stanford: Stanford University Press.

———. 2003b. Reflections on Class Theory. In *Can One Live After Auschwitz? A Philosophical Reader*, ed. R. Tiedemann, 93–110. Trans. R. Livingstone. Stanford: Stanford University Press.

———. 2005. *Minima Moralia: Reflections from Damaged Life.* London: Verso.

———. 2008. *Lectures on History and Freedom*, ed. R. Tiedemann. Trans. R. Livingstone. Cambridge: Polity Press.

Adorno, T.W., and M. Horkheimer. 1972. *Dialectic of Enlightenment.* London: Verso.

Althusser, L. 2001 [1971]. Preface to Capital Volume One. In *Lenin and Philosophy and Other Essays*, 45–70. New York: Monthly Review Press.

Aristotle. 1998. *The Metaphysics.* London: Penguin.

© The Author(s) 2018

263

F.H. Pitts, *Critiquing Capitalism Today*, Marx, Engels, and Marxisms,
DOI 10.1007/978-3-319-62633-8

Arthur, C. 1979. Dialectic of the Value-Form. In *Value: The Representation of Labour in Capitalism*, ed. D. Elson, 67–81. London: CSE Books.

———. 2013. The Practical Truth of Abstract Labour. In *Marx's Laboratory: Critical Interpretations of the Grundrisse*, ed. R. Bellofiore, G. Starosta, and P. Thomas, 101–120. Leiden: Brill.

Aufheben. 2004. We Have Ways of Making You Talk! *Aufheben #12*. http://libcom.org/library/we-have-ways-making-you-talk. Accessed 12 June 2012.

———. 2007. Keep on Smiling: Questions on Immaterial Labour. *Aufheben #14*: 23–44.

Backhaus, H.-G. 1992. Between Philosophy and Science: Marxian Social Economy as Critical Theory. In *Open Marxism Volume 1: Dialectics and History*, ed. W. Bonefeld, R. Gunn, and K. Psychopedis, 54–92. London: Pluto Press.

———. 2005. Some Aspects of Marx's Concept of Critique in the Context of His Economic-Philosophical Theory. In *Human Dignity: Social Autonomy and the Critique of Capitalism*, ed. W. Bonefeld and K. Psychopedis, 13–30. Aldershot: Ashgate.

Balakrishnan, G., ed. 2003. *Debating Empire*. London: Verso.

Banks, M., R. Gill, and S. Taylor, eds. 2013. *Theorizing Cultural Work: Labour, Continuity & Change in the Cultural & Creative Industries*. London: Routledge.

Baran, P.A., and P.M. Sweezy. 2013. Theses on Advertising. *Monthly Review* 65 (3): 34–42.

Bastani, A. 2015. We Don't Need More Austerity, We Need Luxury Communism. *Vice Magazine*. June 12. http://www.vice.com/en_uk/read/luxury-communism-933. Accessed 29 Oct 2016.

Bellofiore, R. 2009. A Ghost Turning into a Vampire: The Concept of Capital and Living Labour. In *Re-reading Marx: New Perspectives After the Critical Edition*, ed. R. Bellofiore and R. Fineschi, 178–194. London: Palgrave Macmillan.

Bellofiore, R., and R. Finelli. 1998. Capital, Labour and Time: The Marxian Monetary Theory of Value as a Theory of Exploitation. In *Marxian Economics: A Reappraisal: Essays on Volume 1 of Capital: Method, Value and Money*, ed. R. Bellofiore, 48–74. London: Macmillan.

Bellofiore, R., and T.R. Riva. 2015. The Neue Marx-Lektüre: Putting the Critique of Political Economy Back into the Critique of Society. *Radical Philosophy* 189: 24–36.

Benjamin, W. 1999. Theses on the Philosophy of History. In *Illuminations: Essays and Reflections*, ed. H. Arendt, 245–255. London: Pimlico.

———. 2004. Critique of Violence. In *Selected Writings Volume 1, 1913–1926*, ed. M. Bullock and M.W. Jennings, 236–253. Cambridge, MA: Harvard University Press.

Benyon, H. 1984. *Working for Ford*. London: Penguin.

Berardi, F. 2009. *The Soul at Work*. Trans. F. Cadel and G. Mecchia. Los Angeles: Semiotext(e).

———. 2013. *The Uprising: On Poetry and Finance*. Los Angeles: Semiotext(e).

Bernstein, J.M. 2001. Introduction to Adorno, T.W. In *The Culture Industry*, 1–28. London: Routledge.

Beverungen, A., A.-M. Murtola, and G. Schwartz. 2013. The Communism of Capital? *Ephemera* 13 (3): 483–495.

Boehm, S., and C. Land. 2009. No Measure for Culture? Value in the New Economy. *Capital & Class* 97: 75–98.

Bolton, M. 2016. The Terrifying Hubris of Corbynism. *Medium,* July 14. https://medium.com/@matatatatat/the-terrifying-hubris-of-corbynism-6590054a9b57#. ftpsvjg87. Accessed 29 Oct 2016.

Bonefeld, W. 1994. Human Practice and Perversion: Between Autonomy and Structure. *Common Sense* 15: 43–52.

———. 2001. *The Politics of Europe: Monetary Union and Class*. London: Palgrave.

———. 2010. Abstract Labour: Against Its Nature and on Its Time. *Capital and Class* 34 (2): 257–276.

———. 2014. *Critical Theory and the Critique of Political Economy: On Subversion and Negative Reason*. London: Bloomsbury.

———. 2016a. Negative Dialectics and Critique of Economic Objectivity. *History of the Human Sciences* 29 (2): 60–76.

———. 2016b. Bringing Critical Theory Back in at a Time of Misery: Three Beginnings Without Conclusion. *Capital & Class* 40 (2): 233–244.

Bonefeld, W., and K. Psychopedis, eds. 2005. *Human Dignity: Social Autonomy and the Critique of Capitalism*. Aldershot: Ashgate.

Bonefeld, W., R. Gunn, and K. Psychopedis, eds. 1992. *Open Marxism Volume I: Dialectics and History*. London: Pluto Press.

Bourdieu, P. 1984. *Distinction: A Social Critique of the Judgement of Taste*. Trans. R. Nice. London: Routledge and Kegan Paul.

Bowie, A. 2010. *German Philosophy*. Oxford: University Press.

Braunstein, D. 2011. *Adornos Kritik der politischen Okonomie*. Bielefeld: Transcript Verlag.

Brown, B.A., and A. Quan-Hase. 2012. "A Workers' Inquiry 2.0": An Ethnographic Method for the Study of Produsage in Social Media Contexts. *tripleC* 10 (2): 488–508.

Caffentzis, G. 2005. Immeasurable Value? An Essay on Marx's Legacy *The Commoner* 10: 87–114.

———. 2013. *In Letters of Blood and Fire: Work, Machines, and Value*. Oakland: PM Press.

Carchedi, G., and M. Roberts. 2013. A Critique of Heinrich's, 'Crisis Theory, the Law of the Tendency of the Profit Rate to Fall, and Marx's Studies in the 1870s'. *Monthly Review*. http://monthlyreview.org/commentary/critique-heinrichs-crisis-theory-law-tendency-profit-rate-fall-marxs-studies-1870s/. Accessed 1 Oct 2014.

Cavendish, R. 1982. *Women on the Line*. London: Routledge.

Clarke, S. 1980. The Value of Value. *Capital and Class* 10: 1–17.

————. 1988. *Keynesianism, Monetarism and the Crisis of the State*. Aldershot: Edward Elgar.

————. 1989. The Marxist Theory of Overaccumulation and Crisis. Presentation Given at Conference of Socialist Economists 1989: Value Crisis and the State Stream. https://homepages.warwick.ac.uk/~syrbe/pubs/CSECONF1989.pdf. Accessed 10 Nov 2014.

————. 1991. *Marx, Marginalism and Modern Sociology*. London: Palgrave.

————. 1992. The Global Accumulation of Capital and the Periodisation of the Capitalist State Form. In *Open Marxism Volume I: Dialectics and History*, ed. W. Bonefeld, R. Gunn, and K. Psychopedis, 133–150. London: Pluto Press.

Cleaver, H. 1992a. The Inversion of Class Perspective in Marxian Theory: From Valorisation to Self-Valorisation. In *Open Marxism Vol. II: Theory and Practice*, ed. W. Bonefeld, R. Gunn, and K. Psychopedis, 107–144. London: Pluto Press.

————. 1992b. Translators' Introductions, Part I. In *Marx Beyond Marx: Lessons on the Grundrisse*, ed. A. Negri, xix–xxvii. London: Pluto Press.

————. 2000. *Reading* Capital *Politically*. Edinburgh: AK Press.

————. 2011. Work Refusal and Self-Organisation. In *Life Without Money: Building Fair and Sustainable Economies*, ed. A. Nelson and F. Timmerman, 47–69. London: Pluto Press.

————. 2014. Genesis of Zerowork #1. *Zero Work*. http://www.zerowork.org/GenesisZ1.html. Accessed 30 Oct 2016.

Cockburn, C., and S. Ormrod. 1993. *Gender and Technology in the Making*. London: Sage.

Cohen, N.S. 2012. Cultural Work as a Site of Struggle: Freelancers and Exploitation. *tripleC: Communication, Capitalism & Critique* 10 (2): 141–155.

Colletti, L. 1973. *Marxism and Hegel*. London: Verso.

————. 1989. *From Rousseau to Lenin: Studies in Ideology and Society*. New York: Monthly Review Press.

Connerton, P. 1976. Introduction. In *Critical Sociology*, 11–39. London: Penguin.

de Molina, M.M. 2004. Common Notions, Part 1: Workers-Inquiry, Co-research, Consciousness-Raising. Trans. M. Casas-Cortés and S. Cobarrubias. http://eipcp.net/transversal/0406/malo/en. Accessed 12 June 2012.

Deleuze, G. 1990. Society of Control. *L'autre Journal* 1. https://www.nadir.org/nadir/archiv/netzkritik/societyofcontrol.html. Accessed 29 Oct 2016.

Dinerstein, A., and M. Neary. 2002. From Here to Utopia: Finding Inspiration for the Labour Debate. In *The Labour Debate: An Investigation into the Theory and Reality of Capitalist Work*, ed. A. Dinerstein and M. Neary, 1–27. Aldershot: Ashgate.

Doogan, K. 2009. *New Capitalism? The Transformation of Work*. Cambridge: Polity.

Elson, D. 1979. The Value Theory of Labour. In *Value: The Representation of Labour in Capitalism*, ed. D. Elson, 115–180. London: CSE Books.

Endnotes. 2010. Communisation and Value-Form Theory. *Endnotes #2: Misery and the Value-Form*. https://endnotes.org.uk/issues/2/en/endnotes-communisation-and-value-form-theory. Accessed 29 Oct 2016.

Fine, B., and A. Saad-Filho. 2004. *Marx's Capital*. 4th ed. London: Pluto Press.

Foster, J.B., and R.W. McChesney. 2013. The Cultural Apparatus of Monopoly Capital. *Monthly Review* 65: 3. http://monthlyreview.org/2013/07/01/the-cultural-apparatus-of-monopoly-capital/. Accessed 10 Sept 2014.

Fuchs, C. 2014. *Digital Labour and Karl Marx*. New York: Routledge.

Fuchs, C., and V. Mosco. 2012. Introduction: Marx Is Back – The Importance of Marxist Theory and Research for Critical Communication Studies Today. *tripleC: Communication, Capitalism & Critique* 10 (2): 127–140.

Fumagalli, A. 2010. The Global Economic Crisis and Socioeconomic Governance. In *Crisis in the Global Economy*, ed. A. Fumagalli and S. Mezzadra, 61–84. Trans. Jason Francis McGimsey. Los Angeles: Semiotext(e).

———. 2011. Valorization and Financialization in Cognitive Biocapitalism. *Investment Management and Financial Innovation* 8 (1): 88–103.

Fumagalli, A., and S. Lucarelli. 2008. Basic Income and Productivity in Cognitive Capitalism. *Review of Social Economics* LXVI (1): 14–37.

Fumagalli, A., and S. Mezzadra. 2010. Nothing Will Ever Be the Same: Ten Theses on the Financial Crisis. In *Crisis in the Global Economy*, 237–272. Los Angeles: Semiotext(e).

Fumagalli, A., and C. Morini. 2010. Life Put to Work: Towards a Life Theory of Value. *Ephemera* 10 (3/4): 234–252.

———. 2013. Cognitive Bio-capitalism, Social Reproduction and the Precarity Trap: Why Not Basic Income? *Knowledge Cultures* 1 (4): 106–126.

Galbi, D. 2008. U.S. Annual Advertising Spending Since 1919. http://www.galbi think.org/ad-spending.htm. Accessed 31 Mar 2015.

Glucksmann, M. 1990. *Women Assemble: Women Workers and the New Industries in Inter-war Britain*. London: Routledge.

———. 2005. Shifting Boundaries and Interconnections: Extending the 'Total Social Organisation of Labour'. In *A New Sociology of Work?* ed. L. Pettinger et al. Oxford: Blackwell.

Gough, I. 1972. Marx's Theory of Productive and Unproductive Labour. *New Left Review* I/76: 47–72.

Graeber, D. 2008. The Sadness of Post-Workerism, or "Art and Immaterial Labour" Conference: A Sort of Review. *The Commoner*. http://www.commoner.org.uk /?p=33. Accessed 29 Oct 2016.

———. 2012. *Debt: The First 5,000 Years*. Brooklyn: Melville House.

Grossman, H. 1992. *The Law of Accumulation and Breakdown of the Capitalist System*. London: Pluto.

Gunn, R. 1987. Notes on Class. *Common Sense* 2: 15–25.

———. 1989. Marxism and Philosophy: A Critique of Critical Realism. *Capital and Class* 13: 1–30.

———. 1992. Against Historical Materialism: Marxism as First-Order Discourse. In *Open Marxism Volume II: Theory and Practice*, ed. W. Bonefeld, R. Gunn, and K. Psychopedis, 1–45. London: Pluto Press.

Habermas, J. 1983. *Philosophical-Political Profiles*. London: Heinemann.

Hardt, M., and A. Negri. 2001. *Empire*. Cambridge, MA: Harvard University Press.

———. 2004. *Multitude*. London: Penguin.

———. 2008a. Sovereignty. In *Reflections on Empire*, ed. A. Negri, 49–59. Cambridge: Polity Press.

———. 2008b. Following in Marx's Footsteps. In *Reflections on Empire*, ed. A. Negri, 173–195. Cambridge: Polity Press.

———. 2009. *Commonwealth*. Cambridge: Harvard University Press.

Harris, J. 2016. Should We Scrap Benefits and Pay Everyone £100 a Week? *The Guardian*. April 13. http://www.theguardian.com/politics/2016/apr/13/should-we-scrap-benefits-and-pay-everyone-100-a-week-whether-they-work-or-not. Accessed 29 Oct 2016.

Harvie, D. 2005. All Labour Produces Value for Capital and We All Struggle Against Value. *The Commoner* 10: 132–171.

Hegel, G.W.F. 1976 [1807]. Master and Slave. In *Critical Sociology*, ed. P. Connerton, 41–50. London: Penguin.

Heinrich, M. 2007. Invaders from Marx: On the Uses of Marxian Theory, and the Difficulties of a Contemporary Reading. *Left Curve* 31. http://www.oekonomiekritik.de/205Invaders.htm. Accessed 29 Oct 2016.

———. 2012. *An Introduction to the Three Volumes of Karl Marx's Capital*. New York: Monthly Review Press.

———. 2013a. Crisis Theory, the Law of the Tendency of the Profit Rate to Fall, and Marx's Studies in the 1870s. *Monthly Review* 2013: 15–32.

———. 2013b. The 'Fragment on Machines': A Marxian Misconception in the Grundrisse and Its Overcoming in Capital. In *Marx's Laboratory: Critical Interpretations of the Grundrisse*, ed. R. Bellofiore, G. Starosta, and P. Thomas, 197–212. Leiden: Brill.

Heinrich, M., and W. Bonefeld, eds. 2011. *Kapital & Kritik: Nach der 'neuen' Marx-Lekture*. Hamburg: VSA.

Holloway, J. 2002a. Going in the Wrong Direction; Or, Mephistopheles – Not Saint Francis of Assisi. *Historical Materialism* 10 (1): 79–91.

———. 2002b. *Change the World Without Taking Power*. London: Pluto Press.

———. 2010. *Crack Capitalism*. London: Pluto Press.

Horkheimer, M. 1976 [1937]. Traditional and Critical Theory. In *Critical Sociology*, ed. P. Connerton, 206–224. London: Penguin.

———. 1992. Nachtrag [Postscript]. In *Kritische und Traditionelle Theorie*, 261–269. Frankfurt: Fischer.

Huws, U. 2014. The Underpinnings of Class in the Digital Age: Living, Labour and Value. *Socialist Register* 50: 80–107.

Jameson, F. 2011. *Representing Capital: A Reading of Volume One*. London: Verso.

Jay, M. 1973. *The Dialectical Imagination, A History of the Frankfurt School and the Institute of Social Research, 1923–1950*. London: University of California Press.

Jones, O. 2016. We Should Be Striving to Work Less, Not Toiling Until We Drop. *The Guardian*. March 3. https://www.theguardian.com/commentisfree /2016/mar/03/retirement-retiring-age-77-strive-work-less-progress-challenge -bleak-prospect. Accessed 29 Oct 2016.

Jorn, A. 2002. *The Natural Order and Other Texts: Reconstructing Philosophy from the Artist's Viewpoint*. Trans. P. Shield. Farnham: Ashgate.

Kant, I. 2007. *Critique of Pure Reason*. London: Penguin.

Kay, G. 1979. Why Labour Is the Starting Point of Capital. In *Value: The Representation of Labour in Capitalism*, ed. D. Elson, 46–66. London: CSE Books.

Kicillof, A., and G. Starosta. 2007. Value Form and Class Struggle: A Critique of the Autonomist Theory of Value. *Capital and Class* 92: 13–40.

Kliman, Andrew, Alan Freeman, Nick Potts, Alexey Gusev, and Brendan Cooney. 2013. The Unmaking of Marx's Capital: Heinrich's Attempt to Eliminate Marx's Crisis Theory. http://ssrn.com/abstract=2294134. Accessed 1 Oct 2014.

Kolinko. 2002. *Hotlines: Call Centre. Inquiry. Communism*. Oberhausen: Kolinko.

Kunkel, B. 2014. *Utopia or Bust: A Guide to the Present Crisis*. London: Verso.

Kurz, R. 1999. Marx 2000. www.exit-online.org. Accessed 7 July 2012.

Lazzarato, M. 1996. Immaterial Labor. In *Radical Thought in Italy*, ed. P. Virno and M. Hardt, 133–150. Minneapolis: University of Minnesota Press.

Lotz, C. 2014. *The Capitalist Schema: Time, Money, and the Culture of Abstraction*. Lanham: Lexington Books.

Mackay, R., and A. Avanessian, eds. 2015. *#Accelerate: The Accelerationist Reader*. Falmouth: Urbanomic.

Marazzi, C. 2008. *Capital and Language*. Los Angeles: Semiotext(e).

———. 2010. *The Violence of Financial Capitalism*. Trans. K. Lebedeva. Los Angeles: Semiotext(e).

Marcuse, H. 1972. *One Dimensional Man*. London: Abacus.

Marx, K. 1845. *The German Ideology*. https://www.marxists.org/archive/marx/ works/1845/german-ideology/. Accessed 29 Oct 2016.

———. 1859. *A Contribution to the Critique of Political Economy*. http://www.ma rxists.org/archive/marx/works/1859/critique-pol-economy. Accessed 15 July 2012.

———. 1861–63. *Economic and Philosophical Manuscripts*. http://www.marxists.org /archive/marx/works/1861/economic/ch38.htm. Accessed 29 Oct 2016.

———. 1970. *A Contribution to the Critique of Political Economy*. London: Lawrence and Wishart.

———. 1975. The Poverty of Philosophy. In *Collected Works*, ed. K. Marx and F. Engels, vol. 6, 105–234. London: Lawrence and Wishart.

———. 1976a. *Capital*. Vol. I. London: Penguin.

———. 1976b. The Critique of Hegelian Philosophy. In *Critical Sociology*, ed. P. Connerton, 51–72. London: Penguin.

———. 1976c. The Fetishism of Commodities. In *Critical Sociology*, ed. P. Connerton, 73–89. London: Penguin.

———. 1981. *Capital*. Vol. III. London: Penguin.

———. 1991. *Capital*. Vol. III. London: Penguin.

———. 1992. *Capital*. Vol. II. London: Penguin.

———. 1993. *Grundrisse*. London: Penguin.

———. 2013. Workers' Inquiry. In *A Workers' Inquiry Reader*. Assembled to Accompany. The Politics of Workers' Inquiry Conference, ed. S. Shukaitis, J. Figiel and A. Walker, 8–15. Wivenhoe: Ephemera.

Marx, K., and F. Engels. 1998. *The German Ideology*. Amherst: Prometheus Books.

Mason, P. 2011. Twenty Reasons Why It's Kicking Off Everywhere. *Idle Scrawl*, February 5. http://www.bbc.co.uk/blogs/newsnight/paulmason/2011/02/twenty_reasons_why_its_kicking.html. Accessed 29 Oct 2016.

———. 2015a. The End of Capitalism Has Begun. *The Guardian*. July 17. https://www.theguardian.com/books/2015/jul/17/postcapitalism-end-of-capitalism-begun. Accessed 29 Oct 2016.

———. 2015b. *Postcapitalism: A Guide to Our Future*. London: Allen Lane.

———. 2016. Corbyn: The Summer of Hierarchical Things. *Mosquito Ridge*. https://medium.com/mosquito-ridge/corbyn-the-summer-of-hierarchical-things-ab1368959b80#.f8e5z4k82. Accessed 29 Oct 2016.

Mezzadra, S. 2010. Introduction. In *Crisis in the Global Economy,* ed. A. Fumagalli and S. Mezzadra, 7–16. Trans. J.F. McGimsey. Los Angeles: Semiotext(e).

Mohun, S. 1996. Productive and Unproductive Labor in the Labor Theory of Value. *Review of Radical Political Economics* 24 (4): 30–54.

Muniesa, F., Y. Millo, and M. Callon. 2007. An Introduction to Market Devices. In *Market Devices*, ed. M. Callon, Y. Millo, and F. Muniesa, 1–13. Oxford: Blackwell.

Napoleoni, C. 1975. *Smith, Ricardo, Marx*. Oxford: Blackwell.

Negri, A. 1992. *Marx Beyond Marx: Lessons on the Grundrisse*. London: Pluto.

———. 2008. *Reflections on Empire*. Trans. E. Emery. Cambridge: Polity Press.

———. 2009. *The Savage Anomaly: The Power of Spinoza's Metaphysics and Politics*. Minneapolis: University of Minnesota Press.

———. 2015. Some Reflections on the #Accelerate Manifesto. In *#Accelerate: The Accelerationist Manifesto*, ed. R. Mckay and A. Avanessian, 363–378. Falmouth: Urbanomic.

Nitzan, J., and S. Bichler. 2009. *Capital as Power: A Study of Order and Creorder*. New York: Routledge.

Noys, B. 2012. *The Persistence of the Negative: A Critique of Contemporary Continental Theory*. Cambridge: Cambridge University Press.

Panzieri, R. 1965. *Socialist Uses of Workers' Inquiry*. Trans. A. Bove. http://eipcp.net/transversal/0406/panzieri/en. Accessed 14 June 2012.

Passavant, P., and J. Dean, eds. 2003. *Empire's New Clothes: Reading Hardt and Negri*. London: Routledge.

Porter, T.M. 1994. Making Things Quantitative. *Science in Context* 7 (3): 389–407.

Postone, M. 2012. Thinking the Global Crisis. *The South Atlantic Quarterly* 111 (2): 227–249.

Reichelt, H. 2005. Social Reality as Appearance: Some Notes on Marx's Conception of Reality. In *Human Dignity: Social Autonomy and the Critique of Capitalism*, ed. W. Bonefeld and K. Psychopedis, 31–68. Aldershot: Ashgate.

Reuten, G. 2005. Money as Constituent of Value; The Ideal Introversive Substance and the Ideal Extroversive Form of Value in *Capital*. In *Marx's Theory of Money: Modern Appraisals*, ed. F. Moseley, 78–92. London: Palgrave Macmillan.

Ross, A. 2003. *No-Collar: The Humane Workplace and Its Hidden Costs*. New York: Basic Books.

———. 2008. The New Geography of Work: Power to the Precarious? *Theory Culture and Society* 25 (7–8): 31–49.

Rubin, I.I. 1972. *Essays on Marx's Theory of Value*. Detroit: Black and Red.

———. 1978. Abstract Labour and Value in Marx's System. *Capital & Class* 5: 107–140.

Ryan, M. 1992a. Translators' Introductions, Part II. In *Marx Beyond Marx: Lessons on the Grundrisse*, ed. A. Negri, xxviii–xxvxxx. London: Pluto Press.

———. 1992b. Epilogue. In *Marx Beyond Marx: Lessons on the Grundrisse*, ed. A. Negri, 191–221. London: Pluto Press.

Saad-Filho, A. 1997. Concrete and Abstract Labour in Marx's Theory of Value. *Review of Political Economy* 9 (4): 457–477.

———. 2002. *The Value of Marx*. London: Routledge.

Scruton, R. 2001. *Kant*. Oxford: Oxford University Press.

Smith, T. 2013. The 'General Intellect' in the *Grundrisse* and Beyond. *Historical Materialism* 21 (4): 235–255.

Sohn-Rethel, A. 1978. *Intellectual and Manual Labour: A Critique of Epistemology*. London: Macmillan Press.

Srnicek, N., and A. Williams. 2015a. #Accelerate: Manifesto for an Accelerationist Politics. In *#Accelerate: The Accelerationist Reader*, ed. R. Mackay and A. Avanessian, 347–362. Falmouth: Urbanomic.

———. 2015b. *Inventing the Future*. London: Verso.

———. 2015c. Remembering the Future. *BAMN* #1. http://www.weareplanc.org/bamn/remembering-the-future/. Accessed 29 Oct 2016.

Standing, G. 2011. *The Precariat: The New Dangerous Class*. London: Bloomsbury.

Stewart, H. 2016. John McDonnell: Labour Taking a Close Look at Universal Basic Income. *The Guardian*. June 6. http://www.theguardian.com/politics/2016/jun/05/john-mcdonnell-labour-universal-basic-income-welfare-benefits-compass-report. Accessed 29 Oct 2016.

Tamas, G.M. 2009. Telling the Truth About Class. *Socialist Register* 42: 228–268.

Thoburn, N. 2001. Autonomous Production? On Negri's 'New Synthesis'. *Theory, Culture and Society* 18 (5): 75–96.

———. 2003. *Deleuze, Marx and Politics*. London: Routledge.

Thompson, E.P. 1978. *The Poverty of Theory*. London: Merlin.

Thompson, P. 2005. Foundation and Empire: A Critique of Hardt and Negri. *Capital and Class* 29 (2): 73–98.

Thorne, J. 2011. The Workers' Inquiry: What's the Point? *The commune.* May 16. http://thecommune.co.uk/2011/05/16/the-workers%E2%80% 99-inquiry-what%E2%.

Turchetto, M. 2003. The Empire Strikes Back: On Hardt and Negri. *Historical Materialism* 11 (1): 23–26.

Uninomade Collective. 2013. *The Logistics of Struggles. Notes on the Italian Case.* Trans. I. Bonnin. http://www.uninomade.org/the-logistics-of-struggles. Accessed 26 Dec 2013.

Veca, S. 1971. Value, Labor and Political Economy. *Telos* 9: 48–64.

Vercellone, C. 2010. The Crisis of the Law of Value and the Becoming-Rent of Profit. In *Crisis in the Global Economy*, ed. A. Fumagalli and S. Mezzadra, 85–118. Los Angeles: Semiotext(e).

Virno, P. 1996. The Ambivalence of Disenchantment. In *Radical Thought in Italy: A Potential Politics*, ed. P. Virno and M. Hardt, 13–36. Minneapolis: University of Minnesota Press.

Vuillamy E. 2001. Empire Hits Back. *The Observer.* July 15. http://www.theguardian .com/books/2001/jul/15/globalisation.highereducation. Accessed 29 Oct 2016.

Wark, M. 2011. *The Beach Beneath the Street: The Everyday Life and Glorious Times of the Situationist International.* London: Verso.

Weeks, K. 2011. *The Problem with Work.* Durham/London: Duke University Press.

Weininger, E.B. 2005. Foundations of Pierre Bourdieu's Class Analysis. In *Approaches to Class Analysis*, ed. Erik Olin Wright. Cambridge: Cambridge University Press.

Wheen, F. 2000. *Karl Marx.* London: Fourth Estate.

White, M.M. 2009. The Politics of Youth. *Adbusters* 82. https://www.adbusters.org /magazine/82/michael_hardt.html. Accessed 29 Oct 2016.

Williams, R. 2005 [1980]. Advertising: The Magic System. In *Culture and Materialism*, 170–95. London: Verso.

Wintour, P. 2015. John McDonnell to Unveil 'Socialism with an iPad' Economic Plan. *The Guardian.* Nov 20. http://www.theguardian.com/politics/2015/ nov/20/john-mcdonnell-to-unveil-socialism-with-an-ipad-economic-plan. Accessed 29 Oct 2016.

Wright, E.O. 1981a. The Value Controversy and Social Research. In *The Value Controversy*, ed. I. Steedman. London: Verso.

———. 1981b. Reconsiderations. In *The Value Controversy*, ed. I. Steedman. London: Verso.

Wright, S. 2002. *Storming Heaven: Class Composition and Struggle in Italian Autonomist Marxism.* London: Pluto Press.

INDEX

A

abstract and concrete labour
expenditure, 7, 26, 27, 30, 31, 33, 37,
38, 41, 44–6, 49, 77, 85, 92, 93,
169, 192, 200, 205, 233, 245,
255
validation, 23, 27, 35, 37, 38, 40, 43,
74, 75, 77, 78, 85, 88, 94, 100,
115, 192, 193, 198, 201, 208,
217
abstraction
determinate abstraction, 11, 78, 79
formal abstraction, 184, 239
mental abstraction, 55, 64, 76
real abstraction, 8, 13, 14, 41, 59, 64,
67–9, 75, 76, 109, 117, 154,
172, 200
Adorno, Theodor, 2–4, 7, 13, 44, 53,
55, 60, 61, 63, 100, 106, 108–13,
115, 116, 118–20, 122–4, 126,
147, 155, 185, 223, 232, 249
affirmationism, 146, 176, 177
Althusser, Louis, 4, 125, 126
appearance, 7, 27, 30–3, 40, 45, 48, 49,
58, 59, 62, 65, 78, 79, 85, 90, 98,
100, 105, 106, 111–13, 115, 118,
120, 122, 134, 146, 156, 179, 183,
202, 215, 223, 255, 257
Aristotle, 57, 76
Arthur, Chris
positing, 44, 93–6
sublation, 91, 96
Aufheben, 81–3, 163, 165, 181

B

Backhaus, Hans-Georg, 4, 119
Bellofiore, Riccardo, 3–5, 24, 25, 38,
45, 53–5, 75–7, 114, 118–20, 143,
212, 249
Benjamin, Walter, 164, 176
Berardi, Franco 'Bifo', 183, 196, 197
Bichler, Shimshon, 222, 228, 229
Bonefeld, Werner
conceptuality and non-conceptuality,
67, 68, 75, 101, 105, 107–9,
115, 178, 213
critique of economic categories, 7, 109
critique of political economy as a
critical theory of society
(CPECTS), 14, 105, 112, 134,
183, 249, 259

© The Author(s) 2018

F.H. Pitts, *Critiquing Capitalism Today*, Marx, Engels, and Marxisms,
DOI 10.1007/978-3-319-62633-8

Printed by Printforce, the Netherlands